When Walls Become Doorways

Creativity and the Transforming Illness

Tobi Zausner, Ph.D.

Harmony Books
New York

*This book is dedicated to the artists whose stories
are told within its pages and to everyone everywhere
who has ever had a transforming illness.*

Library of Congress Cataloging-in-Publication Data

Zausner, Tobi.

When walls become doorways : creativity and the transforming illness /
Tobi Zausner. — Ist ed.

I. Medicine and the humanities.   2. Sickness—Psychology.   3. Artists—
Psychology.   4. Creation (Literary, artistic, etc.) —Psychological aspects.
5. Creative ability—Psychological aspects.   6. Medicine and art.

I. Title.

R702.Z38 2006

6I0—dc22   2006025785

ISBN 978-0-307-23808-5

Printed in the United States of America

Design by Chris Welch

I0 9 8 7 6 5 4 3 2 I

First Edition

Acknowledgments

During the many years of writing this book people have been extremely helpful and I would like to acknowledge them. Starting with the most recent group of supportive individuals, I would like to thank the investigative reporter Marianne Macy, who encouraged me to turn my academic manuscript into a book for everyone, and my agent, Dan Strone, who accepted the book and believed it would be published. I would also like to thank everyone at Random House who took a chance on an unknown author: Kim Meisner for acquiring the book, Shaye Areheart for taking on the project, Josh Poole for his continuing assistance and infinite patience, Maureen Clark for her meticulous copyediting, Sibylle Kazeroid for production editing, Cynthia Crippen for the index, Anne Berry for project coordination, and Ava Kavyani for promotion and publicity.

I would also like to thank the following physicians for their excellent medical information: Garabed Eknoyan for nephrology, Bruce L. Miller for neurology, James G. Ravin for ophthalmology, and Steve Conrad and Ruth Richards for advice on medical research. I would also like to thank Ruth Richards for her comments on psychological theory, the health hazards expert Monona Rossol for her information on toxic exposures during the creative process, the psychologist Sara Denning for her expertise on attention deficit disorder, the psychologist Beverly Conrad for her knowledge of Toulouse-Lautrec, the art therapist Tomar Levine for articles on art and healing, and Clara Claiborne Park of Williams College for articles on autism. The following people have given me very helpful information on artists: Henry H. Sturtevant, who lectures at the Metropolitan Museum of Art; Laura Marmar, a docent at the Philadelphia Museum of Art; and Fred Baker and the late Ron Pisano. I thank Leslie Bauman and Deslie Lawrence for their insightful editorial comments and the librarians in the New York Public Libraries, the Bobst Library of New York University, and the New York Academy of Medicine Library, whose expertise made my research more efficient.

Family and friends have been a great source of support and joy during the writing of this book. I would like to thank my sister, Judith Zausner; my niece, Anneliese Zausner-Mannes; and my nephew, Tavish Zausner-Mannes, for their continued enthusiasm. My friends Phyllis Teiko, Ilene Serlin, Joellen Schumacher, Lyn Lourie, and Miles Lourie have been very excited to see this book completed. Sherrie Smith, Laura Smith, and Alan Lee have been very kind in their continuing good wishes, and Sally Beck Furr and Rich Furr have been very supportive of my idea to include veterans. I am also grateful to the many people who believed in this book over the years and were enthusiastic about it. And finally I would like to thank my cats, Gabriel and Angelica, for their gentle presence and steadfast companionship.

Contents

Preface

*The key to your personal transformation is
the thorn in your side.* —*Rudolph Ballentine*

This book is for everyone—because who among us has never
been sick? Even a cold or a sore throat can be a transforming illness. Although the artists in this book have major
physical problems, any experience that forces us to look deeply within
ourselves and decide what we really want to do can be a turning point
in life. I concentrate on visual artists because they mirror my own experience as a painter whose life and work transformed because of
poor health: in 1989 I had ovarian cancer, yet afterward I completed a
doctoral degree. In addition to painting, I began writing, and it was
through researching the biographies of other artists that I realized I
was not alone.

The artists in these pages—painters, sculptors, printmakers, ceramic artists, fabric artists, conceptual artists, photographers, graphic
artists, quilters, jewelry designers, filmmakers, digital artists, cartoonists, glass artists, architects, engravers, industrial designers, and kimono
painters—use creativity to triumph over challenges and transform their
lives. Some, like Leonardo da Vinci, are famous; others are less well

known contemporary artists. In addition to creating visual art, one of them is an expert in health hazards and others are writers, scientists, poets, art historians, actors, singers, and songwriters. There are a substantial number of women in this group and it is racially and ethnically diverse. Featuring artists of different backgrounds who reflect the composition of our world is very important to me because I come from a family of multiple origins.

Although we combine into one humanity, we are unique individuals, and each person in this book has a story about illness and creativity that is all his or her own. Some who are now world famous never even thought of becoming artists until illness uncovered their creative abilities. Others, who were already established, improved their work in response to poor health. A transforming illness early in life can start a child toward a career in art, and in adulthood it can deepen the art of a practicing professional. When poor health late in life forces people to alter their way of working, they change, and new creativity emerges. Artists will persevere in the face of terminal illness and total paralysis; they share the determination to keep working even under the most difficult conditions.

Any illness can be a transforming illness. It may happen more than once in life, appear in different circumstances, and can even result from the wounds of war. Like most people, I hope for peace, but unfortunately that time has not yet come. To help the veterans of our current wars, I include a section in chapter 15 on artists wounded in battle who transform their lives through creativity.

Although some chapters are devoted to specific conditions, such as quadriplegia, artists with these challenges are discussed in other chapters as well. The book is arranged in five sections: an explanation of the transforming illness; turning to creativity because of poor health in childhood; how learning disorders and problems with vision and hearing shape the lives of artists; the effect of illness and accidents in mid and later life; and the ways that artists respond to illness by changing their lives and the lives of others. Artists with transforming illnesses are heroes of creativity and role models for us all. Working despite innumerable hardships, they shape the essence of our culture and create great beauty in our lives.

Introduction

My Story

Sweet are the uses of adversity,
Which, like the toad, ugly and venomous,
Wears yet a precious jewel in his head
—*William Shakespeare*

It was one of those beautiful mornings when you have the feeling that nothing in the world can go wrong—and then it does. I had just awakened to see sunlight streaming through the windows as my large, gentle, white cat, Bianca, softly walked across the quilt. "What a lovely day," I thought as I started to get out of bed. Then, just as I was pulling the covers away, my hand accidentally brushed across my lower left abdomen. To my surprise, I discovered a large, bumpy, uneven mass. It wasn't painful but it wasn't normal, and it felt awful to the touch.

Ovarian Cancer

That bumpy growth was ovarian cancer, but I didn't know it then. Even though I looked and felt extremely healthy, I had begun to notice that my previously flat stomach was starting to protrude. In a strange way, perhaps I was fortunate to have such a bulky, fast-growing tumor. A smaller growth might have been undetectable, but this large tumor propelled me into action. I went to the doctor, who ordered a sonogram and a CAT scan, and scheduled a date for surgery. An operation in December 1989 found the most aggressive kind of ovarian cancer—moderately to poorly differentiated clear-cell carcinoma. This type of tumor grows so rapidly that its cell walls barely form. An eight-and-a-half-centimeter tumor had already left the pelvic area and was growing into my abdominal cavity at such enormous speed that I could see my stomach getting larger. It had grown to that size in just two or three months, and if left untreated would have given me only another few months to live.

My gynecologist/surgeon, Dr. Michael O'Leary, didn't think I would last a year, even with surgery and chemotherapy. Each time I visited him after the operation, he was extremely surprised—and delighted—to see me still alive. From that time to today, I go to my oncologist, Dr. James Speyer, for regular checkups. After he gives me a complete roster of all the latest tests and they come back normal, I like to say, "So, I'm still too mean to die."

I am also grateful to be alive and I work at keeping it that way. In addition to standard medicine, I also benefit from alternative care. During chemotherapy I began practicing Soaring Crane Qigong, a set of five gentle exercises followed by a meditation, all specifically aimed at strengthening the immune system. These ancient Chinese exercises were compiled into a modern form by Master Zhao Jin-Xiang of China, and I learned them from Ronger Shen and her husband, Master Woo.[1] When Master Zhao came to New York, I studied with him, too. When I began doing Soaring Crane Qigong, my face was gray from chemotherapy, but as I continued, the ashen face staring at me in the mirror grew pinker week by week and my tiredness lessened. After a while, I noticed that during the meditations I had the experience of pulling the illness out of my body.

Even with exercise and meditation, the heavy doses of chemotherapy were still so exhausting that for three years after treatment I would cry from tiredness. Improved nutrition and extra vitamins helped but not enough. Then friends recommended Master Alan Lee, a Qigong healer and retired electrical engineer who is also a Grand Master in martial arts. Master Lee's healing sessions restored the energy I lost in chemotherapy, and they help me stay healthy to this day.

Despite my poor prognosis and even during my worst moments, I was determined to survive. I read books on overcoming illness and watched videos about people who had cancer and lived, treasuring every bit of information about anyone who became well again. When you see someone alive, you realize survival is possible. Through writing this book, I hope to become the same kind of role model that others have been for me.

Transforming Illness

Having ovarian cancer transformed my life. I had already started graduate school before I became sick, but as I recovered I completed an interdisciplinary doctorate in art and psychology. I am still an artist, but now I also write and speak about the psychology of art. Great changes in my life have often come during a time of poor health. I call these experiences transforming illnesses because afterward life is never the same. Things shift and new opportunities appear. Whenever I am sick now, I ask myself, "What is happening?" because an illness that feels like an impassible barrier can become a doorway to a new and more creative existence.

Ovarian cancer was not my very first transforming illness—that was my extremely poor eyesight. Without glasses or contact lenses I am legally blind. In response to my blurred uncorrected vision, I paint very clearly as a way to compensate for my visual disability. I had another transforming illness in 1972 when I was poisoned by an insecticide. My health was compromised for years, but it transformed my art. I started making large symbolic oil paintings and began showing my work in galleries and museums. My most recent transforming illness was Lyme disease. It began in the early autumn of 1998 and was diagnosed in the late summer of 1999. During that year of tiredness I began to make fine-art prints of my work using a computer. I like the inherent generosity of multiples because many more people can own the art that I have created.

All these experiences of poor health became transforming illnesses because each in its own way changed my art and my life. No two transforming illnesses are the same, just as no two people or no two moments in time are the same. Yet they are all effective. In their different ways they alter our work, they change our lives, and ultimately they transform our world.

Illness has profoundly altered my creativity, but this response is not unique to me. Creativity is a basic human capacity that extends across racial and cultural boundaries. Through their diversity and their determination, the artists in this book show that transforming illnesses are fundamental to the human condition.

Part I

Creativity,
Illness, and
Transformation

Chapter I

What Is a Transforming Illness?

Experts are those who pass through the
forest of thorns. —*Zen proverb*

What is a transforming illness and how does it work? Can anyone have a transforming illness? And why is creativity central to its effectiveness and so beneficial that artists choose to be creative when they are sick? I call it a "transforming illness" because the person changes as well as the work. The transforming illness is found throughout humankind, and we see it in shamans, who are the healers of their tribes. Mircea Eliade, the scholar of comparative religion, finds that shamans are only able to access their full abilities after recovering from an illness that transforms them.[1] The psychologist Henri Ellenberger calls the sickness preceding a breakthrough a "creative illness" since it affects productivity.[2] This chapter presents the components of a transforming illness and shows us how it acts to strengthen our lives.

Transforming Illness

A transforming illness is a time of poor health that profoundly alters your work, your outlook, and your life. It can occur at any age, from early childhood to the very end of existence, and can even happen more than once. It can also take many forms, but whether the transforming illness is a single episode of poor health or a chronic condition, things are never the same afterward. When the transforming illness occurs early in life, it can set the path for a future career; in adulthood it can alter a person's way of living and working. Lawrence Alma-Tadema experienced both stages.

Lawrence Alma-Tadema (English, born in Holland, 1836–1912) wanted to be an artist from his early childhood, but his family insisted that he become a lawyer.[3] The stress of attending academic classes and making art in his spare time took its toll on the boy, and he contracted tuberculosis. Believing the illness to be terminal, doctors told the family that he should be permitted to do as he wished. Once Alma-Tadema was allowed to be creative without feeling pressured, his health returned and he became an artist. A second transforming illness came in 1870, when he was an established painter living in Brussels. None of the doctors there knew what was wrong, so a friend advised him to consult with the famous English surgeon Sir Henry Thompson. While in London to see Thompson, Alma-Tadema met his future wife. Later that year he settled in the city, and it became the place of his greatest success.

Even people at the end of their life are not immune to a transforming illness. Intent on staying creative, artists will produce masterpieces in the face of imminent death. Ill from diabetes, **Paul Cézanne** (French, 1839–1906) wrote a letter to his son just days before he died.[4] "I continue working with pains," he admitted, "but finally something will come of it, and that is all that matters."

Change During Illness

There are as many variations of transforming illnesses as there are people who have them. Everyone is a potential candidate because no one is immune either to illness or to change. Sometimes during illness change occurs in a split second of insight, that moment of epiphany when the veil drops away and your path becomes clear. At other times it is a gradual transition to a completely new life. Usually the creativity that starts during a transforming illness begins in convalescence, when the acute phase is over and extended rest produces a need to fill the empty hours. Changes can even begin before an illness, but then poor health accelerates the transformation. Specific illnesses can also pose their own problems. To overcome these obstacles, artists like Janet Sobel and Consuelo González Amezcua change their mediums and alter their creative process in order to keep working.

Janet Sobel (American, born in Ukraine, 1894–1968) was an abstract artist who made drip paintings in the 1940s at the same time as Jackson Pollock.[5] When Sobel became allergic to paints, she changed her medium to crayon and pencil. Expressing herself through colorful drawings, she left a large body of work. **Consuelo González Amezcua** (American, 1903–1975) also changed mediums because of her health.[6] She was a sculptor who carved limestone into intricate designs by mixing imagery and abstraction. Amezcua developed breathing problems from inhaling rock dust, so she turned to drawing. By working on paper, she discovered her gift for color.

Physicians have recognized and written about the connection between illness, creativity, and self-transformation. In his book *Creativity and Disease*, the surgeon Philip Sandblom says, "In artists, the passion to create generates a will power strong enough to defy the worst disease."[7] And in his book *Radical Healing*, the psychiatrist Rudolph Ballentine writes, "Illness gives you the gift of helplessness, the overwhelming awareness that your way of being has, at least in some respects, failed."[8] He believes that an awareness of this situation offers opportunities for renewed health and fundamental change. Whenever a transforming illness occurs, it is a turning point in life, leaving you a different person from the one you were before. But this time of change before the new life begins may feel chaotic.

Illness as Chaos

Whenever we are sick and every time we are stressed we are in a state of chaos. The situation may not always look chaotic, but emotional and physical stress produce turmoil. And turmoil is chaos. Ilya Prigogine, who won the 1977 Nobel Prize in Chemistry for his work on chaos theory, describes chaos as a state of turbulence in which things may appear disordered, but actually have an inherent structure that can produce new order.[9] The transforming illness also looks disordered, but it, too, holds the seeds for a new existence. Illness appears to act like chaos in two ways. In an acute illness, a time of chaos comes, reorganizes our world, and leaves. In chronic illness, the chaos is ongoing, but artists like Dory Coffee persevere and their output increases.

Dory Coffee (American, b. 1942) has eye problems that impair her vision: pseudoexfoliation (flaking of the lens), glaucoma, and cataracts.[10] As a result she has so many floaters in her visual field that they collect, forming cloudy spots. Resilient and persistent, Coffee fights her floaters with blinks that temporarily move them away. Her joyful, bright paintings reveal nothing of this constant struggle. "It's a daily challenge," she says, "but I continue to paint more than ever."[11]

Chaos brings in the new. Our noisy, chaotic New Year's Eve parties usher in the new year, and in Hinduism and the Judeo-Christian Genesis, there is a period of chaos before the new world takes form.[12] We mirror creation through chaos whenever we are so upset that we feel impelled to change. During this period of inner chaos, which can be an experience of poor health, we are uncomfortable, but we also have a window of opportunity. Chaos theory is part of the science of nonlinear dynamics, but the transforming illness can also be explained using concepts from psychology.

Creativity as a Coping Mechanism

In psychology, the method we use to deal with a stressful event is called a coping mechanism. Using creativity to cope during poor health is a positive response to a difficult situation. Making a hard time more bearable is what the psychologist Salvatore R. Maddi calls transformational coping.[13] It is central to a transforming illness.

The portrait and landscape artist **Karen Koenig** (American, 1938–1994) coped by using creativity in two separate ways. She was diagnosed with von Hippel–Lindau disease (VHL) in her late twenties.[14] This rare genetic disorder affects the brain, eyes, spinal cord, kidneys, and, in its late stages, other parts of the body as well. At first she used painting to cope with the stress of illness. Even with diminishing sight in her left eye, Koenig continued to work using her right eye. When her right eye became impaired in 1992 and she could no longer paint, Koenig coped by writing poetry. "My art has been taken from me. . . . How could I endure?" she asked in a poem and then realized, "I could learn to cope."[15] She proudly stated, "I'm a fighter," while creating poems about life, her family, her medical treatments, and her cat, Parpie. "I have somehow coped," she wrote. "We will find ways. Life will still be good. Life will be different. But there are discoveries to be made at every juncture."[16]

There are both positive and negative coping mechanisms. For example, improving nutrition in response to an illness is a healthy coping mechanism; substance abuse is an unhealthy strategy. But even creativity itself can become a negative coping mechanism when it is used as an escape from reality to the detriment of your health; that is, if you ignored early warning signs of an illness and made art instead of going to a doctor. Creativity is an adjunct therapy that does not take the place of medical care; rather, it supplements that care in the pursuit of wellness. As creativity helps us cope through stress reduction and we make a difficult time more tolerable, we increase our hardiness.

Hardiness

Hardiness is the strength that helps us thrive despite obstacles. Maddi believes that hardiness has three components: commitment, control, and challenge.[17] Although Maddi did his psychological research in the corporate environment, his findings relate to creativity. Commitment, which is involvement, is an artist's commitment to work. Control is inherent in the decisions about what will or will not appear in the work of art. And challenge is a constant in the creative process, where problems are continually met and solved in the course of a work. Because creative activity contains the three components of hardiness, I believe that it can not only increase hardiness but produce hardiness as well.

Creating hardiness through commitment, control, and challenge is very important to people who have suffered prejudice. For them, creativity can build a sense of self-worth. **Sylvia Fragoso** (American, b. 1962) is an artist with Down syndrome who paints at the National Institute of Art and Disabilities (NIAD) in Richmond, California. Founded by the psychologist Elias Katz and his late wife, the art teacher Florence Ludins-Katz, NIAD has a spacious studio where challenged people make art and also have a chance to sell their work.[18] Painting at NIAD has given Fragoso both hardiness and self-esteem. "I am an artist," she says and sees herself as a practicing professional.[19]

Hardiness is especially important during illness, when adversity can be a constant companion. According to the American Psychological Association, hardiness helps both our physical and our mental health and is the key to resilience.[20]

Resilience

Resilience is our ability to adapt to new circumstances when life has changed in ways we could not have predicted and would not have chosen. It is the development of strength during a time of hardship. Resilience is our capacity to thrive despite major life stresses that could seriously threaten us. In their study of children born to underprivileged families on Hawaii's island of Kauai, the psychologists Emmy Werner and Ruth Smith show that even in the face of great risks, there are still individuals who will have successful, rewarding lives.[21] They are the resilient ones. Despite multiple problems at home, in school, and in the workplace, they overcome their difficulties and thrive. The artists portrayed in this book use creativity as a tool for resilience, to overcome adverse physical conditions.

Ezekiel Gibbs (American, 1889–1992) said his father came from Africa "around the end of slavery times" and his mother was a Cherokee.[22] Originally a farmer, Gibbs started painting at the age of eighty-three and spoke about resilience in the face of physical exhaustion. "Sometimes, when I think I'm just about played out, I sit down and rest awhile," he explained. "Then I just go to it again. You just have to keep on doing whatever you are doing."[23] It worked for him. Gibbs continued to paint until his death at age 103; he was believed to have been the oldest self-taught artist living and working in America.

The psychiatrist Michael Rutter describes resilience as a dynamic process containing protective mechanisms that modify the response to risk, lessen vulnerability, and generate turning points in life.[24]

Using Rutter's model, we see that creativity is also a dynamic process that can be used as a protective mechanism, generating turning points in both life and art. It also modifies the response to risk and lessens vulnerability because it releases stress and builds strength. It releases stress by allowing you to enter the world of art, where physical problems seem to diminish, and it builds strength through the achievement of goals met and tasks accomplished.

Self-Efficacy and Mastery

Because it is a dynamic process, creativity is not only a tool for resiliency, but can also generate what the psychologist Albert Bandura calls "self-efficacy."[25] Self-efficacy is the way we perceive ourselves and our belief that the things we do make a difference. These beliefs inspire motivation and determine our behavior. The best way to strengthen our sense of self-efficacy is through success and the experience of mastery. Mastery is success in performing a task or in the outcome of a situation. The artists in this book achieve self-efficacy through the experience of mastery by creating art despite physical challenges. The sculptor Michael Gregory acquired this ability through effort.

Michael Gregory (American, 1951–1995) believed he had to work twice as hard to succeed because of the prejudice against him. "One, I'm legally blind since birth," he stated, "and two, I'm black." Unable to see well, he worked with clay, a medium he could feel. Through effort and talent Gregory went from can collector to prize-winning sculptor featured on television and in newspapers. "If you don't try," Gregory insisted, "you don't know what you can do."[26]

According to Bandura, people find stress less upsetting if they think they can cope with it. One of the primary ways creativity helps artists cope is through compensation.

Artistic Projection as a Method of Compensation

A compensation response is an act of doing something to make up for something else that is missing. My clear style of painting is my compensation response to the blurred world I see without corrective lenses. But there is an additional aspect of compensation in art that seems magical but is really psychological. It occurs during what I call artistic projection: artists project themselves and what they desire into what they are creating; as a result, they are able to forget their physical condition at the time. Artistic projection differs from Freud's concept of an individual unconsciously projecting his or her thoughts onto another person.[27]

Artistic projection is a powerful experience because the work of art becomes a kind of virtual reality for artists. When artists draw or paint something, a psychological aspect of their being is projected into what they are making, and they actually sense themselves in their creations. When I draw a leg or a hand, I feel that leg or hand as I make it appear: there is a connection between me and what I create. Projecting oneself into a work of art is so intrinsic to artistic experience that it is routinely used in both Eastern and Western art education. My drawing and anatomy teacher at the Art Students League in New York City told us to "feel" the muscles in the bodies we drew. And when the eighth-century painter **Han Kan** (Chinese, d. 780) created a horse, he "became a horse."[28] Classical Japanese painting calls this concept *sei do*, or "living movement," and insists artists must completely feel and experience as reality everything they create in a work of art.[29]

Artistic projection and the need for compensation can fuse in the creative process. Compensation through artistic projection is extremely rewarding because it is so convincing to the artist. There is a stronger experience of compensation when creating a work of art than looking at it after completion. This is because when we paint something we are enveloped in the moment of its creation, becoming what we paint as it appears.

The Intensity of Artistic Projection

The feeling of projection is so intense that it becomes the artist's total world in that moment, blocking out all other stimuli. By forming a protective wall around the artist, artistic projection becomes a shield, creating a place where the outside world seems not to exist. Only what is currently being created seems real to the artist. In this reality the artist controls and partakes of everything, including the desired feeling of compensation. Satisfied, the artist continues to work to extend this experience as long as possible.

After a traffic accident damaged her health, **Frida Kahlo** (Mexican, 1907–1954) sought compensation in her art. "As the accident changed my path," she related, "many things prevented me from fulfilling the desires which everyone considers normal, and to me nothing seemed more normal than to paint what had not been fulfilled."[30] **Henri de Toulouse-Lautrec** (French, 1864–1901) walked with great difficulty, and although he loved horses, he was unable to ride. Instead, he created horses in his art. By drawing a horse, an artist becomes that horse during the creative process. As the horse leaped on canvas, part of Toulouse-Lautrec leaped with it—free if only for a short time from the confines of his physical limitations.

We all want things that are not currently in our lives, things that may even seem beyond our grasp. But compensation through creativity is a way for us to feel they are obtainable. Painting these desires gives our art enormous strength. Without an artist's longing and projection, the finished work is not as strong. There is less caring and less of the artist involved. Compensation and projection inspire masterpieces by bringing intensity and power to a work of art.

The Flow Experience

One of the most enjoyable aspects of the creative process is the experience of flow. The psychologist Mihaly Csikszentmihalyi describes flow as a time when we are totally absorbed and happy in an activity.[31] He connects this to creativity and says it happens when we are in the flow of things, when goals are clear, challenges are balanced by skills, and self-consciousness fades away. People in a state of flow feel motivated and are so deeply involved in their activity that it blocks out distractions from the external world.

The Renaissance artist **Francesco Mazzola** (Italian, 1503–1540), known as **Parmigianino,** gives us an extreme example of the flow state. The year was 1527 and Parmigianino was in his studio and so engrossed in painting that he was oblivious to the Sack of Rome that was going on in the streets outside.[32] He noticed nothing until the Germans were already in his house. They were so taken with his art that instead of pillaging they only asked for some watercolor drawings and left him unharmed.

Although not everyone may be able to block out the Sack of Rome, experiencing flow is a welcome relief for a person who is ill because it can lessen the sensation of pain. Flow shares some of its aspects with artistic projection and compensation, such as the motivation to continue working and the experience of total absorption in an activity. It is possible that these states may overlap. An artist who is experiencing compensation during artistic projection may also be in a state of flow. The experience of flow may be widespread because we are all capable of creativity.

Everyday Creativity and Eminent Creativity

Creativity is possible for everyone because we are inherently creative. It is part of being human. Every choice we make in life is based on a decision, and the decision is a creative response to the conditions at that moment. The psychiatrist Ruth Richards calls this *everyday creativity* and says we use this capacity whenever we improvise or cope with life during our many complex tasks, such as raising children, cooking food, solving problems at work, and landscaping the yard.[33] We can also activate our innate creativity during times of stress like physical illness.

Quentin Massys (Flemish, ca. 1465–1530)[34] and **David Cox** (English, 1783–1859)[35] were blacksmiths who started their careers as painters with everyday creativity. Massys had an illness that required extensive bed rest and Cox broke his leg. As a result, neither of them could work at the forge. But both began making art in response to the boredom of convalescence, not realizing it would become their career. Through continued effort, their everyday creativity turned into eminent creativity, which is the activity of professional artists. Everyday creativity and eminent creativity are not opposites but form a continuum of achievement in the creative process. No one starts by making masterpieces. Beginning work, even for the most eminent artists, is closer to everyday creativity, and it is only through effort that genius can emerge.

When a coping mechanism becomes a tool for personal growth, everyday creativity can change into eminent creativity. The psychologist Celeste Rhodes[36] says that art created to counteract feelings of deprivation can evolve into an achievement of excellence that leads to a more fulfilling life.

Creativity as Both Healing and Necessary

Creative activity becomes a vacation from the negative aspects of our lives. Immersed in a project, we may no longer be aware of our illness or stress. The psychologist Howard Gardner finds that work is so important to creative people that they do not thrive without it.[37] We see this in the lives of George Tooker and Otto Bluemner.

As a child, **George Tooker** (American, b. 1920) suffered from a chronically inflamed appendix and ulcerative colitis.[38] But when he was allowed to make art during convalescences, the symptoms would go away. Although Tooker was given art lessons, his parents wanted him to work in finance like his father, a municipal bond broker. Acceding to family pressure, he went to Harvard and then to Marine Corps Officers Candidate School. There Tooker's ulcerative colitis worsened drastically and in a few months he was discharged. After this serious illness, his parents relented and allowed him to become a painter. Making art dramatically improved his health. George Tooker is now eighty-seven and still painting.

Oscar Bluemner (American, born in Germany, 1867–1938) was not as fortunate.[39] Trained as an architect, Bluemner turned to painting and became a pioneer of modern art. In January 1935, he was badly injured in a car accident, and the next year his heart and his eyesight began to fail. A doctor concerned about Bluemner's poor health made a grave mistake—he insisted that the artist stop painting. Sick, in financial trouble, and forbidden to paint, Bluemner told friends he had lived beyond his usefulness. On January 12, 1938, he took his own life.

Art as Therapy

The healing aspect of creativity forms the core of art therapy. Kerry Smallwood, a breast cancer survivor, called the UCLA art therapy program "the most important non medical thing I did. . . . It was very powerful how the artwork accessed deeper emotions."[40] Making art can also help physical recovery. Through drawing and painting, a person may regain motor skills that had been lost or learn new ones to take their place. For the painter Trevor Wells, creativity that started in a hospital rehabilitation program became the beginning of a lifetime in art.

Trevor Wells (English, b. 1956) was a twenty-one-year-old apprentice carpenter when a rugby accident broke his neck at the fourth cervical vertebra.[41] Paralyzed from the neck down, Wells was a patient in a long-term care facility when someone suggested he try painting. "I had no interest in art," he recalls, but "it would help to pass the time and I agreed to give it a try." As a quadriplegic, he held his brush in a mouthstick. The first two paintings were not very good, "but when I was on my third picture, I was amazed," insists Wells. "I was actually painting."[42] He is now a member of the Mouth and Foot Painting Artists and creates landscapes that have earned him an international reputation.

The artists in this book accomplish their goals one small victory after another, until they add up to a great success. These victories are not triumphs over other individuals but over setbacks that keep us from fulfillment. This is a path open to everyone that hurts no one. We all have the potential for achievement, but it can sometimes lie dormant until illness provides the strength. Then, like Henri Matisse, we can triumph over adversity.

HENRI MATISSE

Few artists have had their life and work so affected by poor health as Henri Matisse (French, 1869–1954).[43] From his early years until his death at eighty-four, five transforming illnesses molded both the artist and his art.

The First Transforming Illness

Matisse's first transforming illness happened when he was a twenty-year-old law clerk. The chronic intestinal problems that had plagued him since childhood flared into an acute attack.[44] Whether it was appendicitis, ulcerative colitis, or a hernia, we will probably never know, but at that time the conditions were inoperable and rest was the only alternative.[45] A man in the next hospital bed recommended that Matisse try his hand at chromos to pass the time. Chromos were an early type of painting by numbers, and although his father disapproved, his artistic mother bought him two small chromos and a box of paints. "The moment I had this box of colors in my hands," revealed Matisse, "I had the feeling that my life was there."[46]

Before then, nothing had interested him, but from that moment on he thought only of painting. On returning to the law office, he would get up at dawn each morning to go to art class before work. Then, after a quick lunch, he would paint at midday, and again after six o'clock in the evening. Finally summoning his courage, Matisse begged his parents for permission to study art in Paris. In her biography of the artist, Hilary Spurling notes that at this point in his life Matisse was seen as a double failure. First, as a sickly child, he was deemed unfit to take over his father's successful grain and hardware business, so his younger brother August was chosen instead. Now he had failed again by not wanting to be a lawyer. His father was furious, but his mother interceded, and Matisse was allowed to go to Paris. As the train pulled out of the station, his father stood there, waving his fists and shouting, "You'll starve!"[47]

The Second Transforming Illness

The surgeon Philip Sandblom finds that Matisse's second transforming illness came when the artist was in his late forties.[48] Matisse was living in the windy town of l'Estaque. "I had caught bronchitis there," he recalled, "and I came to Nice to cure it."[49] Nice is known for its excellent weather, but it rained for a month after Matisse arrived and finally he decided to leave. The very next day the sun came out and it was so beautiful that he said, "I decided not to leave Nice, and have stayed there practically for the rest of my life."[50] Sandblom notes that moving changed Matisse's work, and "a very personal resplendent coloring was brought forth."[51] The bright sun in Nice enhanced the palette of one of the greatest colorists in the history of art.

The Third Transforming Illness

Matisse's third transforming illness, intestinal cancer, came when he was seventy. After an operation to remove the cancerous blockage, he had two pulmonary embolisms, the flu, and a prolapsed stomach, and remained an invalid for the rest of his life. Only able to stand for brief periods of time but unwilling to stop working, Matisse began to make art from his bed and from his wheelchair. While lying in bed he started to draw on the walls. Then he attached a piece of charcoal to a long bamboo fishing pole so he could draw on the ceiling. But these were black-and-white images and Matisse wanted to work in color.

Sitting in his wheelchair with scissors in hand, he began to cut brightly colored pieces of paper into a variety of shapes and sizes. "I call this drawing with scissors,"[52] explained Matisse, who directed his assistants to place the shapes on large sheets of white paper, or on canvases, or sometimes even on the wall. His home became full of colorful forms that soared and danced from room to room. By creating art that moved for him, Matisse compensated for his lack of mobility. With these brightly colored pieces of paper, a part of Matisse was no longer sitting in his wheelchair or lying on his bed. Through artistic projection, he was up leaping and swirling with the dancing paper forms. These cutouts are among the best works of art he ever produced.

The Fourth Transforming Illness

Matisse's fourth transforming illness happened soon after the intestinal surgery. According to Sandblom, the artist developed gallstones, and for over a year suffered from jaundice, fever, and severe pain.[53] Both stoic and stubborn, Matisse remembered his last operation and chose continued pain over the danger of surgical complications. And he kept on working. He was doing linoleum-cut illustrations for a book, and they took him "ten months of effort," said Matisse, "working all day and often at night."[54] Sandblom notes that in only one of these illustrations, *Increasing Anguish*, do we see the artist's suffering. A curving white outline shows the profile of a person in distress. With its mouth wide open and its head thrown back, the figure cries out for an artist who silently sublimates his pain into work. Of all the book's illustrations, this one is the best known.

The Fifth Transforming Illness

In 1942 Matisse had his fifth transforming illness. During the years after the operation his condition was sometimes stable while at other times it was poor. In an article for the *New York Times*, Alan Riding describes a new creative effort that began when the artist was so sick that he needed a night nurse. Monique Bourgeois, a young woman who lived nearby and was planning to be a nun, answered the request to work for him. Five years later, as Sister Jacques-Marie in the Dominican order, she had an idea that a chapel should be built in Vence, a town in the south of France, and asked Matisse to be the designer.

Matisse worked for four years on this project, called the Chapel of the Rosary. A small, exquisite structure, it is only twenty feet wide by fifty-nine feet long and sixteen feet high. He designed its stained-glass windows, a mural for the Stations of the Cross, the altar, and the priest's vestments, and also planned the architecture with the help of one of the Dominican monks, Brother Raysiguier. The artist remarked that he had always lived a very secular life, but now near its end came a project for the divine. Matisse was eighty-one years old when the chapel was complete, and he said, "I consider it to be my masterpiece."[55]

Illness and Determination

When the doctors gave up on him after the cancer operation, Matisse never gave up on himself—and he lived another thirteen and a half years. "Whether you can or not, you hold on," the artist said, and "when you're out of will power you call on stubbornness."[56] He was also grateful to be alive. "The time you live from now on is a gift from life itself—each year, each month, each day." [57]

Matisse felt that art was healing. When his friends were sick, he would have his work hung around their beds, convinced that the vibrant colors would help them get well. He insisted that we should create both from our strength and from our weakness because what we think is our weakness is often our greatest strength. "Only what I created after the illness," revealed Matisse, "constitutes my real self."[58]

Changing a Time of Sickness into a Transforming Illness

For Matisse and for us, poor health may hold the key to insight and evolution. When that happens, we transform. The next chapter explains how to unlock a difficult situation and turn a time of sickness into a transforming illness.

Chapter 2

Turning Poor Health into a Transforming Illness

I merely took the energy it takes to pout
and wrote some blues. —*Duke Ellington*

We can change more things in life than we realize, and one of the things we are most capable of changing is ourselves. One way to do this is by turning a time of poor health into a transforming illness, and this chapter explains the process by which it's done. Greater strength, enhanced creativity, deepened interests, and a stronger determination to keep going and thrive are just a few of the benefits of using a transforming illness to increase our capacity to adjust during stress. And the transforming illness is available to everyone.

Our Response to Illness Is a Source of Strength

The first thing that sets a transforming illness apart from other illnesses is our response to being sick. The way we react to life shapes our world. I have often thought that free will is not the ability to choose what we get but to choose our response to what life gives us. Most people would not select illness, yet it happens, and when it does, we have choices. One choice is to become mired in self-pity; another is to go forward.

"I've come to believe that people succeed *because* of crisis," says **Lisa Fittipaldi** (American, b. 1948), "not in spite of it."[1] In 1993 Fittipaldi developed vasculitis, an inflammation of the blood vessels that damaged her sight and is now affecting her hearing.[2] Before the illness she was a financial analyst in a Texas hospital, and it was only after becoming legally blind that she started to paint. Fittipaldi also writes and has a nonprofit foundation called The Mind's Eye that helps visually impaired and hearing-impaired children. "I want to encourage others to rise to whatever challenges life offers," she insists. "In the process of making lemonade from lemons, we ourselves are transformed."[3]

Acknowledging Feelings

Fittipaldi believes that "stress is a perception, not an event," and says, "It needs to be acknowledged and managed."[4] We can do this by recognizing our emotions, such as the sadness, anger, or fear we may have about being sick. Give those emotions permission to arise fully even though they may be painful. This may look like self-pity, but it is not. Self-pity keeps us caught in the same place. Allowing our feelings to come up will let us move forward in life. Expressing our feelings can be an experience of catharsis, providing us with a profound sense of relief. One way to do this is through creativity.

When **Edvard Munch** (Norwegian, 1863–1944) was a sick child, his aunt told him about the benefits of creativity.[5] As a boy, Munch had bronchitis and three bouts of rheumatic fever, and almost died at thirteen from tuberculosis, the disease that claimed both his mother and his sister. After his mother's death, her sister Karen Bjolstad came to live with the family and help raise the children. Realizing that young Edvard was very distressed, his aunt urged him to be creative.

Bjolstad, who made paintings and collages with the children, believed that fear loses its hold when it is expressed through words or images. Munch took her advice and art became a focus in his life. Bjolstad also persuaded Munch's father to allow his teenage son to change from engineering courses to art. In a diary entry from November 1880, Munch wrote, "I have now decided to become a painter."[6]

Repressing our emotions does not make them go away. According to the psychiatrist Carl G. Jung, they remain hidden in the unconscious where they can negatively affect our life.[7] When unexpressed sadness about a specific experience is not recognized, it can be projected onto other life events and result in depression. By acknowledging our feelings we are released from their grip, because after the feelings come up fully, they will pass. And when that happens we are ready for action.

Illness as a Challenge

Another method of turning a time of poor health into a transforming illness is to see it as a challenge. When artists respond to illness in this way, it activates them. Viewing illness as a challenge gives the impression that it is outside of us in an adversarial position. Perhaps it's an adversary we can banish, but if not, we can turn it into a benefit. When artists refuse to be conquered by poor health that does not diminish or disappear, they will rearrange their creative process and produce entirely new work. In the face of weakening eyesight, **Edgar Degas** (French, 1834–1917) changed from paint to pastel because chalk lines were easier to see, and he made masterpieces.[8]

Artists tend to look for challenges. By constantly setting new goals for themselves in their work, they extend this attitude into their lives. **Chuck Close** (American, b. 1940), who is painting some of his best work sitting in a wheelchair with a brush strapped to his wrist, thinks problem solving is overrated. "Problem creating is much more interesting," he says.[9] After a head-on car collision left her partly paralyzed, impaired her vision, and destroyed her memory, the artist **Ginny Ruffner** (American, b. 1952) remained determined to work, insisting, "It was as if life said to me, you want a challenge? Try this!"[10]

Convalescence and Change

We all have an inner artist, but the activities of life often override our creative potential. If we stop for a moment, it may appear. That is why creativity can emerge during convalescence. After the acute phase of illness is over, creative activity becomes a way to fill the empty hours of a long time of rest, as it did for Matisse when he was a young law clerk. Convalescence may also be an opportunity to assess our life, to look at what we are leaving behind and what new things are coming into view. Busy schedules leave us little time to be quiet and look within. But when we do sit quietly, layers can lift away, clearing the view and making us ready to try something new. Or we may discover that life has already begun to change. When a transforming illness comes after a life change has begun, it can accelerate the process, as it did for Odilon Redon.

The name of the illness that affected **Odilon Redon** (French, 1840–1916) is not known, but he described it as "being struck by exhaustion like a thunderbolt."[11] In childhood, a transforming illness turned him toward art (see chapter 4), but during the winter of 1894–95 another transforming illness accelerated the change in his work. For the first part of his life, Redon worked almost exclusively in black and white but had experimented with color. By the mid-1890s full-color pastels become his main form of expression, and after

1895 they attained their greatest strength. "I am leaving black behind me," said Redon, who became one of the greatest colorists of his time. And he later wrote, "I have married color."[12]

Intention and Determination as Power

With intention, anyone can convert a time of poor health into a transforming illness. What we intend with all of our power makes us act both consciously and unconsciously to achieve our goals. The desire to change may transform us in ways that we could not even imagine. This happened to me. I remember coming home from the hospital after my operation for ovarian cancer and wanting to stay well. I also remember sitting on my sofa and fervently wishing to make a difference in the world—just wanting my life to be of benefit to others. I had no clear idea what this would entail. I was a painter then. It was before I received my doctorate, before I taught psychology of art, and years before I even thought of writing this book. The universe works in mysterious ways.

Intention and determination helped **Pamela Mailman** (American, b. 1948) fight recurrent breast cancer.[13] Mailman, who had two operations, chemotherapy, radiation, and a stem cell transplant, expressed her experiences in art. She made a series of abstract pieces called *Cancer Cuts* about her surgeries, and produced realistic self-portraits showing the effects of her other medical treatments, such as hair loss from chemotherapy. "I'm a fighter," says Mailman about the illness. "It's just made me stronger."

"Perseverance Furthers"

Intention and determination fuel perseverance and "perseverance furthers." These two words are from the *I Ching*, also called the *Book of*

Changes.[14] I say them to myself as encouragement and also tell myself to "just keep going." Artists tend to be persevering. At least this is my experience based on the ones I know and the artists' biographies I have read. Intention fires their perseverance, but it is not always in-born. Like many traits, perseverance can be learned. Despite difficul-ties in the creative process and hardships in life, it keeps us going.

Perseverance is central to **Michael "Nick" Nichols** (American, b. 1952), one of the world's leading wildlife photographers. *National Geographic* magazine, where Nichols works, calls him "the Indiana Jones of Photography" because nothing stops him.[15] He has had at least twenty bouts of malaria and once came down with falciparum malaria (cerebral malaria), hepatitis, and typhoid fever at the same time. He got well and kept going. Bitten by bees, ants, and scorpions, Nichols is sometimes covered with insects while photographing. He perseveres through all of this because of his concern for endangered species. "I'm kind of on a mission," he says about the animals, "working really hard to tell their story, speaking for them since they can't speak for themselves."[16]

Choose to Create

Life isn't easy. And when misfortune tempts us to stagnate in self-pity, know that there is always a choice. We can be self-indulgent or we can create. Even accidents that happen during traveling will not stop artists like Helen Ramsaran, who choose to be productive.

When **Helen Evans Ramsaran** (American, b. 1943) was crossing a street in Ghana, she fell waist deep into an open drain and broke her left ankle. After an operation, she convalesced with the family whose guest she was in Ghana. "I decided I could do two things," states Ramsaran. "I could wallow in self-pity or continue working on my wax sculpture."[17] She chose creativity, saying, "I finished the last half of my work in my room." When the ankle healed, Ramsaran, who is African American, continued her travels. The trip to Africa was important to her, and she visited Zimbabwe, South Africa, and Malawi.

Illness Is Not Necessary for Change

Do not make yourself sick in order to have a transforming illness. It doesn't work that way. People who are in excellent physical health can also experience profound self-transformation. Making yourself sick is a psychological problem, not a path of personal growth. A time of poor physical health marshals all of your strength to deal with a seemingly uncontrollable situation. When people make themselves sick, *they* control the events, and instead of growing through a journey of self-evolution, they spiral into mental illness.

Individuals who present themselves as sick or make themselves sick to receive attention and care may have Munchausen syndrome, or factitious disorder.[18] A variation is Munchausen syndrome by proxy, where another person, usually a child, is presented as sick. The child may be intentionally injured and in some cases may even die because of a parent's need to seem extremely concerned and seek medical attention. People with these disorders require psychological help but may be resistant. For them, self-transformation would be the maintenance and acceptance of their own ongoing good health and the good health of others.

Frida Kahlo (Mexican, 1907–1954) may have had Munchausen syndrome. Although she suffered from genuine health problems, such as spina bifida, polio, and the aftermath of a traffic accident, Kahlo had more than thirty-two operations. Not all of them were necessary. She used these procedures as a way to attract attention and keep her wandering husband, the painter Diego Rivera, by her side. "I'm a champion of the world," she insisted, "when it comes to surgical interventions."[19]

See Yourself in a New Life

Another method to make poor health into a transforming illness is to see yourself and your life in a new way. When I look at my life before ovarian cancer, it actually feels like another existence. It also seems as if a new life began while I was sick, although I didn't realize it at the time. I still have the same name and address—but somehow this is the present and that is the past. When you feel as if you are in a new life, you are more likely to see things differently and try new activities. The painter Lori Schmitt's new life started with art supplies.

"I discovered a love of art at the age of ten," recalls **Lori Sue Schmitt** (American, b. 1969), "when my parents bought me my first art kit."[20] She was born with arthrogryposis multiplex congenita, a muscle disorder that causes contractions of the joints, resulting in very limited movement in the arms and legs. Operations in childhood to help the condition failed, leaving Schmitt a quadriplegic. The art kit that came at Christmas was for mouth painting, and to her great joy, Schmitt discovered she was talented. Even though she was a business major and then prelaw in college, she returned to painting in 1992. Schmitt, who uses an electric wheelchair, paints by holding a brush in her mouth, as she did with her childhood gift. Her husband, Joe, who is also disabled, helps to set up her palette. Now president of her building's managing board, Schmitt also has a bird sanctuary where she cares for injured and stranded birds.

Know That You Can Help Others

Despite multiple disabilities, you can always help others. Service is one of the best parts of a transforming illness, and there are so many ways to be of assistance. Even if you are lying in bed unable to move, smile at someone—it will make his or her day. When we are sick, physical problems feel limiting, but they can be freeing. Carolyn Lyons Horan, an artist and an art instructor, uses them as a bridge for communication.

Carolyn Lyons Horan (American, b. 1957) is dedicated to helping others.[21] An advocate of art education, she has had multiple sclerosis since 1985 and arthritis since 1987. "Art gives children an opportunity to express themselves in a creative way," explains Horan, "and provides an important outlet for communication."[22] While teaching art to seniors, she finds that her own challenges make her more sensitive to their needs. Since she walks with a crutch, she understands their difficulties in moving and standing. Horan's hand tremor becomes a transforming illness as she helps her elderly students be creative despite their tremors. "Transformation," she says, "is taking something from the experiences of life and growing from it."[23] Horan also believes that her challenges strengthen her commitment to art and reminds us that "less than perfect is a lot more interesting than perfect—and a lot less boring."[24]

Creativity in the Transforming Illness

There are many ways to be creative. There are active ways when we are making art, and quiet ways when we are looking at the world as inspiration for our work. Creativity covers an enormous scope of activities, and what defined fine art in the past has opened up to include mediums such as collage and knitting. Creativity is central to the transforming illness, and in the next chapter we come to understand its importance and learn how to adapt it for our lives.

Chapter 3

Creativity and the Transforming Illness

Whoever undertakes to create soon finds
himself engaged in creating himself.
—Harold Rosenberg

reativity is one of the great joys in life—and we are all in-
nately creative. Central to the transforming illness, creativity
is the engine that drives its core. This chapter shows how we
benefit from creativity and the many ways we can be creative. But why
is creativity so important?

Benefits of the Creative Process

Turning to creativity in response to illness gives us an enormous return on our time and effort. By taking our minds off distress and
redirecting our attention to the work in front of us, we lessen the experience of pain. As a rule, our minds can concentrate on only one
thing at a time, so focusing on the creative process makes us less aware
of discomfort. "When I'm making jewelry or knitting," says **Phyllis
Teiko** (American, b. 1948), "my joints don't hurt as much."[1] Teiko
has Sjogren's syndrome, an autoimmune disease that dries her mucous
membranes and produces severe joint pain and stiffness. "I have

fibromyalgia," she explains, "but I'm not conscious of it while making art. The pain feels further away and doesn't bother me as much." Teiko is a fabric artist who makes wearable knitted sculpture and constructs beads from cloth. For pain management she insists that "creativity works better than other activities such as reading, watching a film, or listening to music. They don't have the same effect."

Creativity provides an active rest during which we are awake and alert yet doing something that is stress reducing. It also counteracts the boredom and isolation of convalescence, making it less lonely and more productive. When we are sick and believe we can do so little, creativity imparts a sense of accomplishment that gives us the strength to keep going, keep creative, and get well.

For **Darcy Lynn** (American, b. 1956), creativity became a source of strength in her fight against immunoblastic lymphoma, which is a non-Hodgkin's lymphoma.[2] She made paintings of herself bald from chemotherapy, showing her surgical scar, her Hickman catheter, and the sites of her bone marrow harvest, and then well again after the treatments. Lynn also did portraits of her doctors and nurses, and pictures of the healing purple seals that appeared to her in a vision when she was under oxygen in intensive care. Her experience was so impressive that she was invited to give lectures to medical personnel about the role of creativity in healing. "I fought illness," says Lynn, "with the best weapon I had—my art."[3]

By providing a time of introspection and concentration in an otherwise busy life, illness gives us a chance to look within and uncover talents we never knew we had. It also helps us to move forward by taking those talents out into the world. In addition, expressing our stress through art brings it out into the open where it can be alleviated. Creative activity also restores a sense of control in a life thrown out of control by illness. Lack of control can destabilize the immune system, while restoring control enhances the immune response. You decide what is going to be on the paper or canvas and control the world you create. By compensating for what is lost due to illness, creativity restores a sense of wholeness that can produce a feeling of well-being comparable to restoring wholeness in life.

Creativity is a tool for personal growth. What starts as an effort at compensation can turn into a journey of achievement and self-realization. It is also a way to help others. By creating works of art, we make the world more beautiful and give joy to generations to come. And creativity is healing. By relieving the mind from worry, enhancing the immune response, and reestablishing a sense of wholeness, creativity helps us stay well.

Creativity as a New Experience

Try to be creative, even if this is new for you. Your first attempts may not look like the results you want, but don't be afraid. Everyone makes mistakes. Don't let them stop you: fix the errors, keep going, and you will get better. It is unusual to be excellent at something you have never tried before. With art, as with many things, improvement comes through effort. It did for the painter Peter Paul Drgac, and his progress became motivation.

Peter Paul Drgac (American, 1883–1976) was a retired grocer who began painting at eighty-five. It started when Drgac saw a flower box that he thought needed decorating. Although his first attempt to paint flowers on the box was a failure, he lay in bed that night thinking about how to improve his work. "I felt the assurance that if I would practice," said Drgac, "I would be able to draw those flowers and anything else I wanted."[4] He bought poster boards to make paintings and also began decorating every surface in his house. From that time until his death at ninety-three, Drgac produced hundreds of works of art.

The Many Ways to Be Creative

There are many ways to be creative. Some people can stand at an easel and paint on canvas with oils or acrylics. But it is not necessary to be able to stand to make art. For those who sit, there are easels that adjust to a variety of heights that can easily be used by a person in a chair. Sitting in a wheelchair is just as effective as sitting in any other kind of chair. Working on paper with watercolors or acrylic paints can be done on a table and also takes less energy. For those lying down, it may be easier to draw with pencil, charcoal, or crayons, although Frida Kahlo painted in bed. There are also tabletop easels that can be adjusted for a person lying down. For sculpture, many kinds of clay are available, including those that harden to extend the life of the work. Fabrics and yarns are very versatile, and artists use them for weaving, knitting, embroidery, and sculpture. The idea that only certain materials and methods are suited to fine art has expanded from painting, drawing, and sculpture—to every medium imaginable.

Originally a figurative painter, **Leonilson** (Brazilian, 1957–1993) began incorporating needlework into his art in 1989.[5] After being diagnosed with AIDS in 1991, he left painting and turned more completely to the less strenuous art forms of sewing and embroidery until his death. His fabric work was exhibited at the Museum of Modern Art in New York and the Tate Gallery in London. Leonilson shared his show at the Museum of Modern Art with **Oliver Herring** (German, b. 1964, lives in New York), who exhibited knitted sculptures. Herring is not ill but finds knitting with Mylar to be a method of self-expression. One of his knitted statues, *Wounded Knee,* shows a sitting figure mending its knee. Speaking about the creative process, Herring says, "I think we all want to do stuff that we are too shy to really do, but deep down we have it in us."[6]

If medical expenses are high and purchasing art supplies is not possible, photo collages are an excellent and inexpensive means of self-expression. You can create beautiful and striking compositions by cutting out photographs from newspapers and magazines and pasting them on paper. Popular in surrealism, a twentieth-century art movement, this technique is still used by professional artists today.

Adjustments in Creativity

Creativity is so central to artists' lives that they will make major adjustments in the way they work in order to stay creative. When poor health bars them from their usual creative process, they will find other ways that are more suitable to their physical condition. Some artists will remain in their field but alter the work they do, like Dale Chihuly, while others such as Margaret Bourke-White and Cecilia Beaux find an entirely new form of creative expression.

A 1976 auto accident threw **Dale Chihuly** (American, b. 1941) into the windshield of a car.[7] He needed 256 stitches in his face, permanently injured his right foot and ankle, and lost the sight in his left eye. Even without the depth perception of binocular vision (seeing with two eyes), Chihuly continued to blow glass until 1979, when he dislocated his shoulder while bodysurfing. These two accidents changed his life and his art. No longer able to work as a solitary artist, Chihuly now draws a design and his team blows the glass into a three-dimensional sculpture. With teamwork his art has evolved from small single objects into large complex pieces containing multiple sculptures. Chihuly enjoys team creativity. "It inspires me to be working with a group of people on an idea," he explains. "It's the way things happen for me."[8]

Visual art requires physical effort, and artists who are ill may find they have to leave their field completely in order to stay creative. **Margaret Bourke-White** (American, 1906–1971) was a photographer and a writer. But when Parkinson's kept her from taking photo-journalism assignments, she concentrated on writing.[9] After a fall that broke her hip, the portrait artist **Cecilia Beaux** (American, 1855–1942) could no longer paint. Instead, she started to write and published her autobiography, *Background with Figures.*[10]

Inspiration

There are as many ways to be inspired as there are works of art and those who create them. Some artists look for inspiration in the people and scenes of their daily life, while others find it in poetry and books, or even in news broadcasts. Don't worry about inspiration because you can start without it. I notice that much of my inspiration arises while I work. Inspiration can also come from the materials we use to make art.

"I am always on the lookout for unusual and exotic fabrics," says **Rebecca Abell** (American, b. 1949), "and I like to let the fabric inspire the quilt in many instances."[11] A self-taught artist, she makes large quilts for beds and smaller works of fabric art that are framed.[12] Abell was a registered nurse until 1988, when she was severely injured while lifting two hospital patients in one day. Although she pulled her neck and shoulders so badly that she damaged the nerve complex leading to her arms, Abell still finished her shift. "That was my last day of nursing," she recalls.[13] Diagnosed with brachial plexus nerve damage, Abell turns her dedication to art. "My arms don't work well," she admits. In response, she uses a frame to hold the fabric near to her while sewing. "To some degree I am almost always in pain," she reveals, "but I keep working."[14]

View the World in a Creative Way

By being creative you may think of yourself differently. And when you look at the world, it may be with new eyes, the eyes of an artist. As a creative person, when you see a tree, you may not only appreciate its beauty but also find yourself contemplating how it would look in one of your works of art. Many artists regard the world in this way, partly as objective reality and partly as possible subject matter for their work. Sometimes when I look at something beautiful like a sunset, I will not only stare at it intently but also decide which colors I would use to paint it. This way of looking and analyzing what is in front of me helps commit the scene to memory and makes it available for future use. Looking, as well as painting, is part of creativity. We often take the external world for granted, but if we look at it intently, we may see objects in a new light and discover things we never saw before. Engaging the world with our senses is an aspect of the creative process that is available even to those like Joseph Turner who are very ill.

One day toward the end of his life, painter **Joseph Mallord William Turner** (English, 1775–1851) secretly disappeared from London.[15] His doctor had told him that his heart was failing, and knowing he did not have much time, Turner went to his cottage in Chelsea. There, near the banks of the Thames River, he could be close to the ships and water he loved and that were the subjects of his art. A few months later he died. Due to illness, Turner did very little art in these last months. But even though he may not have been actively painting, he was partaking of the receptive side of the creative process by looking at the boats and the water. His bedroom had a view of the river, and there was also a passage from the bedroom to a balcony on the roof where he could see both sunrise and sunset on the water. By quietly looking, Turner was an observer through whom sensation was being made ready for the canvas, even if he could no longer paint. All creativity has this duality, the dynamic physical work and the contemplative absorption of stimuli. Like the act of painting, seeing and thinking are integral parts of the creative process.

Working with Challenges

Who among us is perfect? Imperfection is a part of being human. It also is one of the things that make us different from one another. Just as no two people are alike, no two people are imperfect in exactly the same way. But sometimes illness can create what we consider to be such large imperfections that we think of them as impediments. Instead, we should regard them as challenges. And challenges can both make and deepen a career. For some people, challenges can act like a gust of wind directed into a tunnel. When wind blows in the open, it can be strong, but squeeze the same amount of wind through a narrow area and it gains a much greater velocity. Talent denied its usual expression can become magnified when forced into an alternate route. This happened to Katherine Sherwood when a situation that seemed to end her career became the start of greater success.

Katherine Sherwood (American, b. 1952) was forty-four and teaching her art class at Berkeley when she had a major stroke that paralyzed her entire right side.[16] Through therapy, Sherwood regained many of her lost functions, but her right hand, which she used for painting, remained immobile. With determination and effort, Sherwood taught herself to paint left-handed. And then something extraordinary happened—her painting got better and brought her greater recognition than she ever had before. "I think my left hand is a more natural painting hand," says Sherwood. "It's also more enjoyable."[17] She firmly believes that painting helped her recover. "Until I went through this experience," admits Sherwood, "I never appreciated how therapeutic art could be."[18]

Protect Your Creativity

Creativity is not only something we are all capable of but also something to cherish and protect. We should not ignore what people say about our work but rather reflect on and evaluate it. While people are rarely intentionally cruel, they may mean well but can be misguided or prying. Edward Burne-Jones learned self-protection at an early age.

Edward Burne-Jones (English, 1833–1898) turned to art as a sickly child confined to his home.[19] His older sister had died before he was born, and his mother died the day after giving birth to him, leaving him to be raised by a father who was severely depressed. Art became the boy's lifeline. Burne-Jones described himself as "unmothered, with a sad papa, without sister or brother, always alone," yet he added, "I was never unhappy because I was always drawing."[20] As a child he was told that it was a sin to call the model city he was building "Jerusalem" because it was not the real Jerusalem. Burne-Jones rebelled and grew up to be a painter of symbolism. He also protected himself against his governess, Miss Sampson, who was a well-meaning person with a prying nature. Whenever she asked him what he was thinking about, the young boy would always answer, "Camels."

Encourage Others to Be Creative

Compassion is one of the most wonderful connections we can make with someone, and it is a welcome bond during the isolation of illness. One of the ways to be compassionate is through encouraging a sick person to be creative. At a time when illness brings weakness, creativity can inspire strength. Be encouraging rather than overly critical, because harshness may discourage creativity. Making art during illness should raise a person's self-esteem, not lower it. Remember, it is unusual for people to excel at something creative the first time. Your patience and positive attitude will allow people to treat themselves the same way. Encouragement brings enjoyment, and it helped Norval Morrisseau begin a career.

When **Norval Morrisseau** (Canadian, b. 1932), also known as **Miskwaabik Animiiki,** or Copper Thunderbird, was nineteen, he contracted tuberculosis.[21] It was a common disease in Native American communities, and he was sent to the Fort William, Ontario, long-term care facility. Morrisseau started to paint in the hospital and also met a woman there who inspired him to continue. Her name was Harriet Kakegamic, and she taught him a form of her native Cree writing. Morrisseau used the Cree writing in his signature on the paintings he made showing the imagery of his Ojibwe tribe. He became a professional artist and Harriet Kakegamic became his wife.

The Benefits of Gifts

Gifts are an expression of caring, and gifts of art supplies can inspire creativity. But before you think of giving art supplies to a sick person, take a moment to find out if he or she has enough food and other necessities. The financial strain of illness can be enormous, and sometimes friends and family don't realize how much this worries a sick person. A few kind questions can determine whether he or she has enough food and money to pay for medical bills. If essential needs have been met, then art supplies can help pass the long hours of convalescence. Sometimes a gift of art supplies can start a career or change the work of an established painter, as it did for Vanessa Bell.

Vanessa Bell (English, 1879–1961) was the older sister of Virginia Woolf and a central figure among the British writers and artists called the Bloomsbury group.[22] On a trip to Italy in 1912, Bell contracted the measles. While she was convalescing in bed, a friend, the painter and art critic **Roger Fry** (English, 1866–1934), brought her sheets of colored paper to pass the time. She cut the paper into small squares and pasted them onto a board, making mosaics. After being sick, Bell had a breakthrough in her art. Formerly a realistic painter, she started to abstract her images, using larger patches of color and sometimes outlining the forms in black, influenced by the colorful paper mosaics she made in bed.

People who are not well enough to make visual art or are not interested in it might prefer writing. This could be a story, an essay, a diary, or some poems. Just as we are all creative, we also have an inner poetry that expresses our unique way of looking at the world. If the person is not well enough to sit at a computer, buy a notebook. The French author Marcel Proust wrote whole novels in bed.

The Transforming Illness in Childhood

When a transforming illness strikes at a young age, it can set a child on a new life path. We see how the careers of the world-famous artists in chapter 4 began during a childhood illness. But they did not do it alone. Family and friends nurtured the sick child by providing encouragement and art supplies, so that young talent was able to emerge.

Part 2

Illness in Early Life

Chapter 4

Childhood Illness as an Opportunity

Difficulty . . . is the nurse of greatness.
—*William Cullen Bryant*

N
o act of human kindness is ever wasted" are the words on the wall of a nursing station in a California hospital's pediatric ward. Kindness is important for everyone, but for a sick child it can make all the difference in the world.

Resilience, Caregivers, and Art Supplies

Kindness and support can promote resilience in a sick child, creating inner strength and a better life. When the psychologists Emmy Werner and Ruth Smith studied children with multiple hardships, they found that some of them had difficulties later in life but that others were very resilient.[1] In spite of poverty and family problems, these individuals, who were originally considered to be at risk, went on to have successful lives. Looking for clues to their resilience, Werner and Smith found that each child was helped by at least one supportive person and that a good relationship is life changing. The artists in this chapter had serious health problems as children that placed them at risk, and they also had the benefit of at least one supportive person: a parent, a sibling, or a friend. But there is also a difference—the people who supported them encouraged creative activity, and some even provided the children with art supplies. These acts of kindness and generosity not only gave the children joy but also changed our world by inspiring acclaimed art. When we use creativity as a tool for resilience, hardships in life become opportunities in disguise.

Art supplies are essential for creativity to blossom. When we give them to a child, we are saying, "You are creative and capable of making something wonderful." Without pencils, paints, or crayons, a child's drawing would remain an unknown wish, a thing of beauty never realized.

ANDY WARHOL

The gifts and attention Andy Warhol (American, 1928–1987) received during a childhood illness shaped the work he made later as an adult. Although they had very little money, Warhol's family bought him art materials and encouraged his creativity, hoping to distract him from the discomforts of illness and help him get well. Little did they realize that their acts of love and kindness toward a bedridden child would influence the course of twentieth-century art.

When he was eight years old, Warhol had rheumatic fever.[2] It was the 1930s, before antibiotics, and the disease progressed to chorea, also called Saint Vitus' dance. This illness of the central nervous system made Warhol's hands shake so violently that he had trouble feeding himself, tying his shoelaces, or holding a piece of chalk to write on the blackboard in class. The other children in his Pittsburgh elementary school, who used to be jealous of him because he was the teacher's pet, now picked on him. Once an excellent student, Warhol grew terrified of school. As the chorea worsened, his doctor prescribed a month of bed rest. When the month was up, a frightened Warhol had to be forcibly carried back to school. The trauma caused a relapse, and he was sent home again. This time the disease turned his skin a whitish color interspersed with brown patches—a coloration Warhol would have for the rest of his life—and the other children starting calling him "Spot." Ostracized as an outsider, he became a keen observer, something that was central to his career as an artist.

Throughout his illness, Warhol's mother, Julia, cared for him with intense devotion. She had lost a baby daughter to influenza and was determined that her son should live. The Warhol family was not wealthy. Andy's father, Ondrej, was a laborer for a construction company, and when he was out of work Julia cleaned houses part-time. She also sold flowers she made from tin cans. As a creative person herself, Julia believed her son would recover through creativity. Two of Warhol's biographers, Victor Bockris and Bob Colacello, discuss the art supplies and attention he received during his illness. Julia bought him coloring books, movie magazines, comic books, and paper doll cut-outs, and his older brother Paul gave him a camera and taught him art techniques. These art supplies and creative activities not only comforted the bedridden Warhol but also shaped the art that made him famous.

Coloring the pages in his coloring books helped Warhol maintain his mental focus during his bout of chorea and also acted as occupational therapy by giving him an incentive to steady his hands. As he returned to health, the boy filled in a stream of coloring books. The silk-screen prints he made years later show their influence. The images in the prints are often drawn in black lines with swatches of color placed on top of them. They appear to be colored in, with colors going over the lines as sometimes happens in coloring books.

Warhol also enjoyed the movie magazines and comic books his mother bought for him. He cut out pictures from the movie magazines and pasted them onto paper, making collages. Julia believed that using scissors would also help to steady his hands. As an adult, Warhol would put multiple images on a single canvas, as he had in the collages he made as a child. Paul helped him write letters requesting autographed photos of movie stars. Years later, portraits of actresses like Marilyn Monroe and Elizabeth Taylor became important images in his work. The magazines also showed him the world of glamour and celebrity that would later become his life.

Paul's gift of a camera was crucial for the young boy's artistic development. When Warhol grew up, all of his art was based on photography. Paul also showed him how to transfer an image from a comic book onto a piece of paper: first they poured wax on the comic strip and then they turned the wax over and pressed it onto a piece of paper, using a spoon to rub in the image. As an adult, Warhol transferred pictures from other mediums onto the canvases of his paintings. He also liked to shine a flashlight through a comic book's page, projecting its form onto another surface. As a professional artist, he projected images onto canvases that he would then paint. Warhol's favorite comic book characters were Popeye and Dick Tracy, and he made paintings of both of them in adulthood.

Even the paper dolls became part of Warhol's later work. When he came to New York, they influenced the advertisements he made for the I. Miller shoe company.[3] In one ad, the shoes have tabs like the paper dolls' clothing, and in another advertisement there is a paper doll whose body, arms, and legs can be cut out and connected. Matt Wrbican, an assistant archivist at the Andy Warhol Museum, told me that the museum owns one of the early advertisements and has assembled the doll.[4] When Warhol recovered, he started taking Saturday-morning art classes offered free of charge at the Carnegie Museum of Art. Classes are important for professional artists. I wonder how many potential Andy Warhols we have lost because their families were poor and there was no free art education available to them.

Children and Creativity

Children delight in creating art, and it empowers them. Making marks on paper or canvas announces both their existence and their creativity. For a child, the world becomes a different place when it contains their creations. During illness creativity takes on extra importance. Children feel better while they are making art, have increased self-esteem whenever they look at their art, and even feel good when the art is not in view, because they are now art-making individuals. It doesn't matter if they become professional artists; all they need is an opportunity to be creative. Creativity imparts a feeling of wellness that helps the healing process.

This happened to me. When I was about seven years old and sick in bed, I received a big box of crayons. I don't remember my illness, but I remember those crayons. Holding them in my hands made me forget I was sick, and I could hardly wait to use them. I got better soon afterward. The psychologist Ernst Kris says that making art during illness is natural for children, because they tend to be creative during times of stress.[5] Creativity brings them into a world of their own making where they feel happier, stronger, and safe. Creativity is in all of us like seeds in the earth, and art supplies are the rains that allow those seeds to sprout and blossom.

ALBERT PINKHAM RYDER

A gift of art supplies changed the life of Albert Pinkham Ryder (American, 1847–1917) when he developed a severe reaction to a childhood vaccination.[6] The vaccine was most likely for smallpox, because it was the only one commonly available at the time.[7] Ryder developed an inflammation of both eyes that became a chronic condition, leaving him with poor vision for the rest of his life. When he became sick from the vaccine, his compassionate father bought him art supplies. Ryder's father knew his son's eyesight was affected, but he also knew that the boy loved to draw. Even though illness had damaged Ryder's vision, his father encouraged him and the boy believed he could become an artist. "When my father placed a box of colors and brushes in my hands," recalled Ryder, "and I stood before my easel with its square of stretched canvas, I realized that I had in my possession the wherewithal to create a masterpiece that would live throughout the coming ages." Then he added, "The great masters had no more."[8]

Ryder was a quiet, gentle boy who showed a love of art from the age of four, when he would lie on the floor totally absorbed in picture books and drawing. Later, when one of his seafaring brothers brought home magazines with reproductions of art from the Louvre, Ryder was so fascinated that he copied the names of the artists into his notebook. After the vaccination, Ryder's eyes remained weak and were often inflamed. He had trouble seeing small details, and bright lights bothered him. Reading was such a strain that he never progressed past grade school. But the weakness in Ryder's eyes became a strength in his painting. When he had difficulty duplicating details in nature that he found hard to see, Ryder gave his paintings the power of broad swaths of color, often working with a palette knife loaded with pigment. Eventually he started painting from his imagination, caring less for realism than emotional expression. Ryder's diminished sight became a foundation for his art.

Eye Problems and Creativity

If Ryder's father had not bought art supplies for his son with injured eyes, we would not have Ryder's paintings today. Like those of the Warhol family, his gifts influenced the history of American art. Often we think we have to be perfect to accomplish something. If this were true nothing would ever be accomplished, because none of us is perfect. If I had been told as a severely nearsighted child that I could not become an artist, I would have been devastated. Like many people with impairments, children with eye problems may want to enhance what is weak or create something to replace what is missing. Disabilities can inspire accomplishment, and confronting challenges through creativity is a way to become stronger. This happened to Mathew Brady.

MATHEW BRADY

"Brady used art," states his biographer Mary Panzer, "to forge a relationship between photography and history."[9] He accomplished this with very poor vision. "A violent inflammation of the eyes"[10] when Mathew Brady (American, ca. 1823–1896) was a teenager left him with diminished sight for the rest of his life. But despite this difficulty, he was interested in art. While traveling in upstate New York to seek medical treatment for his failing eyesight, young Brady met William Page, an artist who gave him lessons and encouragement. Later, when Brady arrived in New York City as a young man in the 1840s, it was most likely Page who introduced him to Samuel F. B. Morse. Although Morse is best known for inventing the telegraph, he was also an established painter who gave instruction in the new medium of daguerreotypes. Brady was so taken with this type of photography that by his early twenties he began to win prizes in national competitions.

With a talent for business as well as art, Brady established a photography studio in New York and another one in Washington. He posed clients for their portraits and arranged the lighting, but with poor eyesight he could neither focus the camera nor adjust its mechanisms. Panzer says that this was well known, yet he was still admired as an eminent artist who employed the best talent in his studio and trained them to be professionals. Images taken by Brady and his assistants have shaped our view of nineteenth-century America. His portraits of Lincoln are very well known, but his most famous work is the series of photographs depicting the Civil War. Brady saw the war as his destiny. "I felt that I had to go," he insisted. "A spirit in my feet said 'Go' and I went."[11]

During the war his poor eyesight gave us an additional benefit. Had Brady been able to manage a camera by himself, he might not have hired so many assistants, but because of his difficulty seeing, he trained a staff of men. Although Brady went to the battlefield himself, most of the photographs were taken by his assistants, who traveled with the Union army. Because many men produced photographs at multiple locations, we have a more extensive record of the Civil War than could have been rendered by one man working alone. Brady's frailty helped record our history.

The Importance of Vision Correction

Sometimes poor eyesight cannot be improved, and artists must find ways to work around their difficulties, as Albert Pinkham Ryder and Mathew Brady did. But correcting vision is important whenever it is possible to do so, even if children resist getting eyeglasses, as I did despite the fact that I could not see well. Today eyeglasses are considered fashion items, and resistance to wearing them has lessened. Seeing clearly can transform your world. Helping a child's health and vision are also ways to promote creativity. Without corrective lenses, some artists could never have fulfilled their potential. One example is the painter Nell Blaine, whose glasses changed not only her vision but also her life.

NELL BLAINE

"There were two things that influenced me to become a painter," said Nell Blaine (American, 1922–1996). "One was making art when I

was a sick child in bed and the other was the improvement in my eyesight from glasses and operations."[12] Before correction, her eye problems were so isolating that Blaine would always have her head turned
to the side because she could not see. The artist was seventy-four
when she told me about her first pair of eyeglasses.[13] It was such a
wonderful experience that the memory remained vivid throughout her
entire life, even though she was only two years old at the time. "I was
so thrilled to have them," she recalled, "that I ran outside and then
ran around for joy." All of a sudden the trees and landscape of her
native Virginia looked beautiful to the little girl, who was born with
multiple eye defects. Blaine said, "Everything seemed so much easier
with glasses."

Being able to see "made for an extra appreciation of the visual
world," she explained, and later it became the subject matter of her
work. As a professional artist Blaine painted what she saw around
her, gaining an international reputation for her landscapes, cityscapes,
and still lifes. But even with her new glasses, there were problems. Besides being nearsighted and astigmatic, Blaine was also cross-eyed and
had five operations to correct this condition. One of the eye operations happened around the same time as her tonsillectomy. "Having
the two so close together," recalled Blaine, "was very frightening."

In addition to having eye problems and a tonsillectomy, she was a
sickly child who had two bouts of scarlet fever and was once out of
school for a whole year because of poor health. Blaine's mother, a former schoolteacher, tutored her at home so she would not fall behind
in her lessons. Bedridden for long periods of time, Blaine turned to
art as a way to fill the empty hours. "With art," she said, "I was always
able to amuse myself." Creativity made her feel less alone. When she
grew up, Nell Blaine moved to New York to become a painter. Eventually, she divided her time between two homes with beautiful views,
a house in Gloucester, Massachusetts, and an apartment on the Upper

West Side of Manhattan. One looked out on a rural landscape and a bay with boats and the other on a cityscape and the Hudson River. Blaine used them both in her art.

Illness as a Time of Increased Sensitivity

Our surroundings are a constant influence in our lives, but during illness this influence can become even more pronounced. A reason for this may be found in chaos theory. With its emotional and physical stress, illness is an inner turmoil that acts like a time of chaos in the life of a human being. Systems in chaos are characterized by turbulence, and scientists have found that a turbulent system is more sensitive to stimuli than a system at rest.[14] For example, an environmental influence that would hardly be noticed by a quiet system can profoundly transform a system in chaos. Because sick children are in a state of internal chaos, external objects and events may have a stronger effect on them. As a result, influences experienced during a childhood illness can affect an artist's work produced later in life.

JEAN-MICHEL BASQUIAT

Hypersensitivity during illness influenced Jean-Michel Basquiat (American, 1960–1988) in two ways.[15] The first was his response to the automobile that injured him and the second was seeing images in a book he was given during convalescence. While playing in the streets of his Brooklyn neighborhood at the age of seven, Basquiat was hit by a car. "I remember it being very dreamlike and seeing the car kind of coming at me," he recalled, "and then seeing everything through a sort of red focus. . . . That's not the earliest memory I have, but it's probably the most vivid."[16] An ambulance rushed Basquiat to the hospital, where doctors operated to remove his spleen. Although the accident happened in childhood, the car and the ambulance stayed with him for life, becoming repeated images in his art.

A gift from his mother also made a lasting impression. His Haitian father was an accountant, but his Puerto Rican mother, Matilde, was artistic. She liked to draw, take her son to museums, and emphasize the importance of learning. When Basquiat was in the hospital, his mother brought him a copy of *Gray's Anatomy:* its technical illustrations of the human body are used by both artists and doctors. Basquiat's biographer Phoebe Hoban thinks the book was meant as an aid to healing. I agree but also believe it functioned like a gift of art supplies. Matilde was encouraging her son to learn and be creative. Basquiat, who had been a compulsive drawer since the age of four, was so fascinated by *Gray's Anatomy* that as an adult he made references to it in his paintings. "I'd say my mother gave me all the primary things," recalled Basquiat. "The art came from her."[17]

Furniture as Inspiration

The heightened sensitivity during illness can be affected by objects as ordinary as furniture in a room. Sometimes a bedridden child will be influenced by gazing at whatever is nearby. Human beings need visual stimulation. We usually receive this stimulation from the variety of objects and events we encounter in daily activities. But a child sick in bed with few distractions may fill this need by focusing on objects in the immediate environment. A piece of furniture can become so important to an immobilized child that it shapes the art produced in adulthood. This happened to Max Ernst when he had the measles and to Tony Smith during bouts of tuberculosis.

TONY SMITH

"The most important fact of my life," stated Tony Smith (American, 1912–1980), "was that I had T.B. at a very early age."[18] His trouble with tuberculosis started at age four and continued until adolescence. When Smith was sick, he was quarantined inside a one-room prefabricated house that his father built for him in the backyard of their New Jersey home. There he was not endangering the health of his sisters and brothers and his parents could still be nearby. Isolated and without much to do, Smith focused on the most significant piece of furniture in the room, a black metal stove. Its geometric form became extremely important to him. "If one spends a long time in a room with only one object," said Smith, "that object becomes a little god."[19]

The adult Smith became known for his large geometric sculptures, many done in black metal like the stove that dominated his room. The early illness had a second influence on his life and work. As a sick, isolated child, Smith would build structures from medicine cartons to pass the time. In 1961, after a serious automobile accident, he developed polycythemia, a condition associated with an abnormally high red blood cell count. Again, Smith, who started out as an architect, made models from cardboard to fill the hours he spent alone. The small models he made during convalescence became plans for his first large sculpture.

MAX ERNST

Max Ernst (German, 1891–1976) was also profoundly influenced by furniture in his room.[20] Bedridden at six with a serious case of the measles, Ernst found himself staring at an imitation mahogany panel on a piece of furniture near his bed. Then he began to hallucinate. The lines of the painted wood started to swim before his fevered eyes and form into a variety of shapes—an eye, a nose, a menacing nightingale, the head of a bird, a spinning top—and they kept on changing. Ernst was so fascinated by this experience that after he recovered, he tried to repeat it by staring at clouds, wallpapers, unplastered walls, and anything else that stimulated his visual imagination. When asked what his favorite occupation was, young Ernst would reply, "Looking."[21] These childhood hallucinations influenced his art as an adult. Ernst made a collage painting of a menacing nightingale called *Two Children Are Threatened by a Nightingale,* and the fascination with changing forms and images within images became an important part of his surrealist paintings.

Illness Intensifies a Commitment to Art

Sometimes when a young person has already chosen an art career, illness can intensify the commitment. Georgia O'Keeffe had this experience after a bout of typhoid fever.

GEORGIA O'KEEFFE

In 1906, after her first year of study at the Art Institute of Chicago, eighteen-year-old Georgia O'Keeffe (American, 1887–1986) came home for summer vacation.[22] She had done well at school and John Vanderpoel (see chapter 5), the leading teacher, ranked her first in his class of twenty-nine female students. But on returning home to Virginia, O'Keeffe contracted typhoid fever. There had already been deaths from the illness that season and her family was very concerned. On the days she was feeling better, they carried her outside to lie in a hammock beneath the big trees. At one point she lost all her hair as a result of the illness, but it eventually grew back. O'Keeffe recuperated for months, and by the next summer she had a new focus in life—studying at the Art Students League in New York. It was a sacrifice for her family to send her there, but they were supportive, and instead of returning to Chicago in the fall, O'Keeffe went to New York, the center of the American art world.

Illness and Isolation in Childhood

A degree of isolation accompanies every illness, but when poor health is compounded by being sent away from your family, the level of stress dramatically increases. It is extremely traumatic for a child to feel both sick and abandoned. Yet this was the experience of Odilon Redon.

ODILON REDON

When he was only an infant, Odilon Redon (French, 1840–1916) was sent far away from his home.[23] He was a sickly child, but what would make his affluent parents hide a baby at Peyrelebade, their wild, deserted estate in the Médoc region of France, when they kept all their other children at home in their house in Bordeaux? The art historians Douglas W. Druick and Peter Kort Zegers believe it is because Redon was thought to have epilepsy, which carried an enormous social stigma in the nineteenth century. At that time epilepsy was viewed not as a medical condition but as a sign of family degeneracy and was thought to be associated with the poorer classes. Fearing this stigma, the prosperous Redons kept their epileptic son a secret. They concealed the child in a place where no one would see him, to be raised by an uncle who managed the estate. In two meticulously researched essays, "Painful Origins" and "Under a Cloud," which appear in the catalog to the exhibition "Odilon Redon: Prince of Dreams," Druick and Zegers present evidence suggesting that Redon suffered from petit mal, the type of epilepsy that produces short lapses of consciousness, rather than grand mal, which is characterized by violent seizures.

When standard medical care was not effective, Redon's parents brought him to the shrine of Verdelais. Like Lourdes, it is a place of faith healing dedicated to the Virgin Mary. Druick and Zegers discovered that Redon is listed there as one of the 133 documented miracle cures between the years of 1819 and 1883. Following a visit at age six, the boy appeared to be symptom free, but his parents were extremely cautious. After repeated trips to Verdelais, they were finally convinced that the child was well, and when he was eleven, they took him home to Bordeaux and his three other siblings. Within a year of returning to his family, Redon won a prize for drawing, indicating that during his stay at Peyrelebade, the young boy had turned to art. His family encouraged creativity, and at the age of fifteen he started formal art lessons. Redon's early sickness and exile affected not only his creativity but also his work as an adult and his emotions for the rest of his life.

"I see myself in those days," he recalled, "as sad and weak."[24] He was a hidden boy who hid himself further at Peyrelebade. "As a child, I sought out shadows," he revealed. "I remember finding deep and peculiar happiness in hiding myself within the large draperies in the dark corners of the house."[25] As a result of his early exile and despite his later success, Redon thought of himself as an outsider for the rest of his life. Even though he liked the good-natured uncle who raised him, Redon remained very depressed. This constant melancholy became the premise of his Noirs, the black-and-white drawings and graphic works that dominate the first half of his career. In them, the sadness and shadows of his childhood become the subject matter and strength in his art. Redon's work also contains mystical themes. Coming from a religious family may have predisposed him to make spiritual art, and there was an interest in spiritualism in France at the time. But it is also quite possible that Redon was influenced by having been listed as one of the miracle cures at the Basilica of Our Lady of Verdelais.

Accidents in Childhood

The next chapter deals with childhood accidents that change artists' lives and work. While illness is often a gradual occurrence, accidents happen quickly. Perhaps because they are so sudden and unexpected, accidents often bring a legacy of stress, but creativity again becomes an aid to resilience.

Chapter 5

Early Accidents as a Turning Point

You cannot live and keep free of briars.
—*William Carlos Williams*

Accidents in Childhood

Even with the most careful planning, life is full of surprises. Who has never had an accident? This is especially true for children, whose desire for action is often stronger than their concern for caution. The artists in this chapter have had serious accidents that fundamentally transformed their lives and work. While accidents can generate artistic development, they often leave an emotional as well as a physical legacy that lingers long past the initial incident. Yet even the most difficult accidents, despite the pain and distress they cause, can have positive results. These artists endure traffic accidents, play accidents, sports accidents, accidents with sharp objects, and accidents with fire early in life, yet they manage to turn a flash of misfortune into a creative career. As a way to express deep emotions, art can relieve stress and also lift the boredom of a long convalescence.

FRIDA KAHLO

When Frida Kahlo (Mexican, 1907–1954) was eighteen years old, a traffic accident changed her life.[1] Her biographer Hayden Herrera says it happened on a gray afternoon in Mexico City just after a light rain. Kahlo was on a small wooden bus that collided with a much larger two-car electric trolley. As the bus shattered into a pile of jagged debris, a twisted piece of metal entered one side of Kahlo's body and came out the other. The impact also broke the lumbar region of her spine in three places, and there were fractures of her pelvis, collarbone, and ribs. Kahlo's right leg had eleven breaks, and her right foot was crushed and dislocated. She never completely recovered.

Immobilized for months in bed, she turned to painting. Kahlo's parents, hoping to make life easier for their bedridden child, encouraged this creativity. Her mother hired a carpenter to build an easel that could be used by someone lying down, and her father, a professional photographer who was also an amateur painter, gave her his cherished oil paints. Lying in bed, Kahlo started to create the paintings that would eventually make her famous.[2] "Instead of studying to become a doctor," she explained, "and without paying much attention, I began to paint."[3]

This accident, which became a turning point, was intensified by two physical difficulties Kahlo experienced earlier in her life: spina bifida and polio. Both had previously weakened her body, and one had already turned her to creativity. Kahlo's first major physical problem was spina bifida, a congenital condition in which the vertebrae of the spinal cord fail to fuse together, leaving a gap in the spine.[4] Although Kahlo had this condition since birth, it was not diagnosed until X-rays were taken when she was an adult. Because the unfused vertebrae could not be seen with the naked eye and were only discovered with X-rays, it appears she suffered from spina bifida occulta, the

most common form of the disorder. In spina bifida occulta the unfused vertebrae lie hidden under the skin, and most people are not
aware of any spinal abnormality, nor do they suffer disability. But
Kahlo's condition was more severe; it eventually produced open sores
on her feet called trophic ulcers.[5] Leo Eloesser, the California physi-
cian who discovered Kahlo's spina bifida, believes this congenital disorder, rather than the traffic accident, produced increasing disability
as Kahlo aged. But her inborn problem was aggravated by the accident; Kahlo's spine had three breaks in her weakened lumbar region,
the site of her spina bifida.

Kahlo's second major physical problem was polio, which she contracted at the age of seven and which left her with a severely atrophied
right leg. Generally, when polio involves a leg, the foot is also affected.[6]
Like spina bifida, this condition intensified the effects of the accident.
Kahlo's already weakened right leg broke in eleven places, and her right
foot was crushed and dislocated. There were no reported injuries to
her left leg or foot, which were not impaired by polio. After this illness,
Kahlo grew closer to her father, who took her on outings with him
while he painted. She started to draw and showed such talent that her
father taught her how to use a camera and retouch photographs.
Although she became a constant sketcher and eventually began an
apprenticeship with an engraver, Kahlo still thought of herself as a
premed student until the accident changed her life.

In addition to its physical discomfort, polio also brought her emotional distress. When Kahlo was young, the other children called her
Peg Leg Frida because her right leg was so thin. She immediately
yelled back at them but still it hurt, and she wore multiple stockings
on her thin leg to make it look fuller. As an adult, she favored long
Mexican skirts, saying they symbolized national pride and pleased her
husband, Diego Rivera. But Kahlo also knew they would cover her
legs. Although most of her art is autobiographical and she repeatedly

shows the wounds from her accident, Kahlo never accurately depicts the effects of polio. Her leg became her secret. Herrera writes that the wounds and sorrow in Kahlo's work are a cry for attention.[7] I agree but also believe they are an attempt at pain management. Painting her troubles gave Kahlo a feeling of control, even if that mastery was only on canvas. As she said, "I paint because I need to."[8]

Accidents with Sharp Objects

Sharp objects are a common cause of accidents, and we are surrounded by them every day: silverware, scissors, pencils, the thousand things that make up the tools of our world. Although useful, they can also be dangerous. I still have a pencil point embedded in my hand, where the top of a sharp pencil pierced my palm in the third grade. Accidents happen when children play unsupervised with sharp objects. But even the loss of an eye can turn tragedy into art, as it did for both James Thurber and Ben Schonzeit.

JAMES THURBER

On a hot August afternoon in Washington, D.C., seven-year-old James Thurber (American, 1894–1961) and his eight-year-old brother, William, were shooting each other in the back with homemade bows and arrows.[9] It was Thurber's turn to be shot, but he was impatient because William was fumbling. When he turned around to see what was taking so long, William had just released an arrow. It hit him in the left eye. Thurber's mother was slow in taking her son to a doctor, and when she did it was to a local doctor, who just bandaged the eye instead of removing it. After Thurber had endured days of pain, his parents took him to an eye specialist, who immediately removed the injured eye. But by then the boy had developed sympathetic ophthalmia, a condition in which the inflammation from an injured eye travels to an uninjured eye, eventually destroying its sight.[10] Thurber was soon fitted with a glass eye, and he was still able to see through his right eye enough to read, write, and draw, but his vision was never good. Despite medical care and operations, the right eye continued to give him problems, and later in life Thurber became blind. The accident also left him with emotional distress; he remained angry with his mother and brother.

"One of the worst things that can happen to a child," he insisted, "an accident affecting its eyes, can and does happen because parents are careless."[11] Thurber blamed his mother for not taking him to the eye specialist right away, and when he was an adult facing a series of eye operations, his mother, distraught over her son's encroaching blindness and perhaps guilty over her inadequate care, wrote to his surgeon offering one of her eyes as a transplant, not realizing the procedure was impossible to perform. Thurber never openly faulted his brother for the accident and even supported him financially when they were adults. But he never invited William to his home. Still, Thurber kept his famous sense of humor. "Last night I dreamed of a small consolation enjoyed only by the blind," he stated. "Nobody knows the trouble I've *not* seen!"[12]

Thurber became a very successful writer, cartoonist, and humorist, well known for his drawings and articles in *The New Yorker*. The artist's cartoon style comes directly out of his vision loss. His limited eyesight required large, rounded forms and clear outlines because they were easier for him to see. But with just a few strokes of his pen Thurber could convey an entire scene, giving us a unique and humorous view of reality.

BEN SCHONZEIT

When Ben Schonzeit (American, b. 1942) was injured, his family was quick to respond.[13] But even with prompt medical care, it was not possible to save his eye. Yet the accident became a turning point in his life.

"There was this new little girl in the neighborhood," recalls Schonzeit, "and I wanted to impress her."[14] So the five-year-old boy found an ice pick and started to carve the bark of a tree. But Schonzeit was carving upward, and the ice pick rammed into his left eye. All the attempts to save his eye failed, and after a series of infections and two operations it was removed. After the accident, he spent months in a darkened room or wearing dark glasses. Despite her son's vision loss and darkened environment, Schonzeit's mother bought him a large box of sixty-four Crayola crayons and also some clay. Knowing that her son was creative, she said, "Go make things."[15]

"Most of the other presents I got, I broke," admits Schonzeit, "but these made me feel special and I was encouraged."[16] By the age of six he decided to become an artist. Schonzeit believes the accident not only impelled him toward art but still influences his work. "The time I spent alone as a sick child," he explains, "gave me the strength and foundation for the hours an artist must spend alone in the studio." It also made him a keen observer: "I wanted to see as much as I could with my remaining eye and to translate what I saw into my art." This childhood wish may be the reason behind Schonzeit's great variety of subject matter and his search for the new. "I abandon success for the new challenge," he says, "for the unknown and perhaps impossible."[17] His attitude may explain why I have met many artists who are athletic but none who do extreme sports. Perhaps it is because, like Schonzeit, we take our risks in our work.

Vision Problems and the Creative Process

Schonzeit's style of painting also appears to be influenced by his early accident. His excellently drawn images may be a compensation for vision loss, showing a desire to see and re-create the world as clearly as possible. Schonzeit works from photographs, usually ones he has taken. When I visited his studio, I asked him why he prefers to work this way. "Perhaps I don't completely trust what I see," he explained. Then he added, "It's easier to look up close at a photograph."[18]

When he said that, I realized I do the same thing because I, too, have severe vision loss. Like Schonzeit, my work contains clearly painted images, and I also use photographs more often than live models. I would not presume that all artists with major vision problems compensate in the same way, but there may be certain methods of working that some of us share. Even though Schonzeit sees adequately with his remaining eye, and my lenses correct my legal blindness to normal vision, we still have an underlying unease about our ability to perceive the physical world. This may lead us to make our images as sharp as possible and to use photographs as models. Holding a photograph, which is a copy of physical reality, up close in our hands provides a feeling of security, because we still don't believe that we can see as well as we do.

Sports Accidents

Sports are a part of our culture and so are sports accidents. As a healthy outlet for childhood energy, sports can be fun, but there are also dangers. Active behavior can produce higher-risk situations than the quieter times of everyday life. Even when children are supervised at school, like John Vanderpoel was, life-changing injuries can happen.

JOHN HENRY VANDERPOEL

In October 1871 fourteen-year-old John Henry Vanderpoel (American, born in the Netherlands, 1857–1911) and his older brothers helped people escape from the Great Chicago Fire.[19] Later that year, in a wrestling match at school, he had a very bad fall. Although no medical records are available, "he probably broke his back,"[20] says Jimmie Lee Buehler, biographer of the John H. Vanderpoel Art Association in Chicago. The injury was severe and he never completely recovered. As a result of the fall, Vanderpoel's back became hunched, and he walked so bent over that as an adult he appeared to be extremely short. Vanderpoel was eventually taken to the hospital, but not immediately after his injury. His family was busy working and none of them visited him there, but the hospital stay changed his life. All alone and with nothing to do, young Vanderpoel asked to be given paper and pencil "to make pictures . . . if it wouldn't be too much trouble."[21]

Vanderpoel's family was poor but they were also artistic. He had art lessons in Holland and again after they moved to Chicago. When the teenager started drawing in the hospital, people were amazed at his ability. Encouraged, he created even more—and then realized he wanted to be an artist. After being released from the hospital, Vanderpoel began working in a wallpaper store, but he was so intent on being an artist that he drew on the backs of the rolls of wallpaper. He was fired.

Returning to public school in Chicago, Vanderpoel received a scholarship to Turner Hall, which in 1880 became the Art Institute of Chicago, one of the foremost art schools in America. After being an excellent student and staff member, he eventually became the school's leading instructor. His reputation was so great that the Royal Academy in London offered him a position as their head instructor. But Vanderpoel refused, and he would remain at the Art Institute of Chicago for more than thirty years.

When he was about thirty-five, Vanderpoel lost the sight in one eye, but he kept working. Meeting challenges with increased determination, he created enormous murals, and in 1908 he wrote *The Human Figure*, a book on drawing and anatomy that is still in print today.[22] In addition to his accomplishments, Vanderpoel was also known for his kindness and generosity. "His childhood accident sensitized him to the needs of others," explains Buehler.[23] And Georgia O'Keeffe, who was his student in Chicago, called Vanderpoel "one of the few real teachers I have known."[24]

Accidents with Fire

Fire is fundamental to civilization but it is also dangerous. Carel van Mander, northern Europe's first art historian, relates the stories of two artists who were severely burned in childhood: Hendrick Goltzius and Ryckaert Aertzoon. Goltzius became an artist in spite of his injury, and Aertzoon became an artist because of his burns.

HENDRICK GOLTZIUS

According to Van Mander, when Hendrick (Henricus) Goltzius (Dutch, 1558–1617) was a toddler, he was "wild and lively" and "very fond of fire."[25] Active and accident-prone, Goltzius had multiple injuries, but his burns were the most serious. When "he could almost walk alone," relates Van Mander, "he fell face down into a pan of hot oil, and both of his hands were burnt on the red glowing coals." The burns were severe, and his mother tried her best to help. She straightened his hands with strips of wood and applied ointments and other remedies.

A woman who lived nearby removed the wood, advising it was better to wrap the right hand in a towel. "Because of this treatment," explains Van Mander, "the sinews of the hand grew together, with the result that, later on, Goltzius was never able to open his hand entirely." Still, he became an artist, one who preferred to use his injured right hand over his less injured left and managed to draw, paint, and make engravings. Goltzius, whose family included generations of painters, showed his talent by filling almost every wall in his home with drawings when he was seven or eight. Despite limited hand movement, Hendrick Goltzius became the most famous painter his family ever produced and one of the most successful artists of his day.

RYCKAERT AERTZOON

Ryckaert Aertzoon (Dutch, ca. 1482–1577), the son of a fisherman, had an accident in childhood that altered his path.[26] His leg was burned so badly that it had to be amputated. Although the accident happened in his home village of Wijk aan Zee, Aertzoon was taken to the city of Haarlem for medical treatment. While convalescing there after the amputation, the young boy would sit near the fire and draw on the white chimney wall with pieces of coal. When he was asked if he would like to become an artist, he was very excited at the prospect. Aertzoon, who walked with a crutch, became a pupil of the painter Jan Mostaert. "He studied hard," notes Van Mander, "and became a good master."[27] A quiet, religious man who sought peace of mind, Aertzoon moved to Antwerp, where he lived until the age of ninety-five.

Problems with Walking

Like Frida Kahlo and Ryckaert Aertzoon, the children featured in the next chapter have problems with walking or cannot walk at all. Yet all of them turn to creativity and go on to have successful art careers. And in compensation for their challenged mobility, they all become travelers.

Chapter 6

Challenged Walking

Courage conquers all things; it even gives
strength to the body. —*Ovid*

R unning, jumping, and playing sports are so central to growing up that children who cannot participate may feel almost
as isolated as if they were bedridden. But the daily difficulties that challenged walking bring can provide the strength for a lifetime of creativity. Most people who are able to walk take walking for
granted. How many of us think twice before walking somewhere, remembering that for others this task is difficult and may even be impossible. Whenever I see ramps in front of a building or ride on
wheelchair-accessible public transportation, I feel grateful. Everyone
deserves to be able to go places, not only those who can walk there.
The urge to travel may be very strong in a person with compromised
mobility. Whether their problems are genetic or result from illness,
the artists in this chapter have something in common—when they
grow up they all travel: some to live in other cities, some for work, and
some just for enjoyment.

When these artists were children, operations that now routinely cure certain leg and foot problems were not available. They lived at a time when polio scourged our population, before the Salk and Sabin vaccines. Yet despite their incurable conditions, they persevered to create a life of art.

Congenital Conditions

When challenges begin at birth, they can profoundly shape a child's self-image, because the child knows of no time when the disability did not exist. It becomes part of his or her intrinsic sense of self. But the individuals in this chapter also have an additional identity—they see themselves as artists, and as artists they are not impaired. This alternative identity is a source of strength, resilience, and talent—and it is the self by which they are remembered.

HENRI DE TOULOUSE-LAUTREC

Perhaps the most famous artist with congenitally impaired walking is Henri de Toulouse-Lautrec (French, 1864–1901)—and he believed this challenge turned him to creativity.[1] "One thing is certain," he insisted, "if my legs had been a bit longer I would never have become a painter."[2]

Scientists now think Lautrec had pycnodysostosis, a rare inherited disorder that produced his brittle bones, impaired walking, and dwarfism.[3] In 1965, two physicians, Pierre Maroteaux and Maurice Lamy, found evidence suggesting Lautrec had pycnodysostosis, and thirty years later researchers located the chromosome for this condition.[4] He was born the count of Toulouse, and birth defects were common in his wealthy but inbred circles, where marriages between relatives were used to keep money and estates within the family. Although Lautrec's mother and father appeared normal, they were first cousins, and he had close relatives with even greater physical problems.

It was possibly because of inadequately fused head bones and abnormal facial bones due to pycnodysostosis that Lautrec suffered painful headaches, severe sinus problems, and serious nosebleeds in childhood. Pycnodysostosis also produces a tendency to develop dental caries, and Lautrec had terrible toothaches. It also impairs bone growth and strength and results in short stature. Lautrec, who was only five feet tall, found walking extremely difficult and at times almost impossible, even when using two canes. At ten he began to experience severe leg pains, suggesting he had hairline fractures in his bones.

An invalid for much of his childhood, Lautrec found great solace in art and began drawing when he was three to four years old. Coming from a family of amateur artists, he learned from his paternal uncle Charles, who was childless and very fond of him. In her biography of the artist, Julia Frey states that when Lautrec made art, "he entered a private world, and nothing could touch him, not his father's neglect nor his mother's whining, nor the fact that no matter how much he might wish . . . he would never be able to dance."[5]

Nor could he ride, and he loved horses. Incapable of being a horseman in line with family tradition, he compensated by drawing horses from every angle, especially in motion. His output was so enormous that in 1880 alone he created three hundred drawings and fifty paintings of horses and other subject matter. Starting as a diversion and a compensation, creativity grew even more important to him after two crippling accidents in adolescence. When he was thirteen years old, Lautrec fell off a low chair onto the floor, breaking his left thighbone; and then, fifteen months later, while walking in a field he fell and broke his right thighbone. Although neither fall was from a great height, his broken thighbones didn't heal well and walking became even more difficult. People with pycnodysostosis tend to have brittle bones that break easily and heal poorly. During his long months of convalescence, Lautrec concentrated on art. He had previously been an excellent student but now, alone all day, he found that academic studies no longer interested him and reading gave him a headache. But "I draw and paint for as long as I can," he said, "until my hand becomes weary."[6]

The first professional art tutor Lautrec studied with as a teenager was René Princeteau (French, 1843–1914), a friend of the family. Born deaf, Princeteau was trained to lip-read and speak, and the two challenged artists formed a close bond. But creativity was not Lautrec's only way to alleviate suffering. He started drinking at the age of ten and by twenty-one he was severely alcoholic. Lautrec was also convinced that despite his title and wealth, no woman in society, such as his cousin Jeanne d'Armagnac, would want him. "I listen to her but lack the courage to look at her, who is so tall and so beautiful," he admitted, "and as for myself—I am neither of these."[7]

Instead, he frequented brothels and most likely contracted syphilis there. Complications from either tertiary syphilis or advanced alcoholism or both probably caused the fatal stroke before his thirty-seventh birthday. Yet in spite of a lifetime of poor health, Lautrec created approximately 600 paintings, 330 lithographs, 30 posters, and thousands of drawings. His father, who thought it was a disgrace for a titled count to have a profession, was furious. But Lautrec persevered, and it is thanks to this strength that we have his art in our world today.

Mobility and Self-Image

Challenged walking is a physical disorder that can bring emotional distress in its wake. With a negative self-image, a child may feel weak and unattractive, as did Ellen Robbins.

ELLEN ROBBINS

"My mother shed tears when she thought of my future," wrote Ellen Robbins (American, 1828–1905) in her autobiography, *Reminiscences of a Flower Painter.*[8] Robbins explained it was because she was the youngest of seven children and a weak child, but the reason was most likely her congenital clubfoot,[9] which at that time was a problem for life. Although Robbins admitted to being born with "a lame foot"[10] that prevented her from taking long walks, she did not describe the condition. It is reasonable to assume it is a clubfoot, because that is the most common cause of congenital lameness.[11] In this condition, the foot is twisted inward, producing a limp because the outside edge of the foot rather than the sole is used as a support for walking. Today, a clubfoot can be corrected either by casts placed on a child's foot or by surgery. But when Ellen Robbins was young, it was incurable.

At the beginning of her autobiography, Robbins tells us she was sickly, thin, plain, and shy but does not mention her "lame foot" until six pages later. By repeatedly saying she was weak and thin rather than blaming her challenged walking as the cause of her mother's tears or her own unhappiness suggests that the subject of lameness was extremely painful for her. Although Robbins could not be an active child, she loved colors and was determined to make art. Her aunt promoted this creativity by giving her twenty-five cents for a paint box, and her family also arranged for drawing lessons with her cousins.

When she was two years old, her father died shortly after failing in business. To support themselves and their mother, Robbins and her sisters did needlework. But she looked forward to evening when the needlework ended, saying, "I was always thinking of the little time after six o'clock when I should be drawing."[12]

Robbins believed an art career was impossible for someone with so little money, but friends and relatives encouraged her creativity. She was self-taught as well as professionally trained, and eventually sold paintings in both America and Europe. Her subject matter was flowers, and Robbins was so knowledgeable about them that when she wrote, she sounded like a naturalist. At a time when watercolors were made on small pieces of paper, Robbins produced larger works, revealing ambition and self-confidence. Despite challenged walking, she traveled to Europe, visited friends in the New England countryside, and commuted by trolley from Watertown to Boston, where she gave art lessons. Success eased her shyness, and though Robbins never married she was surrounded by people, both friends and relations. In her later years, she said, "Few people have enjoyed life more than I have."[13]

Altered Options

Like Robbins's clubfoot, the contracted sinew in one of Charles Rennie Mackintosh's feet could most likely be corrected by modern medicine. Yet his challenged walking led to an interest in art. Had he been stronger and without a limp, he might have joined the Glasgow police force like his father. But work requiring physical strength was not an option for Mackintosh. Yet losing this possibility made him find others. There are many options available in life, but we are not always aware of them until illness forces us to create new choices. These choices are often ones we never would have imagined that lead to lives that we could not have predicted and can be more interesting than anything we ever knew before. When some doors close, others open.

CHARLES RENNIE MACKINTOSH

Life was doubly hard for Charles Rennie Mackintosh (Scottish, 1868–1928).[14] Dyslexia caused him problems in the classroom, and the contracted sinew in his foot made recess difficult as well. The design historian Alan Crawford believes Mackintosh's early interest in architecture started as an escape from the stresses of both the classroom and the playground. Each day on his way to school, he was exposed to good architecture while passing the Necropolis, Glasgow's classical Victorian cemetery set on a hillside; some of its elegant mausoleums looked like child-sized houses. These small structures may have held a special meaning for the boy. As one of eleven children, he saw three sisters and a brother die in childhood.

Mackintosh also turned to creativity during his walks in the country. Because he was not a healthy child, the family doctor recommended the walks to build his strength. These solitary times, says the architectural historian Barbara Bernard, laid a foundation for his future career. While in the country, Mackintosh drew the buildings and flowers he saw there. The buildings formed the beginning of his architectural vocabulary, and the flowers became subjects in his paintings and motifs in his industrial and architectural designs. Flower imagery may also have been a way for Mackintosh to be close to his father. As a weak child he could not bond with his father through physical activity nor could he follow him into the Glasgow Police Department. But his father was an avid gardener, who would fill the family home with fresh flowers.[15] Mackintosh may have sought his approval through painting flowers and using them in designs. As an adult, he saw plants as metaphors for life and art. " 'Life' is the leaves which shape and nourish a plant," he explained, "but 'art' is the flower which embodies its meaning."[16]

Mackintosh took his childhood dreams of becoming an architect and put them into action. By the age of sixteen, he was working as an apprentice in the architectural firm of John Hutchison and taking night classes at the Glasgow School of Art. Art school stressed drawing rather than reading, and Mackintosh became a prize-winning student. One of his many awards was a traveling scholarship to study the architecture of Italy. Later, as an adult, Mackintosh traveled for architecture to Germany and Austria. He also traveled to France to paint, accompanied by his wife, Margaret Macdonald, whom he met in art school. Although he had some success during his life, Mackintosh's fame and influence grew after his death, and he is now respected as one of the greatest architects of his time.

Challenged Walking from a Childhood Illness or Accident

The next four artists were not born with walking difficulties but developed them in childhood. Unlike the previous children with congenital challenges, these artists had normal mobility until a childhood illness or accident profoundly and permanently affected their ability to walk. With altered walking comes a change in their identities—the children now see themselves as challenged. Although this can be painful, the new sense of self that encompasses a disability also contains increased determination. Their weakness produces strength. None of the children ever walks normally again, but they develop the ability to be alone, to work alone, and to become very productive.

CHARLES DEMUTH

Did Charles Demuth (American, 1883–1935) have an illness or an accident in childhood?[17] Opinions differ as to why the boy was left with one leg shorter than the other, wore a built-up orthopedic shoe, and walked with a limp for the rest of his life. Some biographers say Demuth's father dropped him during a time of play and the fall damaged his hip, while others believe he had either Perthes' (also known as Legg-Calve-Perthes') disease or tuberculosis of the hip. Both illnesses can destroy the upper part of the leg that enters the hip socket, resulting in a shortened leg. Whatever the problem was that he developed at age four, his condition was so severe that it required six weeks in traction followed by one to two years of bed rest. To help pass the time, Demuth made art with crayons and watercolors, and after convalescence he took lessons with a local painter. Demuth came from a family with generations of artists, both amateur and professional, but the young boy with challenged walking became the most prominent painter in his family.

A frail child who walked with a cane, Demuth fared better as an adult. Despite his condition, the artist liked to hike, swim, and even dance. Demuth also found ways to make his impairment seem like an asset. He invented a type of ambling walk that other people found very appealing, and his walking cane became a fashion accessory, due to his great sense of style. Despite his achievements, Demuth still saw himself as an outsider and an invalid. An ardent admirer of beauty in the world around him, he felt he lacked that perfection in himself, saying that he was "denied the one thing which would perfect me, truly."[18] This may have been one of the reasons he became a perfectionist in his art, making all of his lines and forms as precise and perfect as possible. Using this style, Demuth became one of the leaders in the precisionist school of American painting.

Demuth's challenged walking affected his work in other ways as well. One of his biographers, Emily Farnham, thinks it was because of Demuth's physical condition that his parents allowed him to become an artist rather than manage the family tobacco shop, which was the oldest in America. She also believes his impairment influenced the size of his work, making it small and easier to manage, and that it affected his choice of materials. "Oil paints are so messy!" exclaimed Demuth, but he said it to hide the fact that he was not able to carry heavy supplies when he worked outdoors away from his studio.[19] Instead, he brought watercolors, which were lighter and more compact. Charles Demuth became one of the finest watercolorists of his generation.

Polio

Until recently, polio was the most common cause of challenged walking. Now almost completely eradicated, this viral disease was a scourge of the twentieth century. Severe cases could bring muscle wasting, paralysis, and death.[20] When polio affects the legs and feet, it can atrophy limbs and leave a legacy of impaired walking or an inability to walk at all. As a child, I remember the fear polio produced every summer until vaccinations were developed to prevent its occurrence. I was told to change out of my wet bathing suit as quickly as possible and not to catch cold in the hopes of staving off an illness that seemed to strike with arbitrary aim at the young and the strong. No one knew who would get polio, and there was no cure. The singer/songwriter Joni Mitchell (Canadian, b. 1943) contracted polio at the age of nine.[21] She had been interested in art before, but the illness deepened her commitment. Although she later focused on music, Mitchell still exhibits her paintings.

Some people who were stricken were put into iron lungs to help them breathe, and not everyone survived. Those who did survive were often marginalized, first by illness and then by lameness. Isolation is difficult at any age, but in childhood it can be exceptionally painful. No longer able to participate in sports or active games, these children are seen as "different" by their former playmates, and in response they may become solitary observers.

Overcompensation: Photojournalism as a Response to Polio

If the ability to walk is compromised in childhood, it can leave a child with an intense determination to overcome what is seen as a weakness. For some artists, this compensation is manifested not only in the imagery of their art but also in their choice of career. Wanting to conquer what they regard as a defect, they will choose the most challenging road. The psychologist Alfred Adler called this "overcompensation" and described it as the determination to turn what is perceived as a weakness into a strength.[22] Stemming from a fierce desire to regain a sense of wholeness after childhood polio impaired their walking, both Dorothea Lange and Matthias Oppersdorff became photojournalists who traveled extensively for their work.

DOROTHEA LANGE

When she was seven, Dorothea Lange (American, 1895–1965) developed polio.[23] The illness made her right leg thin and weak, and her right foot stayed one and a half sizes smaller than the left one. She also had a noticeable limp. Like other people with visible difficulties, Lange was the victim of prejudice. The neighborhood children called her "Limpy," and Lange's mother told her to walk as well as she could when they were seen together in public. "My parents were ashamed of me," said Lange,[24] and throughout her life, she wore long skirts or pants to cover her affected leg even if she could not always hide her limp. Isolated by illness when she was young, Lange turned her ability to be alone into a strength for her work.

Despite the effects of polio, she was an avid walker. The family lived in Hoboken, New Jersey, but Lange went to public school in New York. As she got older she not only walked to school from the ferry terminal but also walked away from school, cutting classes regularly to explore the city. These long walks became a foundation for her career in photojournalism. Lange believed that this early isolation made her look at life like "a photographic observer."[25] She learned about the world by going down streets alone, looking at events and into people's windows and their lives. In spite of her fears, her limp, and her youth, Lange walked through rough neighborhoods like New York's Bowery. As a child, she developed a way to observe discreetly, adopting an expression that would attract no attention. It was a skill that helped her later as a documentary photographer and a method of self-protection she would use all her life. She also believed that polio helped her work.

"Being disabled gave me an immense advantage," explained Lange. "People are kinder to you."[26] Perceived with sympathy rather than fear, she was less threatening, and people allowed her to take photographs of them. Lange also had compassion for those she photographed. Once a struggling, ostracized child, she developed a concern for others in difficult circumstances and wanted to make their plight known. During the Depression, "Migrant Mother," one of her most famous photographs, was published in a San Francisco newspaper along with a commentary by her husband, the labor economist Paul Taylor. People were amazed that this level of poverty existed, and the government sent twenty thousand pounds of food to the Pea Picker

Farm, where the woman and other migrant workers had been living in starvation. "The camera is an instrument," said Lange, "that teaches people how to see without a camera."[27]

Approaching suffering as one who had suffered, she photographed migrant workers in California, farmers emigrating from the dust bowl states, African American sharecroppers in the South, people on breadlines during the Depression, and Japanese Americans interned in camps during World War II. Empathy and compassion became strength in her work.

Empathy and Compassion

Empathy is the ability to see yourself in another person's situation, and compassion is the intense awareness of the suffering of others combined with the desire to lessen their distress. By developing empathy and compassion, we become able to acknowledge other people's humanity and make a deep connection with them. For Dorothea Lange and Matthias Oppersdorff, compensation for the effects of polio influenced their choice of career, but empathy and compassion guided their imagery.

MATTHIAS OPPERSDORFF

"Polio usually appears in the summer," says Matthias Oppersdorff (American, b. 1935), "but I got sick in the middle of winter."[28] He was fourteen years old and had gone to sleep the night before feeling as though he had the flu.[29] When he got out of bed the next morning, there was no strength in his legs and he fell on his face. Diagnosed with polio, Oppersdorff was sent to the hospital immediately. The illness affected his left leg more than his right, but during twelve weeks in the hospital he read something that made him believe he could walk again. It was an article about Bob Mathias in *Life* magazine. Mathias was a seventeen-year-old American athlete who, despite having been a sickly child, won the decathlon at the 1948 Olympic Games. Realizing the similarity in their names, Matthias Oppersdorff decided that if Bob Mathias could win a gold medal, he could walk after polio. Although he spent the spring and summer on crutches, by the time he started school in the fall he was walking on his own.

Oppersdorff managed to walk, but he was unable to run. And because he could not run, he was not chosen for any of the sports teams at school. Instead, he became a loner. Feeling profoundly like an outsider, he began to admire other outsiders, like Lawrence of Arabia and Sir Richard Francis Burton, who made their fortunes in foreign lands. "I wanted to become a world traveler," says Oppersdorff, who sees his childhood experiences as preparation.[30] "Because I felt like an outsider in Rhode Island," he explains, "foreign countries were not as stressful for me as they might be to someone who always had a sense of belonging." As a solitary child, he became an observer, which translated later into an observer with a camera. "My childhood illness did not turn me directly to photography," he states, "but it developed the character strengths necessary for my career."[31]

After college he worked on Wall Street to please his family, but at thirty Oppersdorff realized that for him photography was more exciting than finance. As a photojournalist, he became a professional traveler whose subjects are often nomadic people. "I'm a traveling photographer who photographs travelers," he says, and he has published books about them.[32] Illness and suffering produced compassion in Oppersdorff, who made repeated visits to the people in his books, photographing them over time. As a result, his work has become a visual sociology. In 1997 he was diagnosed with Parkinson's. No longer traveling for photojournalism, he refuses to let illness stop him. Oppersdorff is now experimenting with an early type of camera called a pinhole camera, and his current photographs of the human body are some of the best of his life.

The Sudden Illness

Like Matthias Oppersdorff, Marguerite Stuber Pearson also became suddenly ill. In what seemed like minutes, she was overwhelmed with polio, which completely transformed her existence. It can be extremely traumatic when a sudden flash of debilitating illness is followed by months of convalescence and the difficult realization that the life and dreams we once had are no longer available. But we can start to build a new and different life. When we think we have lost everything, there is always something left that we had not noticed before, some aspect of ourselves capable of creating an entirely new world.

MARGUERITE STUBER PEARSON

It was a summer day, and sixteen-year-old Marguerite Stuber Pearson (American, 1898–1978) was vacationing in Maine with her parents.[33] Going in for a swim at four in the afternoon, she seemed fine, but later when she came out of the water, Pearson collapsed on the beach. Doctors told her parents the polio was fatal and that their only child had three months to live. In despair, the Pearsons took their daughter home to Somerville, Massachusetts, a town three miles north of Boston. Despite all the predictions, Pearson survived. She had hoped to become a concert pianist, but polio put an end to those plans. Almost completely paralyzed and extremely depressed, she lay in bed for months with her face turned to the wall. In an effort to help, her mother asked their Episcopal rector to bring over some illustrated books, because as a young child Pearson loved to draw and look at illustrations. At first she kept her face to the wall, but eventually Pearson began to look at the pictures. In time, some of the paralysis lessened, and "I started painting," she recalled, "when I could first use my hands."[34]

She quickly learned to maneuver her wheelchair, and Rector Richardson arranged for a medical illustrator to give her art lessons. He also told her that since she lived beyond the doctor's allotted time, she must use her life profitably. Because polio prevented her from graduating with her high school class, he started her on a reading program that enabled her to get a high school equivalency diploma. When she began doing portraits of friends, Rector Richardson secured an instructor from the Boston Museum. Pearson continued to show enormous ability, and in 1919 she enrolled at the School of the Boston Museum of Fine Arts. Her work was so excellent that it was exhibited along with that of her teachers. Creativity was a way to forget physical discomfort, because when Pearson made paintings, she said, "I get lost in them."[35]

Eventually moving to Rockport, Massachusetts, Pearson held art classes, did portraits, gave lectures and demonstrations on painting, won numerous medals for her work, was active in philanthropy, and painted until her death at almost seventy-nine. Her home, constructed on one level with a ramp leading to the front door, was accessible for a wheelchair. Usually working indoors, she gained a reputation for her interior scenes. Her outdoor paintings of boats and water were often views from a window or the deck of her house. But they are so well done it looks as if she were working at the water's edge. And like the other artists in this chapter, Pearson enjoyed traveling. In her self-portraits, she never showed herself with a wheelchair. "It was because she wanted people to see her art, not her disability," explains Madith Mantyla, who worked for the artist as a companion and model.[36] But

I believe there is an additional reason. When Pearson painted, she did not feel impaired—she felt whole.

Creativity, Learning Disorders, and Leonardo da Vinci

The next two chapters present people with learning disorders and the ways in which these challenges inspire their work. Chapter 7 focuses on how the learning difficulties of Leonardo da Vinci become the roots of his greatness.

Part 3

Learning, Seeing, and Hearing

Chapter 7

The Learning Disorders of Leonardo da Vinci

Little minds are tamed and subdued
by misfortunes; but great minds rise
above them. —*Washington Irving*

L eonardo da Vinci (Italian, 1452–1519) was an acclaimed genius—painter, writer, engineer, inventor, architect, city planner, geologist, geographer, astronomer, biologist, physicist, botanist, anatomist, mathematician, musician—and a person with learning disorders. His accomplishments are vast, and his work began the High Renaissance in art.[1]

If we think we must be perfect to create something of value, then how much more perfect do we have to be to make a work of genius? Actually, it is often our imperfections that give birth to our greatest creativity, like the dyslexia and attention deficit disorder that shaped Leonardo's brilliance. Dyslexia inspired his profound observations of the physical world, and attention deficit disorder turned him inward to the realm of imagination. Transforming his challenges into strengths, Leonardo used them to make scientific discoveries that were centuries ahead of his time and to create some of the greatest work in the history of art.

Dyslexia

Usually an inherited disorder, dyslexia is characterized by spelling, reading, and writing difficulties in a person with adequate intelligence, visual ability, and opportunities for education. The problem is not with eyesight, but neurological in origin. Abnormalities in parts of the brain such as the cerebellum, the corpus callosum, and the posterior cortex of the left hemisphere all produce different types of learning challenges.[2] Some people with dyslexia have difficulties in recognizing letters or associating words with their sounds. Dyslexics may also reverse letters and numbers or see only part of a word. People with primary dyslexia have reading problems for life, while those with developmental dyslexia find their problems lessen as they mature. Because of the many varieties of dyslexia, some researchers think it should be called "the dyslexias."[3]

Now a recognized learning disorder, dyslexia can be treated with educational programs, but in the past dyslexic individuals were seen as deficient. As a result, they often had feelings of low self-esteem, while in fact dyslexics can be geniuses. Albert Einstein, Woodrow Wilson, Winston Churchill, Thomas Alva Edison, George S. Patton, and William Butler Yeats are some of history's brilliant dyslexics.[4]

Mirror Writing and Dyslexia

When people think of Leonardo and dyslexia, the first thing that comes to mind is usually his mirror writing. Standard writing in the West is from left to right, while mirror writing not only goes from right to left but also reverses the letters, so that they face left as well.[5] If you took a mirror to this type of writing it would look readable. But mirror writing in itself is not proof of dyslexia, because there are nondyslexic people who can also write in mirror script. The difference is that when nondyslexic individuals mirror-write, they will consciously reverse their letters, while dyslexics may be unaware that they are either seeing or writing backward.

Because all of Leonardo da Vinci's notebooks are written in mirror script, we can assume that he realized he was writing this way. But his dyslexia becomes obvious when he writes standard script and unconsciously reverses letters and numbers. Leonardo also reversed images. Sometimes the image reversal also seems unconscious, as in his landscape drawing of the French town of Amboise.[6] But at other times Leonardo consciously used image reversals during the composition of his pictures. The preliminary sketches he made for three of his paintings, *Adoration of the Magi, Madonna of the Cat,* and *Virgin and Child with Saint Anne,* show that Leonardo drew the image facing left and facing right before he decided which way was best.[7] His tendency toward reversals became an aid to his art.

While many people with dyslexia reverse letters, writing completely in mirror script is rare.[8] Some dyslexics, who do write in reverse, say it is more comfortable for them and their thoughts flow more easily that way. This may have been true for Leonardo, whose mirror-written notebooks are a legacy of his ideas. Mirror writing may also have offered privacy and protection for a man concerned that people might steal his discoveries.[9] In addition, writing from right to left could have been more comfortable for the left-handed artist.[10] But of all the reasons that Leonardo wrote in mirror script, the most important appears to be his great difficulty in writing from left to right. Almost everything by his hand is in reverse. In the rare instance when he does write from left to right, his handwriting seems strained and he makes unconscious reversals.[11]

Art historians now believe that Leonardo dictated all of his business correspondence, probably to his devoted and well-educated pupil Francesco Melzi, who then wrote the words in standard script from left to right.[12] This assistance may also have been necessary because of Leonardo's incorrect punctuation and his unusual spelling. One of the classic signs of dyslexia is poor spelling, a problem found throughout his writing.[13] According to the Italian neuropsychologist Giuseppe Sartori, Leonardo's many spelling errors are the kind known as surface dysgraphia.[14] People with surface dysgraphia will spell a word the way they hear it and often create their own way of spelling by doubling, adding, or changing letters. They may also break one word into two or blend two words into one. Such errors indicate the presence of learning disorders and are not found in the general population.

Education and Left-Handedness

With all of these challenges, it is not surprising that Leonardo, like many other dyslexics, found it difficult to learn a foreign language.[15] He never fully mastered Latin, even though he studied it in childhood and again as an adult.[16] Without Latin Leonardo could not work as a notary like his father. Notaries, who were similar to lawyers, drafted legal documents in Latin. Nor was he able to attend a university, because all higher education in the Italian Renaissance was conducted in Latin, the language of scholars. Instead, Leonardo's father recognized his son's talent and apprenticed him to Andrea del Verocchio, one of the most successful artists in Florence. In the workshop tradition of artists, instruction was spoken rather than written, and all of the information was given in Italian.

The learning disorder specialists P. G. Aaron, Scott Phillips, and Steen Larsen think that Leonardo may also have had difficulty reading.[17] Through analyzing his writing, they find that he processes a word as a whole rather than as a string of letters. This suggests a neurological problem with material that is arranged in a sequence, such as the letters within a word, and indicates challenged reading. If this is true, then Leonardo would have been seen as a poor student and might have even been mistakenly labeled as unintelligent, like so many other dyslexics. This may be why he was never trained to use his right hand, although he lived in an age when "lefties" were very strongly pressured to do so.

There is another reason why Leonardo remained left-handed. He was born out of wedlock and so may not have received a standard education.[18] His father, Ser Piero, came from an established family in the northern town of Vinci, while his mother, Caterina, was a poor young woman who lived there. Leonardo stayed with his mother for the first few years of his life but then was taken into his father's household because Ser Piero's wife could not have children. Leonardo did not stay left-handed because he was an artist. Other artists, like Michelangelo, who were also born left-handed, were retrained so intensely to use their right hand that they hardly used their left hand at all.[19] But Michelangelo was not dyslexic[20] nor was he born out of wedlock.[21]

We have no information about Leonardo's earliest school years or any learning difficulties he might have had at a very young age. But like other developmental dyslexics, Leonardo eventually learned to read. When he was ten or eleven, he attended a secondary school called an *abbaco* for children who were going to be merchants. The sixteenth-century art historian Giorgio Vasari reports that Leonardo made great progress in school.[22] In adulthood Leonardo loved books and read widely. He even copied parts of books into his notes as a way to learn their information. But when he transcribed their contents, it was with the same unconscious dyslexic errors that are found in his own writing.[23] Throughout his life Leonardo had an intense desire for knowledge and taught himself with the passion of the self-educated. Despite his learning disorders, Leonardo never stopped learning.

"Man without Letters"

With all his brilliance and self-education, Leonardo still referred to himself as a "man without letters."[24] He said he was not a "literary man" and that because he lacked literary skills people would say he couldn't express himself correctly. It is generally thought that Leonardo was admitting he had little Latin or academic education.[25] I believe this is true but also agree with Sartori,[26] who says Leonardo may in addition have been referring to his problems with writing. He knew that mirror script was not standard communication and that his spelling and punctuation were poor. Otherwise he would not have dictated his business letters to be written by a person without these problems.

But Leonardo took his challenge and turned it into a triumph. He said that while he couldn't quote from famous authors like some scholars, he would rely on something greater—direct experience. This is an excellent example of using another ability to compensate for a condition we must live with,[27] and it is an option available to everyone. Leonardo could not cure his dyslexia, but he could use it to his advantage. Rather than being stopped by a difficulty, he invented a new course for his life and kept going. He insisted that using quotes was like dressing up in other people's ideas. Instead, Leonardo decided to go directly to Nature and become an original thinker. The dyslexia that kept him from learning Latin well enough to get an academic education turned him outward to the physical world. He became a "disciple of experience" and one of the greatest observers in history.

"Disciple of Experience"

For Leonardo, the world was full of wonders and there was something to learn everywhere. His method of investigation was firsthand experience, which he called the "mother of certainty."[28] Carefully looking at the world, Leonardo wrote about what he saw with great courage—even when his observations did not match the beliefs of his day.[29] Centuries before modern science, Leonardo realized that water erodes mountains and that striated rocks are the creation of repeated layers of sediments. During the Renaissance, people thought the biblical flood had deposited the fossils of sea creatures that are found high in the mountains. But Leonardo realized that what were mountains in his day had in ancient times been at the bottom of some great sea. He observed and wrote about the atmosphere, the course of rivers, and the geography of lakes. Leonardo discussed astronomy, noting that Earth is a sphere and how the moon, which has no light of its own, reflects the light of the sun. He also realized that the stars are enormous but only look small because they are far away.

We can all practice Leonardo's mindfulness. Observation is an activity not only for the eyes but for the ears and the nose as well. It is also something that can be done from a wheelchair or while lying in bed. By making an effort to see or hear or smell our world more acutely we realize the richness of life that surrounds us. Awareness allows us to perceive that our everyday world, like Leonardo's world, is a place of wonders. Using his awareness, Leonardo looked at ordinary objects with extraordinary results. By analyzing cracks in walls and buildings, he discovered the source of their structural problems. Leonardo also examined the physics of constructing a building. He looked at the manufacture and safety of arches and supports, discussing the type of soil best for construction and how large a foundation must be in order to support a wall.

Leonardo also drew plans for cities with canals and designed the architecture of castles, palaces, villas, churches, and mausoleums. He investigated the properties of light, sound, and mirrors, and examined the growth of plants. By exploring the world through observation, Leonardo uncovered the timeless patterns of nature. He studied the flight of birds and found that the curvature of their wings helps to keep them aloft.[30] He realized that currents of air are like currents of water. A group of drawings he did late in life called *The Deluge* portrays the dynamics of rushing water so perceptively that they are used to illustrate chaos theory today.[31]

Anatomy and Instructions for Artists

Leonardo also took his perceptions and turned them into instructions for artists.[32] He wrote about light and shadow and how to model forms with direct and indirect light to make them look real. He discussed color theory and gave advice on portrait painting, landscape painting, and figure painting. Leonardo even noticed that artists, without realizing it, tend to reproduce their own face in the paintings they make and he warned them to be aware of this. He spoke about the proportions of the human body and showed how they look different in motion and that these proportions change with age. He analyzed vision and spoke about perspective, explaining that objects far away not only look smaller but are also fainter in color because they become obscured by layers of atmosphere. Leonardo naturally worked across disciplines. For him, painting was a science, and there was no separation between science and art. We see him as a genius in multiple categories, but for Leonardo da Vinci all areas of knowledge were part of the great web of life.

One of Leonardo's most important contributions was in the field of anatomy.[33] For an artist to accurately draw the human body, it is important to know the bones and muscles that make up its shape. But Leonardo went further. Writing and illustrating his anatomical work, he dissected more than thirty cadavers. Leonardo learned not only about the muscles and bones but also about veins, arteries, nerves, and the inner organs. In addition, he dissected animals and made studies of the comparative anatomy between animals and humans. Dissection is difficult work, and during the Renaissance, before refrigeration, it was gruesome. But Leonardo persevered. Observing and recording what he saw, Leonardo da Vinci became one of the greatest anatomists of all time and left us the most beautiful anatomical illustrations that have ever been created.

Leonardo's vision was not limited to directly observing the world around him; he also had an enormous capacity to look inward and imagine. This facet of his genius was also enhanced by a challenge. As dyslexia fueled his observation of the physical world, attention deficit disorder fired his imagination.

Attention Deficit Disorder (ADD)

Like dyslexia, attention deficit disorder is a learning difficulty that is usually inherited. Its general characteristics are distractibility, impulsivity, and restlessness, which are also sometimes stated as inattention, impulsivity, and hyperactivity.[34] Because ADD is associated with problems in the frontal lobes of the brain, people with attention deficit disorder have difficulties with executive functions.[35] This means they may have trouble planning, organizing, realizing the future consequences of their actions, keeping their attention from wandering, and controlling impulsive behavior. Although dyslexia and ADD originate in different parts of the brain, there appears to be a connection between the two. In their book *Driven to Distraction: Recognizing and Coping with Attention Deficit Disorder from Childhood through Adulthood*, the psychiatrists Edward M. Hallowell and John J. Ratey note that while people with ADD do not tend to have dyslexia at higher rates than the general population, people with dyslexia are more likely to have ADD.[36]

Having both learning disorders can magnify problems at school and may be another reason why Leonardo was never trained to use his right hand.

ADD affects ten to thirteen people out of every hundred[37] and comes in varying degrees of severity. Some people have a very mild form that does not greatly affect the quality of their lives, while others are severely impaired. Some individuals with attention deficit disorder are hyperactive, while others appear to be daydreamers and still others have aspects of both. Because of these differences, the American Psychiatric Association defines three categories of attention deficit disorder: (1) a person is predominantly hyperactive and obviously impulsive; (2) a person is predominantly quiet and inattentive; and (3) a combination of (1) and (2).[38]

Leonardo most likely had the combined form of attention deficit disorder that includes hyperactivity and inattention because he showed evidence of both restlessness and daydreaming. Sometimes Leonardo would be quietly lost in thought for hours,[39] but his behavior was unpredictable.[40] He traveled a great deal and also moved from place to place, living in Venice, Parma, Rome, and France, and multiple times in Florence and Milan.[41]

Attention Deficit Disorder and Creativity

Leonardo was not alone in having attention deficit disorder. It appears to be widespread in the creative population. I have ADD, and many other creative people I know have it as well. ADD may be so prevalent in artists because of its many similarities to the creative process.[42] And these similarities can promote creativity. For example, creativity depends on new ideas, and the fleeting focus of attention in ADD both allows and encourages many ideas to come into the mind. Rapidly moving thoughts can be disconcerting, but they can also keep us open to what is original and valuable. In addition, many thoughts provide multiple options for the creative process.

ADD can help creativity through both daydreaming and activity. The creative process has an active component, the physical creation of a work of art and a contemplative aspect when artists quietly assess what they have done or think about new possibilities. People with attention deficit disorder, who can be captured by their imagination like Leonardo, may be very comfortable with the contemplative aspect of creativity and find it's the time when they get their best ideas. The hyperactive element of ADD can be positive as well. Bursts of energy are very useful for creativity, especially during times of extended physical work. When stretching canvas material over the wooden frame that supports a painting or putting in large areas of color, it helps to have an internal boost.

Creative people and those with ADD are also more sensitive to stimulation from their environment.[43] Because of this, it may be difficult to block unwanted distractions. I have to travel with earphones on planes and long train rides to screen out the sounds around me. But the sensitivity that is so distressing can also allow a deeper experience of the world and profound impressions are more likely to find their way into a work of art. Using his extreme sensitivity, Leonardo looks intensely at the environment and then transforms his impressions into creativity.[44]

People with ADD like new experiences, and newness can be fundamental to the creative process. Without new elements, creativity dissolves into repetition. Searching for the new brings originality into art and life. Although the desire for novelty can degenerate into harmful sensation seeking, when used constructively it can change history. By turning ADD into a creative force, Leonardo began the High Renaissance style of art.[45]

Restlessness, Attention, and Creativity

If you do a Web search for Leonardo and attention deficit disorder, the results always bring up the artist's tendency to leave projects unfinished. Not everyone who abandons a task has ADD, but Leonardo's long history of uncompleted work and abandoned activities strongly suggests attention deficit disorder. He was famous for this in his lifetime,[46] and it is a pattern that had been with him since childhood. Vasari says that as a schoolboy Leonardo "didn't stay with any subject very long and asked so many questions that he bewildered his teacher."[47] While quickly changing subjects suggests the shorter attention span of ADD, the psychologist Sara Denning says that curiosity and asking many questions are also hallmarks of the condition.[48] In addition, she notes that people with ADD may ask a second question even before they hear an answer to the first one. Perhaps this is why Leonardo bewildered his teacher.

Although Vasari complains that Leonardo "set himself to learn many things, and then, after having begun them, abandoned them,"[49] he also writes that Leonardo never ceased drawing and that his brain never stopped working. What we see here are two aspects of the restlessness of ADD.[50] There is a restlessness that prevented Leonardo from completing his projects but there is also a restlessness that drove his production.

Restlessness and the shorter attention span of ADD appear to have shaped Leonardo's output in many ways. Painting and sculpture, especially the extremely slow and painstaking method in which Leonardo worked, was less comfortable for his ADD temperament than making a drawing. This may account for the artist's pattern of leaving long-term projects unfinished while producing work that can be done more quickly. Although Leonardo completed only fifteen paintings in his entire life and did not finish any of his sculptures, he left us more than four thousand drawings, which is four times more than any other artist of his era.[51] And there may have been more than twice that many, because so much of Leonardo's work has been lost.

Creating many drawings may also appeal to the ADD temperament because it is a varied experience full of new, short-term events. Novelty holds the attention of someone with ADD longer than sameness, and Leonardo sketched quickly. Carmen Bambach, of the Metropolitan Museum of Art, calls his emphasis on freshness in sketching one of the great innovations of the Renaissance.[52] Leonardo's writing also suggests ADD, because he wrote very briefly on a great many topics. His essays are rarely longer than a page in length and are often just one short paragraph.[53] But his abbreviated style concentrates on the important information and avoids unnecessary material. It also makes his writing more comfortable for another person with ADD, like me, to read.

ADD and Concentration

A hallmark of ADD is wandering attention. One of the ways that people with ADD help themselves focus is through creating a distraction in the environment. It may seem paradoxical, but for individuals with ADD distraction can help minimize distraction. Music and sound from a TV or a radio during work might annoy some people or entertain others, but for those with attention deficit disorder it serves a specific neurological function. It helps concentration. The psychiatrists Edward M. Hallowell and John J. Ratey believe that environmental sounds can keep one part of the brain from sending distracting signals to another part of the brain that is trying to concentrate.[54] In the past, artists who wanted ambient sound and could afford it hired musicians or readers as background accompaniment. Leonardo wrote about the pleasure of listening to music or the words of fine authors read aloud as he painted.[55]

This is still a very popular method of working. Most of the contemporary artists I know listen to either music or words in the background while they work. Do they have ADD? I don't know, but from personal experience I presume a substantial number do. Sara Denning believes that listening to words or music can lower the anxiety of decision making and allow creativity to flow.[56] For me, it seems to capture the conscious mind, letting the unconscious control the hand that paints and the eye that sees. And it is the unconscious mind that brings depth and surprise to a work of art. Even though a person may be only barely aware of the sound, it still helps him or her focus. In fact, there are some artists with ADD who actually prefer working in the midst of a commotion as a way to concentrate. In addition to being a focusing aid, ambient noise can both initiate and stimulate work. People with attention deficit disorder often have difficulty switching tasks or starting an action, but music or words can form a bridge from one activity to another and help them begin to work.

I also like to have background accompaniment when I make visual art. Sometimes I listen to music and sometimes to words. This is a very different experience for me than when I am in a public place and not able to screen out unwanted sounds. Somehow the sounds that I allow in the studio when I paint are acceptable rather than annoying. They get me going and working. Then there is that special time. I never know when it will come or how long it will last. It's when my concentration is directly on the work and all I know is the work. That is when I cease to hear all sound. The world becomes astonishingly silent. Somehow the words or music in the studio cease to exist, and all other sensory input seems to stop. I hear nothing. The painting always improves during that period. All I know is that despite any sounds, there is only the work and complete silence. It's my favorite time.

Impulsivity and Lateral Thinking

Another characteristic of ADD is impulsivity, and like so many things it has both positive and negative aspects. Using impulsivity to fight boredom can lead to reckless behavior, but used creatively it can encourage invention. We see impulsivity in Leonardo's lateral thinking. This is a type of thought pattern often found in people with ADD. Lateral thinking occurs when someone breaks off in the middle of a train of thought and makes a lateral connection to another idea (or ideas) that has just occurred to him or her.[57] For years I have noticed this in myself and in other people with ADD. I also call it tangential thinking, because after starting a topic, a person might suddenly go off on a tangent and bring in something else that seems related. Although this may be confusing in conversation, it can be excellent for creativity. Instead of proceeding conventionally in a straight line or sequence of ideas, an individual may think sideways, find a new association, and follow it to a more creative conclusion. Sometimes lateral thinking leads to a string of thoughts going nowhere, while at other times it is a flash of brilliance.

Leonardo's lateral thinking benefitted him, but it also got him in trouble with Pope Leo X, who hired him to do a small painting.[58] Because lateral thinking can generate pieces of inspiration out of sequence in a project, Leonardo started making a special varnish to complete the work before he even began the painting. The pope became so exasperated that he said Leonardo would never achieve anything because he thought of the ending before the beginning. And he gave the artist no further commissions.

We also see Leonardo's lateral thinking when he impulsively breaks off in the middle of some beautiful anatomical drawings of the hand and writes that he must create a book on the mechanics of movement in humans and other animals.[59] It shows us how Leonardo's creativity in one field propeled him to work in another. By sparking his creative impulse, lateral thinking revealed the workings of Leonardo's mind. It is a way he makes connections across disciplines. Unable to remain in one field, Leonardo mastered many, and ADD may be one of the reasons he is considered to be a universal genius.

Inconsistent Attention and Hyperfocus

Some researchers think that attention deficit disorder should really be called inconsistent attention disorder because of its various types of concentration.[60] ADD can manifest as brief periods of work before one project is abandoned for another and also as hours lost in thought rather than physical action. A third aspect of ADD is the ability to hyperfocus, to concentrate on one thing for an extended period of time to the exclusion of everything else. This combination of fleeting efforts, absorption in thought, and extreme concentration was evident during Leonardo's work on his large mural painting *The Last Supper*, in the Monastery of Santa Maria delle Grazie in Milan.

Matteo Bandelli, who was one of the monks in the monastery, gave us a firsthand account of the artist's variable behavior.[61] Sometimes, he said, Leonardo would arrive at dawn and paint until dark, without stopping to eat or drink. Then for three or four days he would be deep in thought for hours at a time, examining the unfinished mural and not painting at all. On still other days the artist would leave the huge sculpture of a horse he was working on in a different part of the city and come to the monastery. But then, after putting a few brushstrokes on *The Last Supper*, he would suddenly be gone.

Leonardo's variable behavior distressed his clients no end. He was also always experimenting: instead of using the classic technique of fresco painting to create the mural, Leonardo kept inventing new processes. He worked on this project from 1495 to 1498, but unfortunately his new methods weren't successful, and by 1517 the mural started to disintegrate.[62] Yet even with its fading paint and despite Leonardo's erratic schedule, the mural is a masterpiece. There had never before been such a profound depth of interaction among figures in any previous painting of the Last Supper or such a dramatic portrayal of space. Leonardo's *Last Supper* is one of the great landmarks in the history of art.

ADD: Low Arousal

In some people with attention deficit disorder, there is decreased blood flow to the frontal cortex of the brain.[63] As a result, they have reduced activity there, along with lower glucose utilization. Glucose is a sugar that brains cells use as fuel. When a smaller amount of glucose is consumed, the cells are less active. Because of this, the frontal brain of a person with ADD may seem "sleepy" or chronically underaroused. To increase their level of brain function and maintain attention, some individuals search for high-stimulus activities. This is why certain people with ADD may engage in risky behaviors, such as skydiving or gambling. During these intense activities, they don't feel nervous; they feel alert.

The need to arouse a sleepy ADD brain may be another reason why artists listen to music or words while they work. Experiments indicate that certain types of music or words can actually stimulate the brain and improve spatial abilities. Called the "Mozart effect,"[64] it comes from research demonstrating that similar groups of neurons fire in the cerebral cortex during both music recognition and spatial tasks, such as the ability to visualize an image and rotate it in your mind. Because of this similarity, scientists theorized that listening to music might stimulate the neurons active in spatial abilities. In an experiment, they found that Mozart's *Sonata for Two Pianos in D Major*, K. 448, significantly raised people's test scores on spatial performance as measured by the Stanford-Binet intelligence test. Other lively pieces of music were also found to be effective. But silence, relaxation sounds, and music that was slow or repetitive did not improve spatial intelligence. Further tests showed that people's spatial abilities were enhanced most while listening to what they preferred, either music they liked or spoken words about something that interested them. The underlying factor appeared to be a stimulus that provided the optimum level of arousal.

In their studios, artists listen to what they prefer, and I believe they realize intuitively which sounds are arousing and benefit their work. Many of the artists I know sometimes listen to music and at other times to words, depending on their preference of the moment. Although the experiments measured spatial abilities on intelligence tests, spatial aptitude is central to creating visual art. None of the experiments mentioned whether any of the people tested had ADD. It would be interesting to find out if the auditory stimulus of either words or music makes a greater difference in the spatial performance of individuals with ADD as compared to those without the condition. Perhaps someone will design an experiment to measure this effect.

ADD: The Excitement of Daydreaming

While some individuals with ADD act out with risky behavior to excite an underaroused brain, I believe that others act "in" to achieve similar results. By this I suggest that instead of skydiving or gambling, people with the inattention or combined form of ADD may go inward and use the rich fantasy world of their daydreams as a way to maintain optimal brain arousal. They may be stimulating their brains through the creation of vivid fantasies. For them an extensive inner life might be as exciting as vertical skiing is for a physical athlete. If their fantasies do result in better brain arousal and sustained attention, it could be a reason why people like Leonardo stay in reverie for hours. Daydreaming, which is considered to be inattention, might be more aptly viewed as attention directed to another source.

It is possible that Leonardo, who could be lost in contemplation for half a day,[65] used his daydreams as arousal mechanisms. He even spoke about "arousing the mind to various inventions."[66] Like other artists and inventors, Leonardo's mental imagery was most likely very vivid. We do not know his personal fantasies, but when we consider that he invented a human-powered flying machine/glider, a submarine, a parachute, and a tank, among other things, it is possible that the subject matter of his creative reveries may have been as exciting to him as extreme sports are to someone else. And it was in daydreaming that Leonardo got his ideas. But of all Leonardo's habits, it was his daydreaming that exasperated his clients the most.

The Benefits of Reverie

Like tangential thinking, daydreaming can evaporate into nothing or become an experience of inspiration. It all depends on a person's ability to bring ideas from his or her imagination into reality. Some individuals with ADD are unfortunately blocked in this way and unable to realize their thoughts in the physical world.[67] Yet for others like Leonardo, reveries are the groundwork for genius. But while he found inspiration, his clients found exasperation. During the time Leonardo worked on *The Last Supper*, the prior of the monastery kept pushing him to paint rather than daydream.[68] Finally, the prior became so angry that he complained to Duke Ludovico Sforza, the ruler of

Milan. Leonardo answered the duke by saying that sometimes people accomplish the most when they seem not to be working. Then, he explained, the mind is at its most creative. The brain must first invent what the hands will later express.

Leonardo believed so strongly in the power of daydreams that he recommended them as an aid to the creative process.[69] He said that if one stares at stains on a wall one may begin to see landscapes, strange faces, figures in battle, or other images that can be used as subjects for art. Inspired by reverie, Leonardo's stream-of-consciousness associations are seen as a breakthrough in creative thinking.[70]

Imagination and Inventions

Leonardo's reveries became not only art but also inventions. After taking inspiration from the physical world, Leonardo imagined objects that would fill a need, such as his flint lock that produces a spark. Afterward he turned them into drawings. Designing machines in his mind is a trait Leonardo shared with another inventor, Nikola Tesla (1856–1943). Tesla, who is also thought to have had ADD,[71] had such a vivid imagination that he could construct machines in his mind, start them running, and then later check on their functioning to see if they needed improvements.[72] Leonardo may have had similar abilities. Many of his machines, like the spring-driven car, were designed in his mind and then drawn, but never built in his lifetime. Yet centuries later, when constructed from his drawings, they work perfectly.

According to the historian of science Ritchie Calder, Leonardo made more discoveries than Edison.[73] A partial list of Leonardo's inventions includes a helicopter, a submarine, a human-powered flying machine/glider, an air-cooling system, a bicycle, a car, a parachute, a telescope, a toilet seat, musical instruments, a mechanized harpsichord, an underwater breathing device, a swimming flipper, a dredging machine, a lifesaver flotation device, movable bridges, water locks for boats, a paddle boat with gears, a canal system, a crane, a pile driver, a machine gun, a tank, an ideal city with two-level walkways and suburbs, an olive press, prefabricated houses, machines for the textile industry such as the gig mill or teaseling machine, a shearing machine, and a needle-sharpening machine.[74]

There are presumably many more of Leonardo's inventions than we currently know of, because through the centuries much of his work has been lost. His mirror-written manuscripts may have been discarded by people who didn't realize how they could be read. But over the years, additional works by Leonardo have surfaced and we can only hope more will be discovered.

Ahead of His Time

Leonardo lived at a time when the printing industry was starting, and he even contributed a weight-loaded spinner and a screw to improve the flatbed printing press.[75] But he never published his inventions. His only published works are illustrations for a book on mathematics by his friend Luca Pacioli. As a result, the great majority of Leonardo's discoveries remained unknown to the general public, and over the centuries they were reinvented by other people.

Calder notes that Leonardo's double-winged glider was reinvented four hundred years later by Otto Lilienthal, the German aviator whose designs influenced the Wright brothers' plane.[76] Leonardo also discovered the fundamental principle describing the movement of objects through air that two hundred years later Newton identified as a law of physics.

Self-Esteem and Depression

Despite his genius, Leonardo had a poor opinion of himself. Throughout his writing, he repeated the phrase "Tell me if anything was ever done?" He also lamented, "I have wasted my hours," and tried to compensate by pushing himself. "No work shall tire me," he insisted. "Death before weariness," said Leonardo. "God, sellest us all good things at the price of labor."[77] Although low self-esteem and depression are associated with ADD,[78] Leonardo's negative self-image is a lesson for us all. The way we see ourselves can be completely different from the way others perceive us and may have little to do with reality.

Challenges and Genius

Leonardo's challenges fueled his genius. The dyslexia that turned him away from literature to observation of the physical world and the ADD that promoted his internal reveries profoundly influenced his art, his science, and his body of inventions. Without these learning difficulties, Leonardo might have had a classical education, entered an established profession, and enjoyed the self-esteem that comes from following an accepted course. But he might not have discovered the origin of striated rocks or the reason that fossils of sea animals are embedded high in the mountains. He might never have invented a helicopter or a submarine, designed bridges, or studied anatomy. And our world would be without the *Mona Lisa*.

Challenges and Perfection

Leonardo's challenges seem less like imperfections and more like creative inspirations. Leonardo da Vinci and the artists featured in the next chapter were all born with learning challenges that became a basis for their creativity. They show us we don't have to be perfect to create art. We don't even have to be perfect to be one of the greatest artists of all time, like Leonardo. I also think we don't have to be perfect to be a great person, friend, or relative. Perfection is unattainable. What is important is to try our best. When we do our very best, amazing things can happen, often with unimagined success. Our best is perfection for all of us.

Chapter 8

Artists and Learning Difficulties

*A problem is a chance for you to do
your best.* —*Duke Ellington*

It is no surprise that we are born with what seem like imperfections, because even our universe was born that way. Scientists tell us that as a result of the big bang, the enormous event that started everything, there was an uneven distribution of matter and energy in the universe. But it was this imperfect distribution in the initial explosion that later caused the formation of galaxies, stars, and our Earth. Without unevenness, the universe might have sprung into being as a vast, undifferentiated, and lifeless place. So we have cosmic imperfections to thank for our existence.

Like our universe, we are also born with imperfections that prove to be beneficial. In this chapter, artists take what looks like a disability—difficulty reading, an inability to recognize faces, autism, or Down syndrome—and use it in the service of their art.

Dyslexia

One of our most widespread challenges is language-based learning difficulties. According to the way they are defined, learning problems affect 10 to 30 percent of our population.[1] Of all of these challenges, the most prevalent is dyslexia. Affecting both males and females in nearly equal numbers, dyslexia occurs in every socioeconomic and ethnic group.

On the lists of famous people with dyslexia, we often see the artist Walt Disney (American, 1901–1966, born Walter Elias Disney), but he did not have learning difficulties.[2] In grade school Disney's paper route required him to get up at 3:30 in the morning, often making it hard for him to stay awake in class, and in high school he was more interested in trying to enlist in World War I and creating art than in his schoolwork.

Six of the artists in this chapter do have dyslexia, and each one does something different with his or her reading problem. But for all of them it is important to their work. With excellent visual talent despite learning difficulties, the artists are examples of the psychologist Howard Gardner's theory of multiple intelligences. He defines intelligence as "the ability to solve problems, or to create products, that are valued within one or more cultural settings."[3] According to his theory, we are capable of different types of intelligence, which explains why dyslexic people with difficulty in linguistic (language-based) intelligence can excel in the spatial intelligence needed for art.

One of the reasons dyslexia interests me is because I am dyslexic. Occasionally I transpose letters and numbers and sometimes do not even see a letter or a number at all. This has not been a big problem with words, because it's possible to guess a word with a letter or two missing, but not seeing every number in an equation produces a sum with vastly different results. Had I been able to see every number, I would have become a mathematician or a physicist rather than an artist and a writer. Writing is a struggle for me, because I write more slowly than a person without dyslexia. But it also helps me to write clearly. I rewrite my words many times until I understand them easily as a dyslexic. Then I know others will understand the words, too. Over the years, by observing friends and students, I have noticed that artists tend to have a higher degree of dyslexia than the general population. I haven't found any statistics on this as yet, but it may be because dyslexics have good visual-spatial ability and can be very creative. Also, if the perception of words or numbers fails you, images may become your chosen path.

ROBERT RAUSCHENBERG

"Probably the only reason that I'm a painter," admits Robert Rauschenberg (American, b. 1925), "is because I couldn't read."[4] Because he is severely dyslexic, words sometimes look backward or upside down to him. In school, while other children were reading their books, he was drawing in the margins. "I grew up being reassured every day that I was inferior,"[5] recalls Rauschenberg about his painful early years. "I excelled at poor grades."[6] Later the dyslexia that hampered him in school became an asset to his career. In his art Rauschenberg will repeat images, sometimes reversing them and also turning them upside down, which is the way he sees letters. The art historian Robert Mattison believes this adds to the richness of Rauschenberg's imagery. He says it captures the complexity of modern life by showing us that we live in a world of multiple viewpoints.[7]

Rauschenberg is a printmaker as well as a painter, and dyslexia also helps him in the print workshop. In the process of making a lithographic print, an artist must create an image that will be reversed when it is printed on paper. Because of this reversal, most artists make multiple trial prints called proofs in order to see how their art will look in its final form. But as a dyslexic Rauschenberg doesn't have to go through this process. He knows instantly how the reversed images will look in the final work of art. "I already see backwards," explains Rauschenberg. "So printing is an absolute natural for me."[8]

Like Leonardo and many other creative people, Robert Rauschenberg appears to have attention deficit disorder. But again, he uses the challenge to further his art. Instead of being derailed by the constant distractions of ADD, Rauschenberg turns them into inspiration. The artist enjoys the sudden insights that arise from lateral thinking and encourages comments from studio assistants.[9] Rauschenberg also incorporates the way light happens to fall on a canvas as an influence in his art and utilizes items he hears on the news while working. Accepting his varying attention span, Rauschenberg works in a way that allows him to quickly switch from one project to another or concentrate on only one piece for a long time. His work hours also vary, sometimes extending throughout the night. By accommodating the fluid time frames inherent in attention deficit disorder, Rauschenberg lessens his frustration and improves his production.

Rauschenberg is one of those people with attention deficit disorder who likes to work in the middle of a commotion. In addition to having assistants in the studio and the TV turned on, he is often surrounded by family, friends, and pets. "I love a kind of social chaos," he says. "It stimulates me."[10] Rauschenberg's preference for company and closeness with people shows in his work through the numerous pieces he has done in collaboration with others. It is also apparent in his many acts of charity.

PABLO PICASSO

Dyslexia was influential in turning Rauschenberg to art, but it is likely that Pablo Picasso (Spanish, lived in France, 1881–1973) would have become an artist even without his reading difficulties.

Picasso's father, a professional painter, was his first teacher and a role model. As a child, Picasso created art well before he could read, but difficulties in the world of letters made visual creativity even more important to him.

According to family legend, Picasso loved art in his infancy and was drawing before he could talk.[11] His mother said the first sound her son made was *piz* for the word *lapiz*, which is Spanish for pencil. As a young child, Picasso drew happily for hours, but school was not such fun. Picasso hated school so intensely that he would throw tantrums before going and often had to be dragged there screaming and kicking. Although he started school at five, Picasso said that he could not remember when he finally learned to read and write, but that it was not before he was ten. Arithmetic was also very difficult for him, and he had trouble telling the time. His spelling was poor and his handwriting was a scrawl. Frustrated and angry with schoolwork, young Picasso sought refuge in his father's studio. Here, creating art, he felt at home. Although Picasso's father was afraid his son might grow up to be nearly illiterate, he also recognized the child's enormous talent.

Part of the art lessons he gave the boy were instructions on how to draw pigeons. These beautiful drawings of birds are some of the earliest work we have by Picasso's hand. But it was through his drawings of pigeons that Picasso began his understanding of math. He realized that the eye of the pigeon looks like a round zero and that the bird has two eyes, two wings, and two legs. Another pencil sketch from childhood shows how Picasso tried to incorporate numbers into images in a further attempt to make them real in order to understand them. In a drawing of two men he makes the eyes of one in the shape of the number 7 and the eyes of the other like the number 8. Near the figures, the numbers from one to nine are written several times. Numbers eventually served Picasso well. Later, as one of the most successful artists of the twentieth century, he carefully calculated all the commissions that art dealers made on his work. In adulthood Picasso also wrote poetry, but his spelling remained unusual, and he still could not remember the sequence of letters in the alphabet.

Dyslexia and the Tangible World

Associating numbers with images is a way to make them concrete and easier to grasp, and connecting written symbols with the tangible physical world is one of the methods currently used in teaching dyslexic individuals to read. Picasso invented his own way to do this and so did Monona Rossol.

MONONA ROSSOL

"They told me I was slow because I couldn't read," says the ceramic artist and health hazards expert Monona Rossol (American, b. 1936).[12] "I was a very verbal child and in kindergarten I was an excellent student," she recalls, but in the higher grades, as reading became central to learning, Rossol was placed lower and lower in class. "Finally they put me with the worst students in my grade and I was very angry," she relates. The anger started fights and Rossol became a behavior problem. It was not until high school that she discovered a way to cut through the dyslexia.

Rossol's invention is an alphabet in which every letter has its own color. "*A* is red, *b* is a light yellow brown, *c* is a pale yellow, *d* is a darker brown, and so forth," she explains. Without their colors, the letters jump around in total confusion and even reverse before her eyes. But when the shape of a letter is assigned a color it stays in place. "Color has no up, down, or backward," states Rossol, "so it holds the meaning of the letter steady." The instant she sees a letter, she remembers the color and it is the colors that give her the word. Rossol also assigns colors to numbers and it helps her to remember them. Her method works very well when reading text in black and white, but computer monitors are in color. Rossol can easily handle colorful icons but has difficulty with colored Web language. After transposing it into black and white and then using her own color alphabet, "I read as quickly as a person without dyslexia," she says.

"My system is based on synesthesia," explains Rossol. This type of thinking is found in a small percentage of the population. According to the neurologist Richard E. Cytowic, synesthesia is an experience that is felt in more than one sensory mode.[13] People with synesthesia, he states, can taste shapes and hear colors, and while their ability is unusual, it is not abnormal. Rossol gives an example with the phrase "the yellow pain." "For most people," she explains, "this phrase would be poetic license, but for a person with synesthesia, it is the reality of their experience." Seeing letters and numbers as colors, she processes the enormous amount of scientific data necessary for her work as a health hazards expert and says, "I use synesthesia every day."

Dyslexia: Its History and Future

What are seen today as learning difficulties may be so prevalent in our society because it is only recently that we have made an effort toward widespread literacy. For much of the time that modern human beings have existed, most of us did not learn to read. Even kings could be illiterate, relying on scribes to read and write for them. When literacy was restricted to a minority of individuals and the vast majority of us could not read or write, most learning difficulties went undetected. And because they did not impact on daily life, they were not recognized as problems. There is another reason why dyslexia is still with us: the many talents associated with dyslexic people.[14] Thomas G.

West, who writes on dyslexia, says people with this condition are frequently intuitive and good speakers, can be entrepreneurs, have excellent memories, and are often gifted visually and spatially, which is why they may become artists.[15]

AUGUSTE RODIN

Like many other dyslexics, Auguste Rodin (French, 1840–1917) enjoyed speaking, was gifted spatially, and had severe reading problems. There is an institute named in honor of Rodin's father, Jean-Baptiste Rodin, because he was so concerned about his son's academic failures. Called the Rodin Remediation Academy, it is part of the Institute of Medical Psychology at the University of Munich and encourages research in the diagnosis and treatment of learning difficulties.[16]

Rodin was nearsighted as well as dyslexic, and his poor vision intensified his problems with reading.[17] His education began in a neighborhood school run by Brothers of the Christian Doctrine, and although the monks had an excellent reputation for teaching, the young boy learned almost nothing. Instead, he preferred to make art. One of his favorite pastimes was copying pictures from the illustrated newspapers used to wrap the grocery packages his mother brought home. Despite their limited means and the boy's academic problems, his parents sent him to a small boarding school run by his uncle to ensure their son would receive a formal education. Rodin eventually learned to read there, but he could never master spelling, mathematics, or Latin. After Rodin had attended boarding school for four years, his parents realized that their son would not have a career in civil service or the professions, and they allowed him to study art.

One day as a beginning art student, Rodin happened to open the door to a sculpture class—and experienced a revelation. "I saw clay for the first time," he recalled, "and I felt as if I were ascending into heaven."[18] From that moment on, sculpture was his focus, and he eventually became the leading sculptor of his age. Later in life Rodin mused over not having learned Latin. As a poor person, he said that Latin would have enabled him to become a teacher. But then we might not have his sculpture today.

Multiple Challenges

Sometimes a person with multiple learning difficulties can integrate them all in making art. Each of Chuck Close's challenges complements the other and enhances his creativity.

CHUCK CLOSE

"Art saved my life," says Chuck Close (American, b. 1940), who has dyslexia, attention deficit disorder, and prosopagnosia.[19] Reports cards he received during his childhood in Tacoma, Washington, said he was unintelligent and lazy and didn't pay attention.[20] In fact Close is extremely intelligent and worked so hard because of his learning problems that he devised his own way to study. He would fill the bathtub with hot water and then lay a board across it to hold a book. In the darkened room, Close would shine a spotlight on each page and read it out loud five times. By hearing the information, he could remember it. Using the ADD capacity to hyperfocus, he stayed in the tub half the night reading pages out loud, until his skin was wrinkled as a raisin and he had learned enough to pass a test.

Jan Greenberg and Sarah Jordan, who wrote about Close's learning challenges in their book *Chuck Close Up Close*, believe that the extreme discipline the artist developed in school laid the foundation for his adult work. I agree and also think that concentrating on one page at a time and trusting that the information from all the pages will add up to a unified whole is similar to the way Close paints a canvas. He fills in a grid of multiple small squares that combine their bits of information into a large, recognizable image. "Learning disorders," states Close, "shape every aspect of my work."[21]

Because of Close's difficulties in school, his teachers advised him to go to junior college. He did and then transferred to the University of Washington and on to Yale for graduate school. Like many other dyslexics, Chuck Close was uncoordinated and could not play sports. But he excelled at art and his parents encouraged him with art supplies and lessons.[22] When a serious kidney infection at eleven kept him in bed for months,[23] it deepened his commitment, but he had already started art lessons at the age of eight. "I learned to draw from nude models," he says, and "it made me the envy of all my friends."[24]

Chuck Close has another neurological difficulty—prosopagnosia, also called face blindness.[25] "I have trouble recognizing faces," he admits, "particularly in three dimensions."[26] Ruth Daniels, a professor of education, notes that in compensation for prosopagnosia, the artist's work is composed exclusively of faces, some of which are nine feet tall.[27] Spending three to fifteen months on one of his large canvases, Close accepts no commissions and only portrays the people he cares about, his family and friends. Using his photographic memory for flat images, he remembers their faces by painting portraits of them. "I commit to my memory," explains Close, "people who are important to me."[28]

I believe that Close's prosopagnosia has an additional effect on his work. Most people perceive and recognize faces as a whole, but according to the neurologist Oliver Sacks,[29] individuals with prosopagnosia are not capable of seeing an entire face at once. Instead, they perceive faces more indirectly as a composite of many separate and seemingly meaningless features. But they perceive these bits of information more acutely than a person without face blindness. By combining many small areas of information, people with prosopagnosia can identify a face. This is an exact description of Chuck Close's art. He creates his images the way a person with prosopagnosia sees a face, as an aggregate of seemingly meaningless small bits of information that when combined create a very meaningful whole. "I'm overwhelmed by the whole," reveals Close. "How do you make a big head? How do you make a nose? I'm not sure! But by breaking the image down into small units . . . eventually I have a painting."[30]

Because of this, all of his works have something in common. They are created from a group of small squares that form an underlying grid in his portraits. For centuries artists have used grids as a way to transfer images from a drawing onto canvas. By dividing the smaller work into a grid of squares, they could use the information in each square to redraw the image inside a corresponding larger grid created on canvas. But the grid was just a convenience and not an end in itself. For Close, it is the basis and structure of his work and refers to his mode of seeing.

First he draws a grid on a photograph he has taken of a person's face and then transfers the information from each square in the photograph to its corresponding square on the paper or canvas. Because of prosopagnosia, Close's awareness of the small bits of information in each square is much more acute than the perception of an average person, so he can translate the information from each square into a small abstract design that still retains a complete relevance to the whole image. When you stand very near one of his paintings, the squares appear to be small, separate abstract works of art, but from a distance they build a perfectly constructed face. Close manages these small bits of information so well that he has on occasion painted with his fingertips instead of using brushes. And yet these faces created from fingerprints are both realistic and recognizable.

Animals and Art

Rosa Bonheur and Raymond Hu are two artists with learning difficulties who love animals and identify with them so strongly that it becomes central to their creativity and a source of personal strength. Each of them is an *animalier*, which is the classic art historical term for an artist who specializes in painting animals. Although they live a continent and a century and a half apart, both artists show the dignity of animals and portray them as vehicles for the emotions that human animals and nonhuman animals share.

ROSA BONHEUR

"Couldn't I become famous by just painting animals?" young Rosa Bonheur (French, 1822–1899) asked her painter father.[31] And he replied, "Of course."[32] Bonheur would almost certainly have become an artist even without learning difficulties, because her father, like Picasso's, was a painter and her role model. In a portrait he made of her when she was four, she is shown holding her doll in one hand and a pencil in the other. When her father painted portraits of people, she sat her little doll in a chair and started drawing it. Bonheur's mother encouraged her painting and also taught her daughter to read. Reading was more difficult than art for the young girl, but an interest in animals helped her overcome dyslexia.

"Lessons always gave me a hard time," admitted Bonheur. "Beads of sweat would collect on my forehead while my mother wore herself out trying to drum the alphabet into my head." Then one day her mother had an excellent idea. "She told me to draw an ass next to the letter *A*, a bull next to the *B*, a cat next to the *C*," recalled Bonheur, "and so on right up to *Z* for zebra." Bonheur began to read. "This intelligent object lesson," she said, "was a revelation for my infant brain."[33]

Bonheur also began using animal images to interpret the world. By the age of ten, she was drawing animals in the parks outside Paris, and as an adult she gained an international reputation for her paintings of animals. Bonheur's most famous work, *The Horse Fair*, is an eight-by-sixteen-foot oil on canvas that was completed in 1853. Now in the collection of the Metropolitan Museum of Art in New York, it was one of the most celebrated paintings of its day. In reward for her excellence and achievement, Rosa Bonheur became the first woman in France to receive her country's highest decoration, the cross of the Legion of Honor.

Visible Challenges

When individuals are visibly challenged in addition to having learning difficulties, they can experience a double prejudice: first, because they do not look like the average person, and second, because they have difficulty learning. The reaction of people who are prejudiced toward visibly challenged individuals is a xenophobic response. Xenophobia comes from the Greek words *xeno*, meaning foreign or strange, and *phobos*, meaning fear, so it is a fear of someone who is perceived as different.

Our minds often categorize out of fear, as if labeling the stress will provide a safe distance from it. This fear can sometimes be irrational, such as thinking that a person's difficulties can affect us, even though we know they are not contagious. As a result, all too often people are labeled as their condition, which robs them of their humanity. We can counter xenophobia toward challenged individuals by acknowledging their inner life. When we realize that they, too, have their own thoughts and outlook on living, the visibly challenged become people to us rather than conditions. A way to recognize this humanity is by looking at their art, such as the work of Raymond Hu, a gifted painter with Down syndrome.

RAYMOND HU

"I usually start with my heart," says Raymond Hu (American, b. 1976) about his work. "That's where the imagination is—in the heart."[34] Through heart, art, and talent, Hu expresses his profound feelings for animals and the environment.[35] Despite learning difficulties from Down syndrome, he is an accomplished, exhibiting painter, with a website that shows his vivid watercolors of animals. Creating a unique fusion of Eastern and Western techniques, Hu paints with bamboo brushes on rice paper using inks and watercolors, traditional Chinese materials, but his expressionistic style is Western. He began painting in 1990, when his parents were studying classical Asian painting with the San Francisco artist and art professor Lampo Leong. They wanted their sons, Raymond and his younger brother, Jason, who does not have Down syndrome, to learn as well.

The physical limitations of Down syndrome, such as impaired motor control, made painting difficult at first for Hu, but he persevered. Occurring as the result of an extra chromosome in a person's genetic makeup, Down syndrome can cause mental retardation, reduced muscle tone, distinctive facial features, small stature, vision problems, and other difficulties.[36] Because Hu's eyesight cannot be completely corrected with glasses, he puts his face a few inches away from the paper when he works. In spite of all obstacles, Hu's art has made him a celebrity. He has been the subject of a book and a PBS documentary, and August 20, 1997, was declared Raymond Hu Day in Oakland, California. "I like the popularity," he admits, "and the national spotlight."[37]

Hu paints endangered species and infuses the animals with humanity. They become his voice and he becomes their champion. Using photographs of animals from wildlife magazines as models, he begins with the eyes and then draws the face and form in ink, which he fills in with color. Hu identifies with the animals he paints, in both their dignity and their vulnerability. When I spoke to him on the telephone, he told me that he is very much like the wolf, one of his favorite animals. Hu says, "Wolves are intelligent and superior, show good leadership and good sense, are stubborn and demanding, have determination, learn from experience, and love their children."[38] But there is another reason. His mother, Margaret Hu, in a separate, private part of the phone conversation, said her son also likes animals because they are not critical and do not judge him for having Down syndrome. Instead of becoming angry from prejudice, Hu transforms his suffering into compassion and art. "I want people to recycle more and protect our earth," he insists, "and try to balance the human population with the animal population."[39]

Autism and the Savant

Another condition that can come with learning difficulties is autism, now often called autism spectrum disorders because of the wide range of symptoms and capabilities in people with this condition.[40] Some individuals with a severe type of autism called Kanner's syndrome may be mentally retarded and incapable of functioning on their own, while others with a milder form of autism called Asperger's syndrome can be highly successful professionals. In autism, certain parts of the brain, such as the cerebellum, the corpus callosum, and the brain stem, may be an abnormal size or not function properly. As a result, autistic people have impaired abilities for communication and social interaction. They can also have learning disorders, very restricted interests and activities, repetitive behaviors, and fixations on inanimate objects, such as dials, meters, or machines.

Despite the limitations of autism, approximately 10 percent of autistic people demonstrate abilities so far above those of the average person that they seem superhuman. These individuals are called savants. This aspect of autism became known to a wide audience through the movie *Rain Man,* in which Dustin Hoffman played a man who could not manage his daily affairs, yet had extraordinary mathematical abilities. Temple Grandin, an autistic artist and scientist, says while some areas of the autistic brain are diminished, other parts may be enhanced.[41] That is why autistic people, who may be lacking in social or verbal skills, can show extremely high aptitudes for math, music, or art and may also have photographic memories. By demonstrating these capacities, autistic savants do us a service: they reveal the extraordinary potential inherent in humankind. Jessica Park and James Castle are autistic savants. Neither artist is capable of living alone, but both combine strength in geometry with a photographic memory to create excellent art.

JESSICA PARK

"Very pale," says Jessica Hillary Park (American, b. 1958), "mint, lavender, and yellow."[42] She is referring to subtle color differences in the multiple shades of delicate pastels in her art.[43] Park's ability to distinguish color is so heightened that in the area she is describing, an average person might see only white. Now an accomplished painter, Park was born with the severe autism of Kanner's syndrome. As a seemingly unreachable child, she gazed through people as if they were glass. Her mother, Clara Claiborne Park, who devoted herself to Park's education and social skills, wrote two books about the experience. She called her first book *The Siege* because it felt as if she were attempting to break into a locked fortress of autism. The title of the second book, *Exiting Nirvana,* refers to Park's empty serenity of repetitive activities, making it seem as if she is in Nirvana, a state of bliss.

Clara Park realized this was a false, vacant Nirvana and that her daughter must leave it in order to grow and change.

Realizing that Park liked images, her mother taught her to speak while they looked at picture books and drew shapes. Words were so hard for Park that for years she communicated mainly through images. Even as an adult, she finds speech difficult. Reading and writing did not come easily, either. Her parents, both professors at Williams College, have been very encouraging, and so have her three older, nonautistic siblings. In addition to being an artist, Park has been a mail clerk in the Williams College mailroom for twenty-five years. An excellent worker, she can be much faster than her nonautistic coworkers, especially with numbers.

Park is also a mathematical savant, and the geometry of her paintings' composition gives force to their imagery. Her work usually shows detailed views of buildings, rooms, and bridges with every brick, window, and steel girder carefully rendered and painted in rainbow hues against a darker background. The autism that causes her difficulties in life becomes strength in her art. She can paint from sketches, photographs, or her photographic memory. Like other autistic artists, Park easily draws in perspective and can rotate images such as buildings in her mind to increase the drama of her compositions. As a result, some of her buildings are painted from a viewpoint she has never physically seen. Park does this by visualizing the building perfectly in her mind's eye. Then she mentally rotates the structure and paints it from the angle she decides is best for her art. On May 25, 2003, Park's creativity was greatly acknowledged when the Massachusetts College of Liberal Arts presented her with an honorary doctor of fine arts degree at their commencement ceremony.

Different Environments

Jessica Park lives in an extremely supportive environment. She has a caring family and is well liked in her New England community, but not everyone is that fortunate. James Castle did not have a supportive environment. His main biographer, Tom Trusky, shows that although the artist was adequately fed and clothed, prejudice was a constant part of his life.

JAMES CASTLE

Unable to speak or hear, James Charles Castle (American, 1899–1977) was called "dummy" even by his family.[44] He was also called C.J., for "Crazy Jimmy," because of his autistic personality and mannerisms. Castle's hearing difficulties may have come from an autistic impairment that prevented him from adequately processing sound, or he may have been physically deaf. But the two conditions that brought him great difficulty in life became cornerstones of his creativity. Deafness turned him to art, and autism provided the brilliance for the geometry in his work.

Castle started drawing at an early age. "As soon as he could get up and grab a pencil," said his sister Julia.[45] In addition to having a farm, Castle's parents ran the local post office and general store. Frustrated by a deaf son who refused to do chores, they put him in a downstairs room with cast-off papers from the post office to occupy his time. For Castle, these were art supplies. At the age of eleven, he was sent to the newly opened Gooding School for the Deaf and Blind in Boise, Idaho, but was expelled within a year. The school said the boy was incapable of being taught and that he only wanted to draw. At school, Castle learned to sign his name and some very rudimentary reading and writing skills. But he never acquired speech or American Sign

Language. Instead, he communicated through simple signs created at home and with his art. Making his own art supplies with soot and spit, he used sticks as brushes and drew on discarded pieces of paper. Almost completely unable to read yet with a fascination for words and books, Castle made his own books using letters of the alphabet as design elements. He also did collage and created cardboard sculptures, some of which were life-size figures that his family called his "friends." Their silent company eased his loneliness. But the most extraordinary pieces of James Castle's art are his drawings that show perspective.

Perspective in art is a way of representing a three-dimensional space on a flat surface, such as paper or canvas, that gives it a feeling of depth and reality. As a savant, Castle created not only perspective drawings of his current environment but, using his photographic memory, he made perspective drawings of rooms he had not seen for decades. He drew these rooms from multiple angles with correct perspective for each point of view. By doing this, Castle showed that he had the capacity to rotate complex three-dimensional objects in his mind while correctly recording the geometry for the different angles. Despite his extraordinary abilities, people only saw James Castle as a deaf man who could not speak, read, or write. They called him "dummy," but he showed extraordinary abilities.

Autism, Perspective, and Perception

Like James Castle, Jessica Park could draw in perspective without being taught and so can other savants. The autistic artists Stephen Wiltshire (English, b. 1974),[46] Dane Bottino (American, b. 1990),[47] and Nadia (English, b. 1967 in the Ukraine)[48] also drew in perspective at a young age without being taught. But why are these artists able to give a believable illusion of space when almost all nonautistic people have to be trained to draw this way? The answer appears to be in two parts: first, most nonautistic people draw what they know, while autistic people draw what they see, and second, most people only see what they know, while autistics are more likely to see what is there.

If nonautistic people are asked to draw the roof beams of a barn receding into the distance, most of them will depict the beams as parallel to each other because they "know" the roof is built that way. As a result, there will be a flat, unrealistic picture. An autistic person, such as Castle, unhampered by "knowing" the beams are parallel, will be free to see them converge to a vanishing point in the distance as they actually do in our vision. As a result, he will have a drawing done in perspective that gives the illusion of depth. Unknown in medieval times, perspective was one of the great accomplishments of Renaissance art.[49] But Renaissance artists used mathematical formulas to draw in perspective. This method ensured they drew what was correct rather than what they presumed was correct.

The formulas were helpful because most people only see what they know and what they expect to see. In other words, not only do people draw what they think is reality, they also see what they think is reality. This is because we tend to organize our world into mental constructs called schemas that become a framework for understanding reality. Schemas let us grasp a situation quickly, but we pay a price for this ease by seeing a world we already know instead of a possibly more accurate view of an existing situation. For most of us, expectation alters perception. We see what we expect to see. Because the construction of schemas starts in childhood,[50] creative people who say they want to see the world through the eyes of a child might more accurately desire to see a world without schemas.

In a famous experiment by Daniel Simons at the University of

Illinois, people watching a video of a basketball game are asked to count the number of passes made by a specific team. As they are counting, a woman in a gorilla suit walks into the video, looks at the camera, and beats her chest. Half of all the people watching the game don't see the gorilla. According to Temple Grandin, who cites this experiment in her book *Animals in Translation,* an autistic person would probably see the gorilla.[51] The autistic mind is different. It is, as Clara Park described her daughter Jessy's mind, "free of conventional perceptions."[52] It is a mind unframed by schemas. This allows vision without cognition, or seeing without knowing. It lets autistic people see what is there and not what they think should be there.

Artists with Savant Abilities

Jessica Park and James Castle not only see what is there, they use what is there, and change what is there to improve their art. By visualizing images from different angles, they find the one that works best. Park takes houses in which she notices every detail and then paints them in colors she creates against backgrounds that she invents, and over the years her work has become more complex. Although Castle drew in perspective, Tom Trusky discovered that he spent years perfecting this ability. As a result of practice his compositions have greater impact. These individuals are not autistic savants who happen to make art, but artists who use savant abilities as tools in their work.

Acquiring Savant Abilities

Can nonautistic people acquire savant abilities? Allan Snyder and his associates at the University of Sydney believe they can.[53] While brain damage through illness or accident may in rare cases result in savant capacities, these scientists have temporarily produced savantlike skills in normal individuals. Nonautistic people tend to think in concepts and see things as meaningful combinations, while savants have immediate access to raw details before they are assembled into a whole. By applying magnetic pulses to the left anterior temporal lobe of the brain, these scientists have temporarily freed people from thinking in concepts, thus allowing them to see literal details more accurately. During brain stimulation, nonautistic individuals showed marked improvement in numerosity (correctly counting large numbers of objects), proofreading, and drawing.

Vision and Visual Art

Just as artists can have learning disorders, they can also have vision problems. Some artists have excellent eyesight, but not all of them do. Like the general population, creative people have a wide range of visual difficulties. Yet despite their visual challenges, and sometimes even because of them, artists continue to make art.

Chapter 9 ⌐

Vision Challenges and Visual Art

One eye sees, the other feels. —*Paul Klee*

For most of us sight is our primary means of knowing about the world. About 80 percent of the information we receive comes through our eyes. Eye problems can alter our vision, and when our vision is altered our world seems to change. We literally see things differently. For artists, this means that they make art in a different way. Vision is such an integral part of visual art that there are two excellent books by ophthalmologists on art and the eye and how the eye problems of artists affect their work. The most recent is *The Eye of the Artist,* edited by Michael F. Marmor and James G. Ravin, and the earlier book is *The World through Blunted Sight,* by Patrick Trevor-Roper. I refer to these books throuhout the chapter.

It may seem paradoxical that someone who cannot see well would become a visual artist, yet we all long for wholeness. Triumphing in a field in which we are challenged gives us a sense of accomplishment that makes us feel whole. Beginning as compensation for something we lack, creativity can become a path to strength we never knew we had. Art is communication and a connection with other people. By creating a form of beauty even with our impairments, we become able to share that beauty with others. Through art we can communicate something of the essence of ourselves.

Temporary and Permanent Vision Problems

Sometimes an eye problem is temporary, as in the case of Edvard Munch. But the other artists in this chapter, like Charles R. Knight, have permanent vision loss. Yet working with severely impaired and diminishing sight, they, too, create art.

EDVARD MUNCH

In 1930 Edvard Munch (Norwegian, 1863–1944) developed a hemorrhage inside his right eye.[1] The condition was very difficult for the artist, because his right eye was the stronger one and he was not able to paint using his weaker left eye alone. The hemorrhage took almost a year to heal, and as he regained his sight, Munch made a series of drawings and paintings showing the shadowy blockage and how it appeared in his visual field until it vanished. In one of his drawings Munch maps the blockage in a grid to illustrate it clearly and follow its progress. The ophthalmologist Michael Marmor, who believes the grid was Munch's invention, says, "it was well ahead of the medical practice at that time."[2]

CHARLES R. KNIGHT

Many decades before the film *Jurassic Park*, people learned about dinosaurs through the work of Charles R. Knight (American, 1874–1953).[3] An artist, a writer, and a naturalist, he was the first person to visually re-create the prehistoric world. Knight, who was born in

Brooklyn, came to this interest through a love of animals. Like Rosa Bonheur and Raymond Hu, his passion was animals, and they became the subject of his art. When Knight was three years old, the first full sentence he spoke was "Look at that black chicken,"[4] and as a child, he would come to attention any time he heard the word *animal*. In response, Knight's father brought him books with beautiful color plates of animals and took him to the American Museum of Natural History, in Manhattan.

Knight also started to draw. His stepmother, who was artistic, encouraged his talent until she became jealous because he was a better artist. In spite of her anger, Knight persevered. He went to art school, drew careful sketches of plants and animals at the zoos and parks in New York City, and also learned anatomy by dissecting animals at the American Museum of Natural History. Using his knowledge and skill, he became an illustrator for natural history magazines.

Living in New York at the turn of the twentieth century, Knight was at the right time and place for his work. Skeletons of dinosaurs and other extinct animals were being excavated in different parts of the world, and Henry Fairfield Osborn, a paleontologist at the American Museum of Natural History, was looking for someone to recreate them in art. He hired Knight, whose understanding of animals, plants, and anatomy, combined with a vivid imagination, allowed him to create the first images of the prehistoric world. Knight's paintings were so excellent that they won fame for him and drew people to the museum.

He accomplished all of this in spite of severe vision problems. Knight, who had astigmatism and was extremely nearsighted, said he inherited poor eyesight from his father. As he grew older, the condition progressed, and he became legally blind without his glasses. In addition, when he was young, a neighborhood child carelessly threw a pebble in his direction, striking him in the right eye. As he aged, his injured right eye weakened, leaving Knight's left eye to do the work of two.

Artists with severe vision problems often work from photographs, because they bring the subject matter closer into their visual field. But there were no photos of dinosaurs. So Knight made clay models of dinosaurs from the scientific evidence available. This way he could view them close up and also see how light and shadow fell on their forms. His way of working was not only easier for a nearsighted person, but it produced such realistic images that paleoartists still work this way today. Knight created murals of the prehistoric world for museums across the country and also wrote books and articles on the subject.[5] Many came after him as painters, sculptors, and filmmakers, but Charles R. Knight was the first person to bring the dinosaurs back to life through his art.

Macular Degeneration

The artists Edgar Degas and Georgia O'Keeffe also had a serious eye problem, macular degeneration. This disease of the retina is the most common cause of vision loss in older people.[6] The retina is a layer of tissue in the back of the eye containing cells that are sensitive to light. Without a retina, we cannot see. When the central part of the retina, called the macula, is damaged, there is a loss of central vision, leaving a person with only peripheral sight. There are two types of macular degeneration: the dry form, which is more common and less harmful, and the wet form, which can quickly lead to severe vision loss. Laser therapy is helpful, but it was not available to either Edgar Degas or Georgia O'Keeffe. There is a hereditary aspect to macular degeneration: both Degas's first cousin and O'Keeffe's grandfather appeared to have this condition.[7]

EDGAR DEGAS

One of the most popular Impressionists, Edgar Degas (French, 1834–1917) spent his adult life facing increasing blindness, probably from macular degeneration.[8] The condition usually occurs in people over fifty-five, but the artist noticed his first symptom at thirty-six. It was in 1870, during the Franco-Prussian War, and Degas, who was a member of the National Guard, realized he could no longer see a rifle target using his right eye. Eventually his left eye gave him problems as well.

Degas said it was agonizing to make art because all he had left was peripheral vision. He continued to work, however, even though he was not able to see what he was looking at directly, but could see only around it. He also had trouble with bright light and was unable to paint out of doors like the other Impressionists. Instead of creating landscapes, Degas worked mainly indoors, concentrating on portraits, interior scenes, and the images of ballet dancers that made him famous. Realizing his condition was progressive and irreversible, Degas said, "I shall remain in the ranks of the infirm until I pass into the ranks of the blind."[9]

But he did not go gently or acquiesce to the impairment. Through work and willpower Degas produced masterpieces. When his eyesight became so limited that it was hard to see the fine lines his brush made on canvas, Degas turned from painting to pastel as his primary means of expression. He could use large pieces of chalk, which make thicker lines that are easier to see. Degas also found that working from photographs brought images more easily into the range of his limited vision. As the years wore on and his eyes continued to worsen, he made pastels with increasingly thick lines and less detail. The pastels Degas produced due to failing eyesight are his most popular works.

Eventually the artist's sight became so poor that it was even difficult to see chalk lines on paper. At that point he turned increasingly to sculpture, creating works he could feel. Helping his failing eyes with his sense of touch, Degas made statues of ballet dancers and horses. It was the need to make the statues rather than exhibit them that drove his creativity.[10] For Degas they were not public pieces, and he never sought to show them. The statues are molded out of wax and clay, which are impermanent mediums. During his lifetime Degas cast just two of them and then only in plaster. After his death, a group of these beautiful statues was cast in bronze for posterity.

GEORGIA O'KEEFFE

In her later years Georgia O'Keeffe (American, 1887–1986) noticed that her sight was failing.[11] Previously, she'd had excellent eyesight but now macular degeneration was blurring her world and obscuring her central vision. According to the ophthalmologists James Ravin and Michael F. Marmor, O'Keeffe had wet macular degeneration, the most severe type of this condition.[12] They also find additional problems in her left eye, because a vein occlusion caused the rupture of small capillaries in the retina, further damaging her sight. Although it became increasingly difficult to paint, O'Keeffe was determined to remain creative.

Just as O'Keeffe modified her exercise from steep walks high in the mountains to shorter walks on her own property because she wanted to stay active, so she changed her way of making art in order to keep creative. Vision loss simplified the forms in her paintings, but they still maintain a sense of presence and power. At times O'Keeffe worked from photographs, as she did in *Road Past the View*, a painting done in 1964, the year she noticed her severe vision loss.[13] The artist was also able to create from memory. "You paint from your subject," she explained, "not what you see."[14]

O'Keeffe also began to make pottery. Like Degas, she used her sense of touch to aid her weakening eyes. When asked about her ceramics, she replied, "It could become still another language for me."[15] But painting remained her favorite medium. To compensate for vision loss, O'Keeffe tried working with an assistant, but that didn't go well for her and she returned to painting alone. "Painting is like a thread," she said, "that runs through all the reasons for all the other things that make one's life."[16]

Cataracts

One of the most common eye problems is cataracts. They are the primary reason for blindness in the world and are also on the increase as our population ages. A cataract is the clouding of the lens of the eye, leading to a loss of vision. We are very fortunate to live in an era in which cataract surgery is both commonplace and usually extremely successful. When my mother had cataract surgery on both eyes, she marveled that such a simple procedure could restore her sight so well that she no longer needed glasses. But this was not always the case. Before modern medicine, cataract surgery was very dangerous. In spite of this, there are artists who have chosen an operation when it was available in an effort to maintain their sight and their ability to paint accurately. As a cataract grows, the progressive clouding of the lens dims the vision and changes the perception of color. Cool colors like blues, violets, and some greens are unable to penetrate the cloudy lens, while reds, yellows, and browns are often seen more easily. Artists with the altered color sensitivity of advanced cataracts tend to produce art with distorted colors, making paintings that emphasize red.

ANTONIO VERRIO

The early murals Antonio Verrio (Italian, worked in England, 1639–1707) painted for the English court are beautiful, but the colors in his later work are very red because cataracts altered his perception.[17] The ophthalmologist Patrick Trevor-Roper discovered that Verrio underwent what he believes was a cataract operation in the early eighteenth century. The procedure was unsuccessful and Verrio did not regain his sight. In the early twentieth century, Claude Monet was more fortunate.

CLAUDE MONET

The Impressionist painter Claude Monet (French, 1840–1926) did some of the best work of his life when a cataract operation and glasses restored his vision.[18] James Ravin tells us that Monet's eyesight was not a problem until 1908, when the artist realized he had difficulty distinguishing colors. The paintings Monet made at that time distressed him so much that he tore some of them to shreds. He could not bear the frustration of producing poor work. Another time, utterly disgusted with what he had done, Monet decided to give up painting altogether and threw his art supplies into a river. I think of all the pollution that those paints, brushes, oils, and turpentine spread in the water.

Monet's vision continued to decline, and in 1912 he was diagnosed with cataracts in both eyes. The artist began to consult a series of ophthalmologists, but he was too frightened to have surgery. In an effort to keep working, Monet would check the names on his tubes of paint to help him select colors. He also arranged the paints on his palette in a set order so he could choose the right paint by memory, since he was no longer able to distinguish colors by sight. Despite all his efforts to be productive, Monet realized he wasn't doing well and in frustration destroyed his work again. "I would be seized by a frantic rage," he revealed, "and slash all my canvases with a penknife."[19]

A reason Monet may have hesitated to have surgery is because he knew that Mary Cassatt (American, lived in France, 1844–1926) gave up painting after her failed cataract operations.[20] Ravin believes

Cassatt's case may have been complicated by diabetes and the radiation therapy she was given to combat the illness. Finally, in 1923, Monet had a two-stage operation on his right eye, which was almost completely blind. Unfortunately, he developed complications and had to have a third procedure. He refused to have an operation on his left eye and could not adjust to the glasses he had to wear after surgery. Again he was so frustrated that he destroyed his art. "I burned six canvases," exclaimed Monet, "along with the dead leaves from my garden. It's hopeless."[21]

Modern cataract operations fit a new synthetic lens inside the eye, but in the past this procedure was not available, and special glasses were prescribed. Monet got two pairs of glasses in 1924 but neither corrected his eyesight.[22] Finally, in 1925, the third pair of glasses that came was successful. All the years of stress and frustration from his cataracts were over, and in response the artist was bursting with creativity. He had been struggling with his *Water Lilies* series for years but now he could see and the work was going well. "I have recovered my true vision," declared Monet. "I am happily seeing everything again and am working with ardor."[23] These large paintings are considered to be among the greatest masterpieces of his life.

Vision and Art

The many vision problems that we have as human beings affect artists as well as the general public. In the next chapter, color blindness, one of the most common visual impairments, influences the creativity of masterpieces, and we will also discover that even the blind can create visual art.

Chapter 10

Art and the Way We See the World

I see every thing I paint in this world,
but everybody does not
see alike. —*William Blake*

The way we see the world influences the way we portray the world in our art. One of the fundamental aspects of our perception is color vision. Color is such a part of everyday life that we rarely stop to realize that people see colors differently. Some individuals have an acute sense of every color, while others are not able to recognize certain colors, and there are a few who cannot see any color at all. Even in the visual arts, where color is a primary means of expression, we find a great range of color sensitivity. Some artists like Titian, Vermeer, Matisse, and Gauguin in the Western tradition and Nobuzane, Sharaku, Ch'iu Ying, and Wang Yüan-ch'i in the Eastern tradition are great colorists. But there are other artists with a reduced sense of color who have used their color vision deficiency as an aid to their work.

Color Vision Problems

Color vision defects, also called color blindness, usually result from problems with the photoreceptor cells in the retina of the eye. Photoreceptor cells convert light received by the eye into electrical impulses that are accepted by the brain. We have two types of photoreceptor cells: rods around the exterior of the retina that allow us to distinguish light from dark and cones in the center of the retina that let us see color. Cone cells are further specialized to recognize specific wavelengths of light. Some cones are sensitive to red light, others to blue light, and still others to green light. The combination of these three wavelengths of light gives us the full spectrum of color that we see as human beings. Unlike people, birds have additional cones that receive ultraviolet light.[1] Compared to birds, all humans have color vision deficiency. If we had these extra cone cells in our eyes, our art would most likely extend into the ultraviolet spectrum.

When cone cells are missing or damaged, we are unable to distinguish certain colors. A small number of people cannot recognize blue or yellow, but the great majority of individuals with color vision deficiency have problems with red and green. The degree of color deficit ranges from a minor impairment in which colors are slightly altered to a profound incapacity to distinguish one color from another. It may seem paradoxical that a person with color vision deficiency could become a famous artist, yet it has happened more than once, and even to Rembrandt, one of the greatest painters of all time.

REMBRANDT

The work of Rembrandt Harmenszoon van Rijn (Dutch, 1606–1669) is a symphony of shades in which colors play a minor role. A painter of human intimacy, he uses light and shadow to convey the great emotional depth of his work. The humanity of his figures and the gradations of his tones are so impressive that his reduced color palette becomes less noticeable. But the sensitivity to light and shade that gives Rembrandt's work great power may be due in part to a difficulty with color. I first became aware of Rembrandt's possible color vision difficulty when I read an essay on his etchings by A. Hyatt Mayor of the Metropolitan Museum of Art.[2] Mayor notes that if Rembrandt was not completely color deficient, he was still not a colorist like Vermeer or Monet. But Mayor also realizes that Rembrandt's lack of color perception makes him more sensitive to the gradations of light and dark.

Rembrandt appears to have two types of color vision difficulties: one that he was born with and another that he acquired as he aged. Although not extremely color-blind, Rembrandt may have had some degree of red or green color vision deficiency. This is just a hypothesis because, as the ophthalmologist James Ravin points out, there were no clinical tests done on Rembrandt's eyes or his color vision, and pigments in paintings can change over time.[3] But from the appearance of his paintings, it seems possible that Rembrandt has a type of red or green color vision defect. This inherited condition is the most common kind of partial color blindness.

Like the painter John Constable (English, 1776–1837), who the ophthalmologist Trevor-Roper believes had partial red-green color perception deficiency,[4] Rembrandt hardly ever uses a true green color, even when he depicts foliage, and his reds are most often brownish reds. When he uses full color in his paintings, he tends to use a blue, yellow, and brown palette. This is also seen in the work of the painter Charles Méryon (French, 1821–1868), whom the ophthalmologists James Ravin and Philippe Lanthony find to be red-green color-blind.[5] Even in Rembrandt's very earliest work where he tries to be more colorful, his color range is limited and awkward. It was only in his mid-twenties, when he discovered how to paint with light and shade and a minimum of color, that the Rembrandt of greatness emerged.[6]

When I spoke to James Ravin about Mayor's writing on Rembrandt's possible color deficiency, Ravin agreed with Mayor and gave me further information.[7] He noticed that Rembrandt's color perception decreased as the artist became older, probably due to a common age-related condition that causes the lens of the eye to turn a yellow-brown color. When this happens, the lens becomes a yellow filter, blocking out cool colors such as blue and violet while allowing warmer colors such as yellow and brown to be visible. As a result, an artist will paint using these colors. But even with limited choices of increasing color deficiency, Rembrandt made masterpieces. "Seeing the world more or less in browns," says Mayor, "freed him to calibrate luminosity with a delicacy as expressive as any palette of colors."[8]

The Benefits of Color Deficiency

Mayor's theory about Rembrandt's possible color deficiency and the benefits it gave him in perceiving light and shade matches later research by the neurologist Oliver Sacks. In his book *An Anthropologist on Mars*,[9] Sacks discusses the case of Jonathan I., an artist who lost his color vision in a car accident. The brain damage he sustained left him with a type of achromatopsia, which is a complete lack of color perception, making his world look like a black-and-white photograph. But as a result of becoming completely color-blind, Jonathan I. finds that he has an enhanced perception of textures, tones, and patterns. This ability of color-deficient people was acknowledged during World War II, when the Allies recruited people with extreme color deficiency to analyze reconnaissance photographs and to serve as bombardiers. Undistracted by color, they were better able to see through camouflage.[10] We can see from paintings by Jonathan I. that are reproduced in the book that his work after the accident is much better than the work he did before. Losing his color vision became a transforming illness.

Oliver Sacks continued his work with total color vision deficiency in a 1997 book, *The Island of the Colorblind*, by visiting the small Pacific island of Pingelap.[11] Although complete color blindness is a very rare condition worldwide, in this isolated community about 10 percent of the inhabitants have an inherited type of achromatopsia. Like Jonathan I., they are completely color-blind and their world looks like a black-and-white photograph. But as Mayor notes in the work of Rembrandt, color deficiency can enhance the perception of tones. The people on Pingelap with complete color deficiency perceive light and dark better than those on the island who see the full range of color. Their acute sense of light and dark serves the community well; they are the night fishers. With a heightened perception of luminescence and shadow, they can more easily identify the pale glimmer of fish as they swim underwater.

When people see the world differently, their art reflects their eyesight. This is evident in the work of the best weaver on Pingelap, a woman with achromatopsia, who learned the skill from her completely color-blind mother. Working in the dim light of her hut, she weaves beautiful mats in fine gradations of light and dark. People with achromatopsia prefer dim light because bright light hurts their eyes. Her delicate woven designs that can be easily seen indoors almost vanish in broad daylight. The Norwegian scientist Knut Nordby, who traveled with Sacks to Pingelap, told the weaver about his sister Britt. Both Nordby and his sister also have achromatopsia. He said Britt knitted a jacket in such subtle patterns of light and dark that they could hardly be seen by a person with normal vision. Britt calls it her "special secret art" and explains, "You have to be completely colorblind to see it."[12]

I wonder if a person with color deficiency could see more tones in Rembrandt's work than a person with normal color vision. Perhaps it is like birdsong. Just as there are many more notes in a bird's song than our human ears can hear, so there may be tonal modulations in Rembrandt's art that people with color deficiency might be better able to perceive. According to Mayor, the color deficiency that made Rembrandt more sensitive to nuances of light and dark also helped him with his etchings.[13] In the seventeenth century, when Rembrandt turned to etching, it was a new medium. Unlike the color etching we have today, in his time it was done entirely in black and white. Rembrandt may have been attracted to etching because it was an art without color and also because he excelled in light and shade. The art historian K. G. Boon says that in his etchings Rembrandt created "an alternation of tints between gray and black such as his contemporaries had never dreamed of."[14]

The Prevalence of Color Vision Problems

Total color blindness is very rare but partial color vision deficiency is not. Almost always inherited, it affects about 10 percent of males and about 0.5 percent of females.[15] Approximately 99 percent of all color vision difficulties involve the perception of red or green. This trait is located on the X chromosome. Women have two X chromosomes, and the trait must be on both of them in order to be expressed. Because of this, they must inherit the trait from both parents to have color vision difficulties. Males, with only one X chromosome plus a Y chromosome, need to inherit the trait from only one parent to be color vision deficient. I have two first cousins who have problems distinguishing red and green. One of them is a woman. Therefore, it is possible that even though I see the full range of colors, I, too, may carry the trait for impaired color vision.

Although I have not found any statistics to support this hypothesis, it is likely that the rate of color vision deficiency may be lower among visual artists because a percentage of people with color problems may choose other fields. Also, it is rare to find a woman with color vision deficiency, but a woman artist with this difficulty is even more unusual. Yet Kaethe Kollwitz appears to have had this condition, and, like Rembrandt, she turned it to her advantage.

KAETHE KOLLWITZ

Known for her powerful black-and-white images, Kaethe Kollwitz (German, 1867–1945) depicts human emotions and the plight of the poor.[16] Kollwitz, who came from a family deeply interested in social causes, started drawing at the age of five or six and by thirteen she was taking formal lessons. Her parents encouraged her creativity by sending her to an art school for women in Berlin when she was seventeen. There Kollwitz excelled in drawing and also learned etching, which at that time was still a black-and-white medium. Her teacher Karl Stauffer-Bern recommended that she see an exhibit of Max Klinger's etchings about social oppression. "It excited me tremendously," recalled Kollwitz. Stauffer-Bern recognized her gift for drawing and also probably realized her problems with color. "I wanted to paint," said Kollwitz, "but he kept telling me to stick to drawing."[17]

After Berlin, Kollwitz studied painting in Munich with Ludwig Herterich. But this teacher emphasized color over drawing, and she had to admit, "I did not see colors the way he did."[18] For the first time Kollwitz realized she had a problem. "In the painting class I made no progress," she revealed. "Color was my stumbling block."

Although she excelled in drawing and tones of light and dark, Kollwitz declared, "I suddenly saw I was not a painter at all," and she abandoned working with oil on canvas. From Kollwitz's statements about her difficulties, it is likely that she had a degree of color vision deficiency. The exact type of problem is hard to identify, because there is no record of clinical tests on Kollwitz's eyes or her color vision, and the very small amount of color work she did shows a palette even more limited than Rembrandt's. Kollwitz's problems with color led her to work in black and white. But what began as a necessity turned into a triumph.

There was a school competition, and for her entry Kollwitz illustrated a scene from Émile Zola's novel *Germinal*, showing the struggle of coal miners. Her black-and-white work was so unanimously acclaimed, it restored the faith she had lost in herself because of her difficulties with color. Kollwitz focused almost exclusively on black-and-white and brown-and-white imagery for the rest of her life. In her drawings, etchings, and lithographs, the drama of tones strengthens her work and emphasizes its themes of poverty and suffering.

In an age in which women had to choose between marriage and a family and a successful career, Kollwitz managed to have both. Her husband, Karl, was a doctor who specialized in medical care for the poor, and they lived in Berlin with their two sons, Hans and Peter. After her son Peter was killed in World War I, Kollwitz was so distraught that she sculpted a memorial statue to express her grief. Kollwitz continued to make sculpture; it was another medium without color in which she could convey the depth of human emotion.

Color Vision Deficiency and Visual Expression

Charles Méryon (French, 1821–1868) also switched from painting to black-and-white mediums because of color vision deficiency.[19] In praise of Méryon's work, the writer Victor Hugo said, "His splendid etchings with nothing but shadow and brightness, light and dark, have dazzled me."[20] Another artist with color vision difficulties is Paul Manship (American, 1885–1966). After problems in painting with color, he became one of the most celebrated art deco sculptors.[21] The ceramic artist Michael Wainwright (American, b. 1964) freely acknowledges he has color vision deficiencies.[22] By limiting his color palette and focusing on gold and platinum, Wainwright produces beautiful ceramics, and has also expanded his designs to flatware, textiles, and other products for the home.

Color vision deficiency was first detected in ancient Greece, but it was not until 1798, when the British chemist John Dalton noticed his own difficulties in perceiving red and green, that the condition was formally recognized.[23] He called it Daltonism.

The earliest artist I found with evidence of a color vision deficiency is Jacques de Gheyn (Flemish, 1565–1629).[24] His father, Jacob Jansz van de Gheyn, was also a painter. Most likely because he realized his son's difficulty with color, he urged him to concentrate on engraving, a black-and-white medium. But de Gheyn was determined to paint. To help distinguish colors, he made a chart of one hundred squares, each numbered and filled with a color and its related shadow tones, along with careful written notes on how to use the colors in painting. Although de Gheyn became a successful painter, he continued to be an engraver and his pupils were engravers.

Working only in black and white or with reduced color is not enough to suggest problems with color perception. Both Chuck Close and Odilon Redon, who are excellent colorists, worked in black and white for the first half of their artistic careers. Caravaggio (Italian, 1573–1610), born Michelangelo Merisi, also had an excellent sense of color but chose to work with a reduced color palette that emphasized light and shadow. His dramatic style of painting influenced Rembrandt and changed art history.

Black-and-White Painting in Asian Art

Even though a reduced color palette is not always evidence of color vision deficiency, there is a tendency for artists with color vision problems to work in black and white. Just as there is a higher incidence of color vision deficiency in Western artists who work in monochrome, I cannot help but wonder if this true for Eastern artists as well. It would be interesting to know if this occurs in styles of Asian art that favor monochrome images, such as Sung landscape painting, Ch'an Buddhist painting, and bamboo painting.

There are also individuals within these schools of painting who focus strongly on monochrome work. Wang Wei (Chinese, 699–759) is considered to be the originator of black-and-white ink painting.[25] He preferred to work in monochrome and is known for his richness of tone. Li Lung-mien (Chinese, ca. 1041–1106) never used color except when he was copying older paintings.[26] Lin Liang (Chinese, Sung dynasty), who was called Rinro in Japan, also preferred to paint in monochrome.[27] Wen T'ung (Chinese, d. 1079), one of the great artists in the monochrome tradition of bamboo painting, was known for his excellent tonalities of ink wash.[28] Did any of these individuals have diminished color sensitivity? Or were they perhaps like Caravaggio in the West, an artist with excellent color vision who preferred to work in light and shade?

Drawings and the Blind

Creativity is so important to artists that they will make art in spite of the most severe challenges—even blindness. It may seem surprising that blind people can create visual art, but according to the perception and cognition psychologist John Kennedy, we have images of the world in our brain whether our eyes see them or whether we gather information through our sense of touch.[29] "Where a sighted person looks out," says Kennedy, "a blind person reaches out, and they will discover the same things."[30] In his book *Drawing and the Blind: Pictures to Touch*, blind individuals create line drawings of the world they experience through touch. These drawings are completely understandable by sighted people. To make their art, the blind use a raised-line drawing kit. This is a board covered by a special type of plastic sheet that produces a raised line in response to the pressure of a ballpoint pen. By touching their raised-line images, blind artists can know what they create. The philosopher Jacques Derrida says the experience of making lines without seeing is like having an eye open at your fingertips.[31]

People who are completely blind have drawn houses, animals, other people, and even wheels in motion. Kennedy finds that both blind adults and blind children have the ability to portray the world around them. One child was so proud of her work that she wanted to take her drawings home to show her parents. And in another instance a parent said, "Now our child can have her drawings up on the wall like everyone else."[32] Just as sighted people make better drawings with practice, so do the blind, and Kennedy believes they should have art lessons.

Blindness and Visual Art

The Braille Institute in Los Angeles also believes in art classes for the blind, and some of their students have become professional artists. Another organization in Los Angeles, the View from Here, promotes the work of visually impaired and blind artists. Its director, Christine Leahey, who is a seeing advocate for art of the blind, curates exhibitions of their work that travel across the country. Leahey points out that by looking at the work of these artists, you can't tell they were created by a blind person. She says that at art fairs, the pack of Seeing Eye dogs is the only way to know that her booth features work by visually impaired and blind people. Helen Fukuhara, Alice Wing-wall, John Dugdale, Alison Ulman, and Michael Richard are five of the artists she represents.

HELEN FUKUHARA

"If it weren't for the Braille Institute," says Helen Fukuhara (American, b. 1948), "I wouldn't have done art at all."[33] Completely blind, she lost her sight in the hospital as a premature baby when she was given too much oxygen. Fukuhara, who is a graduate of Hofstra University, taught daily living skills to blind children at the New York State School for the Blind.[34] After moving to California, she started making fine art prints at the Braille Institute of Los Angeles, working exclusively through her sense of touch. Touch conveys experiences of beauty for the artist. Fukuhara remembers feeling a duckling come out of its shell in a high school biology class. She says, "It was the best moment of my life."[35]

To create her prints, Fukuhara places objects such as lace, burlap, and string on a metal plate. After covering the plate with a sheet of paper she runs it through a press. The pressure of the press forces the paper to capture the objects on the plate as raised areas that Fukuhara can feel. She runs the plate containing the objects through the press multiple times until she achieves her final composition, which Fukuhara again judges through touch. Her compositions are excellent, and every print is a monotype, which means it is one of a kind.

Sighted assistants at the Braille Institute suggest some colors but she also chooses her own colors. Fukuhara has an excellent memory for what people say about colors, and because each color is stored in a different-shaped bottle, she can choose the one she wants through feeling its container. Speaking about her father, Henry Fukuhara, a well-known watercolorist, she says, "I inherited the genes for artistic talent from him."[36] Fukuhara is also a poet and an accomplished musician.

ALICE WINGWALL

Alice Wingwall (American; birth date not available) is legally blind because of retinitis pigmentosa.[37] An inherited disease, it destroys the retina and the optic nerve. After having retinitis pigmentosa for most of her adult life, she now can distinguish only light and dark. Wingwall was an artist before the illness, and as she lost her sight, she was determined to keep working. When people ask her how she can be a photographer, she answers, "Any photograph begins with an idea in the brain."[38]

Ideas for photos constantly come into her mind. She describes them to assistants, who help her keep her automated camera pointed in the right direction. In some of her photographs there are images of her guide dog with architecture. Wingwall also does sculpture and has driven a backhoe to clear ground for an outdoor installation piece. In 2000 she codirected an award-winning film with Wendy Snyder MacNeill on her art and life called *Miss Blindsight/The Wingwall Auditions.* It shows the artist in her daily life making tea and making art with a sense of humor and a determination to remain creative. "You can have bad days," says Wingwall. "You can sit there and cry. Then you think there's always something I want to do. Better get up and load the film."[39]

JOHN DUGDALE

Ever since John Dugdale (American, b. 1960) received his first camera at the age of seven, he has been taking photographs.[40] In adulthood Dugdale became a very successful commercial photographer. Although he always wanted to do fine-art photography, the lure of receiving $30,000 for two weeks of work was difficult to turn down. The jobs were challenging, but still he felt guilty about not creating the art he had originally meant to. Then Dugdale contracted AIDS and a host of opportunistic illnesses that can come with this condition.

After viral pneumonia, viral meningitis, cytomegalovirus retinitis, toxoplasmosis, cancer, and a stroke, he lost half of his hearing and most of his vision. Cytomegalovirus retinitis, which is a herpes infection of the eye, caused total vision loss in his right eye and an 80 percent loss in his left. Dugdale says he sees the world as if he is looking through six Baggies.

As each illness happened, Dugdale made it into a gift. Instead of complaining about the noise from his deafness, Dugdale says, "Now I have the sound of the universe in my ear." He believed it was the only way to live, because all around him people were dying. Like the aftermath of a war, he lost a whole circle of friends. One day his agent called with a freelance job offer from a major commercial client. "What should I tell them?" she asked. "Give me one minute," replied Dugdale, "and then call me back." When the agent called back, Dugdale said, "Tell them that I'm HIV-positive, I'm paralyzed from a stroke, and I'm losing my sight." When Dugdale hung up, he had a great feeling of freedom, because he knew he had transformed his life. He could be a fine-art photographer. "In illness," says Dugdale, "there is an unbelievable opportunity for freedom and change."[41]

Now that he is creating fine-art photography, Dugdale says his work is about transformation through loss. With limited vision, he concentrates on close-up views that convey the quiet, intimate aspects of life. Using only his family and friends as models, Dugdale works with a large-view camera from the nineteenth century. He also prints in an antique method. His cyanotype and platinum photographs convey a timeless tranquillity. An assistant helps him focus the camera and with some aspects of printing, but the ideas for the photos, the lighting, and the composition are all his. Since his illness, Dugdale has had seventy-nine shows around the world and has also learned to play the piano. "The mind is the essence of your sight," says Dugdale. "It's really the mind that sees."[42]

ALISON ULMAN

Despite being legally blind, Alison Ulman (American, b. 1955) works in a wide range of mediums. Ulman has ocular histoplasmosis syndrome, an eye condition that blocks the center of her vision. The illness was caused by inhaling spores of the fungus *Histoplasma capsulatum*, which can migrate from the lungs to the eye and damage the retina. Although she was exposed to the spores in childhood, the symptoms did not appear until her twenties. "As my central field of vision is affected," she explains, "I piece together the world with my peripheral vision."[43]

As difficult as the illness is, it has given intensity to Ulman's work. One of her pieces is a mahogany coffee table. On the tabletop Ulman has carved books, magazines, and a photo album. But there are no images in the album or words in the books or magazines. They are accessible only through touch. What Ulman has done through wood carving is to visibly show us what the world of a blind person feels like through the sense of touch. In another sculpture she presents a metaphor for inner strength in the face of adversity. It is a teacup tilting on a broken saucer. The liquid is still in the teacup despite the tilt and the fractured saucer, as the artist's inner strength remains in her despite the difficulties of life.

Ulman has an extensive exhibition record, won an Outstanding Artist Award, and is also a California state-certified massage therapist. While her father was dying, Ulman made a sculpture called *Spirit Movement* that shows a cow's skull set behind shimmering iridescent glass. It captures both physical and spiritual essence. The sculpture is a fountain, she says, and the "energy is moving/transforming/enlightening."[44]

MICHAEL RICHARD

When Michael Richard (American, b. 1947) became blind, he had no idea he would return to making art.[45] Richard was born with amblyopia in his left eye. Unlike strabismus, or "lazy eye," where the eye sometimes turns out of alignment, in amblyopia the eye is constantly turned away, and the brain does not recognize the images it sees.[46] Richard depended on his right eye for vision until 2002, when surgery to remove a malignant tumor from behind the eye left his right eye blind. Richard, who can now use only his left eye, says he sees as if he is looking at the world through a glass covered with petroleum jelly.

Richard had previously been a documentary and scenic photographer, but he never expected to make visual art again. Then, on impulse, while visiting the Braille Institute in Los Angeles to learn how to use his white cane, he signed up for their photography course. Now an acclaimed photographer, who calls the camera his eyes, Richard develops his film and makes his own prints. His wife drives him to possible photo sites in Los Angeles where he paces the distance between himself and what he photographs, using a magnifying glass to help him adjust the settings on his camera.

Because it is so difficult for Richard to see, the forms he does see are very dramatic and translate into the powerful imagery of his work. Richard's condition also inspires his personal philosophy. He believes that the blurred boundaries of his vision reveal the basic interconnectedness of our world. Richard, who is also a musician, is now an assistant photography instructor at the Braille Institute of Los Angeles. "To think," he says, "that a visual impairment could stimulate a photographic career."[47]

Art and the Mind's Eye

The previous five artists—Fukuhara, Wingwall, Dugdale, Ulman, and Richard—have had the benefit of lessons, but Esref Armagan is self-taught. He draws, paints, and works in color, although he is completely blind. Armagan visualizes his work in what we call the mind's eye. All artists who think about what to do next in their work also visualize in the mind's eye. But these visualizations originate from what they have seen—Armagan cannot see at all.

ESREF ARMAGAN

Using color, shadow, and perspective, Esref Armagan (Turkish, b. 1954) paints realistic landscapes, butterflies, people, and fish, although he has never seen them.[48] Armagan started drawing when he was six years old despite being blind from birth. Coming from a poor family, he never received any schooling. Instead, isolated by blindness and unable to play with other children, he began to draw. Armagan started by taking a nail and drawing on cardboard boxes. Then he tried pencil and paper, and at the age of eighteen began to paint with oils. Later he switched to acrylics because they dry more quickly.

Armagan draws on a surface that produces a raised line that he detects with his fingers. As he draws with one hand, the other hand follows the line, checking it as he creates it. Using fingers instead of brushes, Armagan feels the lines and fills them in with color. He learned about color, shadow, and perspective through the comments of sighted viewers and by asking people. The artist has never seen the sky as blue or the grass as green, but he remembers people saying they are and he can paint them that way. By arranging his colors in a specific order, he chooses them by memory rather than sight. He also memorized which colors go together and which colors clash. Armagan's realistic images are not only pleasing to the public but also amazing to scientists. He can not only draw objects on request but also rotate them in his mind and depict them from different angles with accurate three-dimensional perspective.

In 2004 the neurologist Alvaro Pascual-Leone and his colleagues from Harvard, along with John Kennedy from the University of Toronto and a team of scientists from Boston University, examined Armagan. Alison Motluk of *New Scientist* magazine was also there, and in her article she says that after determining that Armagan was completely blind the scientists did brain scans to discover how he made art. They found he uses his visual cortex, the same part of the brain that receives information from our eyes. In sighted people, the visual cortex is active in seeing and less active while imagining visual images. Looking at his scans, the scientists discovered that Armagan's visual cortex was also less active during imagination, but when he painted, it lit up as brightly as though he were seeing. This is an example of neural plasticity, the alteration of the brain to suit specific needs. "Lacking sight, the brain draws on information from the other senses," explains Pascual-Leone. "Even in the absence of vision the visual cortex is involved in creating images."[49] This means that although Armagan has no vision, he still has a mind's eye.

Deafness and Visual Art

Just as there are artists with visual difficulties, there are also artists with hearing impairments. Deafness, whether congenital or acquired, can profoundly affect the process of making visual art. We will see in the next chapter how the deafness of one artist becomes an example of strength to another who is losing his hearing. The deaf have also created a culture for those without hearing, and there are artists within that culture who celebrate their community.

Chapter 11

Deafness and the Creative Process

It is not because things are difficult that
we do not dare; it is because we do not
dare that they are difficult. —*Seneca*

eaf people are visual people," says the psychologist Harlan
Lane, who sees this as an advantage to being deaf.[1] He cites
studies that find deaf individuals have more of their brain
devoted to vision than people who can hear. Because our brains are
not static and can change in response to life situations, a region dedicated to sound in hearing people can be used as an additional area for
vision in the deaf.[2] Lane believes that this may be a reason for enhanced visual perception in the deaf. Using sign language, which is a
visual communication, also increases visual ability.[3] So it is not surprising that today and throughout history, there are excellent artists
with challenged hearing.

Another reason for the existence of deaf artists is that hearing difficulties are very widespread, and people with these challenges form a
substantial minority. Currently in the United States, more than 20 million people are hearing impaired.[4] This group, which includes both
the deaf and the hard of hearing, makes up about 8.6 percent of the

total population. And these are just the statistics in one country among many. Some of the artists in this chapter were born deaf; others developed hearing disorders as a result of illness or genetic predisposition. Those who were born deaf or became deaf very early in life often used drawing as a way to communicate with the hearing members of their families. Ninety-five percent of all deaf individuals are born to hearing parents.[5] Like visual difficulties, problems with hearing can profoundly influence both work and life.

The artists show a great range of responses to deafness. Some feel it is a prison, while others use it as a political platform. The sculptor Duane Hanson (American, 1925–1996) saw deafness as a refuge. While working, he would remove his hearing aids to eliminate distractions and improve his concentration.[6] For still other artists, the deafness that closes a door to certain professions during their lifetime can open a path to creativity and fame that lasts for centuries.

JOHN BREWSTER

The portrait painter John Brewster (American, 1766–1854) was born deaf into a prosperous and established New England family.[7] In his biography of the artist, Harlan Lane tells us that Brewster's father and brother were physicians, but at that time medicine and many other professions were closed to those who could not hear. Brewster might have hidden behind what he called "his unfortunate situation"[8] and lived an idle life, but instead he became a painter, a field in which a deaf person could succeed. Brewster was a limner, a type of artist whose style combines the flatness of folk art with excellence in drawing and composition. With great natural talent, Brewster was mainly self-taught, but in his mid-twenties he took art lessons from the Reverend Joseph Seward. Seward said Brewster could "write and converse by signs so that he may be understood in many things." He also remarked that the young man had "a genius for painting."[9]

Brewster was active during a time the art historian Deborah Sonnenstrahl calls the golden age of portrait painting.[10] It was after the American Revolution and before the invention of photography, when the newly prosperous merchant class wanted images of themselves for posterity. Brewster, who created excellent likenesses, painted his subjects with a quiet dignity. Although he had no known children of his own, the children in his paintings often have a beautiful, ethereal quality. In Brewster's time most of the population lived in rural areas. Because of this, people offering services like portrait painting were often on the road. Brewster traveled the New England coast in search of clients and also advertised in newspapers. Successful in his day, he is now considered one of the leading folk artists of nineteenth-century America. Brewster's paintings not only bring enormous prices at auctions but are also a record of our history.

Ear Trumpets

Brewster was probably completely deaf, because there appears to be no record of him using an ear trumpet, which helped the hard of hearing at that time. Ear trumpets are devices that people with hearing difficulties held at their ears until battery-operated hearing aids became available in the twentieth century.[11] Originally employed by sailors and people who had to speak across long distances, they were later adopted by the hearing impaired. Ear trumpets, which come in a variety of shapes and materials, have one end that is flared and another end narrow enough to fit near the ear opening. When a person speaks into the flared end, the sound amplifies as it reaches the narrow end and the ear. With an artistic sense of style, Joshua Reynolds used an elegant silver ear trumpet. But on February 4, 1785, London's *Morning Herald* newspaper reported that when Reynolds was using his ear trumpet in a theater, a woman asked him, "What is the name of that instrument you appear to play upon by means of your ear?"[12]

JOSHUA REYNOLDS

Although Joshua Reynolds (English, 1723–1792) was known for his ear trumpet, in a famous ca. 1775 self-portrait he shows himself cupping his hand to his ear in an effort to hear more distinctly.[13] Reynolds used his partial deafness as an excuse to avoid people he didn't like.[14] If the artist thought a person unworthy of communication, he immediately became harder of hearing. The most common account of his hearing loss is that as a young man he caught a bad cold on a trip to Italy, where he was studying art. But his family shows a tendency to hearing problems. Six of his relatives also became deaf at a young age.

Despite his hearing difficulty, Reynolds was very active in London social circles and the most successful portrait painter of his day. He not only painted the current celebrities, they became his friends and he also introduced them to one another. Realizing that in his time paintings were seen only by the wealthy, Reynolds wanted to open a museum to make art available to the general public. King George III gave support to the project, and in 1768 Reynolds, along with other leading artists, opened the Royal Academy. As its founder, he was appointed the academy's first president, and later Reynolds also became Painter to the King.

CHARLOTTE BUELL COMAN

Another artist who used an ear trumpet is Charlotte Buell Coman (American, 1833–1924).[15] Known for her sense of humor, Coman believed deafness had its advantages. She said it protected her from attacks by critics, because they were too embarrassed to shout negative comments into her ear trumpet. Coman, who was born in upstate

New York, moved with her husband to Iowa City, which was then a western frontier town. Seven years later her husband died, and Coman returned east to her family. At that time she began to lose her hearing. Becoming almost completely deaf, but refusing to give in to self-pity, Coman looked for a new direction in life and found it in art. In her thirties, she began to take lessons, and she later went to Europe to study painting in France and Holland.

Creating art may have enormous appeal for someone like Coman who is losing the ability to hear, because it can make the absence of sound less painful. For a person with encroaching deafness, there is the uncomfortable silence of not hearing the spoken word, the sound of music, or the noise of everyday life. But through the strong silence of visual art, painting can provide a counterpart to an increasingly noiseless environment. Art is a deliberately quiet world in which sound never appears to be missing because it is not needed. As the ancient Greek poet Simonides said, "Painting is silent poetry."

Coman may have taken the silent world she experienced due to hearing difficulties and translated it into the quiet peacefulness of her landscapes. Originally trained in the French Barbizon tradition that emphasized light and atmosphere, she became one of a group of American painters who conveyed a mood of "quietism" in their work. In response to the ravages of the Industrial Revolution, these artists portrayed the tranquil beauty of a vanishing countryside. Exhibiting widely, winning many prizes, and working until her death at ninety-one, Coman is considered to be the dean of women landscape painters in America.

The Response to Deafness

Just as we are all different from one another, so our responses to life's difficulties vary as well. Even when the challenge appears to be similar, such as deafness in a previously hearing person, individuals react from their own points of view and life situations. Joshua Reynolds had already decided to become a painter, and while becoming deaf must have been stressful, it did not deter him from his goal. Charlotte Buell Coman turned to art in response to her hearing loss, and her work seems to reflect the peacefulness of pervading quiet in the world. Francisco Goya became enraged at his loss of hearing, but his unwanted condition transformed his art.

FRANCISCO GOYA

In 1792 Francisco Goya (Spanish, 1746–1828), also known as Francisco de Goya y Lucientes, realized his health was deteriorating.[16] He was having blackouts and hallucinations. When Goya received an invitation and art commission from his friend Sebastian Martínez in Cádiz, he wanted very much to go, but on this visit he would lose his hearing. Martínez said that Goya arrived at his house already ill and then became worse. The artist's symptoms were deafness, partial paralysis, vision problems, noise in his head, confusion, and a loss of balance. He was in bed for months, deaf, half paralyzed, and intermittently delirious. Most of these problems were temporary, but his deafness was permanent. The only sound Goya could hear for the rest of his life was a buzzing and roaring in his ears. Forty-six years old and profoundly deaf, he now communicated through hand signals and writing.

We may never know Goya's exact diagnosis, but there are many suggestions. Some possible explanations are acute otitis (an infection of the middle ear) that severely damaged his Eustachian tube; Ménière's syndrome, which can cause vertigo and noise in the ears; syphilis; botulism; neurolabyrinthitis (inflammation of the inner ear); typhoid fever; malaria; and lead poisoning from years of exposure to the white lead pigment in his paintings.

Goya felt that he barely escaped with his life, but after the ordeal his art transformed and he created his best work. The challenge itself may have galvanized him into action. Artists seek challenges, or else they wouldn't choose creativity with its constant demands. Working also gave him strength. Goya said the group of paintings he made shortly after his recovery were not only for income but "to occupy my imagination, which has been depressed by dwelling on my misfortune."[17] Goya's deafness was not a world of silence but rather a barrage of unwanted sound. Because of this, he may also have used painting to divert himself from the constant inner noise.

Difficult as it was, the illness became a turning point and afterward his production increased. Perhaps the deafness that limited his social interactions forced him to concentrate on art, thus making him more prolific. Goya previously painted on commission and now he painted more for himself, resulting in a greater variety of subject matter. Before being sick, Goya made brightly colored paintings, but afterward dark shadows appear, giving his images greater structure and power. He continued painting portraits, but his work became stronger.

He also began to make political art such as *The Third of May, 1808*, his famous painting that shows the tragedy of indiscriminate executions in response to an uprising against the Bonaparte regime. Goya's last large project is the series of paintings he made for his home outside of Madrid. Known as the *Black Paintings*, they are scenes of fantasy and the macabre. Works that artists create for themselves reveal their innermost nature. Social amenities are dispensed with and the unconscious becomes visible. Beginning as an eighteenth-century rococo painter of colorful and pleasant pastimes, Goya changed the essence of his work after his deafness. He became a romantic painter and one of the great forerunners of modern art.

Centuries later Goya has become an important role model for artists. His triumph in the face of deafness inspires contemporary deaf artists. But perhaps he was helped by a role model of his own who lived more than two hundred years earlier, the artist Juan Fernández de Navarrete (Spanish, 1526–1579), who is known as El Mudo (the Mute).[18] Navarrete, who became deaf from an illness in early childhood, began his formal art education in the northern Spanish town of Logroño, where he was born. Afterward, he traveled to Italy, studying in Rome and then in Venice with Titian. Navarrete's paintings have the beautiful colors of Venetian art. In 1568 Philip II called Navarrete back to Spain and appointed him Painter to the King, which was the country's highest honor for an artist. Goya was also Painter to the King, and perhaps Navarrete's great success as a deaf artist in a hearing society may have encouraged Goya to believe that he, too, could succeed.

The Importance of a Role Model

Role models are very important. As children we learn through mirroring the actions of our parents, both consciously and unconsciously. Role models can also be crucial in a crisis situation, such as poor health, when we not only learn from the behavior of other people who have been through similar difficulties but see by their existence that survival is possible. Knowing that someone else has triumphed proves it can be done and makes it possible for you. One of the main goals of this book is to provide many role models.

DAVID HOCKNEY

When David Hockney (English, b. 1937, lives in America) was going deaf he found strength by taking Goya as his role model.[19] At first, Hockney was so depressed by his hearing loss that he thought of suicide. But then he remembered Goya, accepted his condition, and went on working. Hockney says he has an explanation for the improvement in Goya's work after the onset of hearing difficulties. Hockney believes that deafness clarifies and intensifies vision. "I actually think the deafness makes you see clearer," insists Hockney. "If you can't hear, you somehow see."[20]

David Hockney was born with normal hearing that began to diminish in adulthood. His father and older sister also have hearing impairments. By 1979, he could no longer deny that he was having difficulty understanding what people said. Formerly extremely social, Hockney wore two hearing aids and began to avoid parties, dinners, restaurants, and the opera. This was a great hardship on the artist and also on his work. One of Hockney's main interests is designing for the stage. But as his deafness increased he avoided theatrical design, because he could no longer hear the productions. Over the years, Hockney created sets and costumes for eleven operas. "When I go to the opera," he says, "I want to have something to look at."[21] In 2003 Hockney returned to the theater with a design for Stravinsky's ballet *Le Sacre du printemps* (*The Rite of Spring*). He had gotten new hearing aids and was excited that he could listen to music in a theater again if he sat in the first row. Since then Hockney's impairment has worsened, leaving him with a love of music that he can no longer hear because he is becoming completely deaf.

In a 2005 film by Maryte Kavaliauskas and Seth Schneidman about his theatrical designs and hearing loss called *David Hockney—the*

Colors of Music, Hockney not only creates stage sets but directs the lighting effects as well. The film shows Hockney as an artist doing his best work in a race against the time of total deafness. His awareness that each theatrical production may be the last gives his art an extra intensity. Hockney, who is a superb colorist, believes that in the theater "you physically take the color into your body as you take in the music."[22] His stage designs have magnificent color. "I think it's possible," says Hockney, "to make the eye hear."[23]

The Deaf Community

Goya has also influenced artists in the deaf community. Like most hearing people, I know that the deaf community exists, but until I did the research for this book, I had no idea that there are and were so many deaf visual artists. The art historian Deborah Sonnenstrahl finds that some deaf artists, like David Hockney, are active in the hearing world but that other artists are part of the deaf community.[24] The work of artists in the deaf community reflects contemporary culture and contemporary deaf culture. It has a great following among deaf people and is usually not seen by the hearing public. I strongly believe these artists should also be shown in mainstream art galleries as well as in exhibitions for the deaf community. Imagery is a universal language, and by learning the meaning this work has for deaf culture, the hearing population can more fully appreciate the world of the deaf.

ORKID SASSOUNI

One way to learn about deaf culture is through the social events of their community. This subject matter is central to the photographer Orkid Sassouni (American, b. 1972).[25] Sassouni, who was born in Iran, fled with her family to Europe after the 1979 revolution. Eventually they settled in Great Neck, Long Island, a suburb of New

York. Even though Sassouni was found to be deaf at three years old, her mother insisted that she attend regular schools. She did not go to the Iran School for the Deaf, and with intensive speech therapy, she graduated from Great Neck High School. As a result, Sassouni thought of herself as the only deaf person in the world.

Then she saw the television coverage of Deaf President Now, the student uprising at Gallaudet University that resulted in the first appointment of a deaf person to head this university for the deaf. After the event, Sassouni very much wanted to attend Gallaudet, but her parents thought it was improper for an unmarried Persian girl to go away to school. She finally convinced them, learned sign language, and graduated from Gallaudet. The interest in photography that Sassouni acquired in college has become a career. Showing aspects of the deaf experience, such as deaf weddings, deaf conventions, and deaf social clubs, her work features the animated hand gestures of sign language and the lively facial expressions found throughout the deaf community. "I wanted to capture the moment," says Sassouni, "when signers express their energy, spirit, and soul in front of the camera."[26]

The Deaf Experience and Sign Language

Like other artists who are a part of deaf culture, Sassouni focuses on what it is like to be deaf. The experience of being deaf is the common thread woven throughout the great variety of art in the deaf community. Some deaf artists feel it is so central to their existence and their creativity that in 1989 they formed an art movement called Deaf View/Image Art, which is also known as De'VIA.[27] Expressing the physical and cultural aspects of deafness through visual art, De'VIA shows a perception of the world through the experience of being deaf.

From my point of view, deafness is a transforming illness for these artists because it inspires their work. But I say this from the perspective

of a hearing person. In the deaf world, deafness is not seen as an illness but as a normal way of being, with sign language as the preferred
communication. The art historian L. K. Elion says that she and other
deaf individuals dream and think in sign language.[28] Signed poems
and stories are to the deaf, she explains, what music is to hearing people. That is why images of signing and, in certain cases, a defense of
sign language are often found in the art of the deaf. For Ann Silver
and Mary Thornley, who are both influenced by Goya, deafness and
sign language is a political cause.

ANN SILVER

Ann Silver (American, b. 1949) uses art as a way to promote the
rights of deaf individuals.[29] Born deaf into a hearing family, Silver
first used art to communicate. Then she learned English. When Silver
was young, deaf children were only taught to communicate verbally,
but later at Gallaudet University she learned ASL (American Sign
Language). Like other artists in the deaf community, Silver refers to
ASL in her work. Her pencil drawing and collage called *Freedom to
Speak Out in ASL* shows a man with his wrists and hands bound. Unable to sign, he stands tied and in shadow. For Silver, signing is an aspect of her freedom. In another work reminiscent of an Andy Warhol
soup can, called *Will the Real Goya Please Stand Up*, Silver shows the front
and back of a can similar to those of Goya brand foods. But this can
is labeled *Francisco de Goya y Lucientes* and shows a picture of the artist
along with statements about his deafness and his accomplishments.
Silver, who helped to start a program for deaf museum visitors in
New York, believes that "art and activism can serve each other."[30]

MARY THORNLEY

Mary Thornley (American, b. 1950) is also influenced by Goya and
she also defends the use of ASL.[31] Using Goya's painting *The Third of*

May, 1808, as a basis for her painting *Milan, Italy, 1880*, Thornley refers to a conference of international educators that met in Milan in 1880 to ban the use of sign language for the deaf. While Goya's canvas shows soldiers executing civilians, Thornley shows soldiers shooting down the letters *ASL*. Thornley, who was born to hearing parents, has one deaf sister and one hearing sister. She began to lose her hearing at four or five years old, and by adulthood was completely deaf. When she started making art as a child, people admired her work but saw it as a compensation for her deafness. This was very upsetting to Thornley because she just wanted to be seen as someone who could draw. In fact, she can draw with either hand; she is ambidextrous. In addition to being an artist, Thornley is an art historian and a curator of deaf art.[32] "I want to make deafness 'visible,'" she says, "and relate it to art history."[33]

Deaf Art and the Hearing World

The work of the contemporary artists in this chapter who are active in deaf culture could be shown in mainstream galleries of the hearing art world. But so far, like the work of other deaf artists, it is rarely seen outside of the deaf community. I hope this practice will change. The communication barrier is one of the main reasons why deaf art has remained invisible to the hearing population.[34] When our next artist, Chuck Baird, tried to sell his work on a busy street, people stopped and were very interested until they realized he was deaf and quickly moved on. By the end of the day, he had sold nothing. This unfortunate situation limits the audience for deaf artists and also deprives the hearing world of their work. There should be an advocate who promotes the art of the deaf in the hearing community, just as Christine Leahey in chapter 10 is an advocate who promotes the art of the blind in the seeing community.

CHUCK BAIRD

I first became aware of contemporary deaf art through the work of Charles Crawford "Chuck" Baird (American, b. 1947).[35] His painterly yet realistic images have an enormous following in the deaf community. Baird was born deaf in Kansas City to hearing parents. He has three deaf sisters and a hearing brother. Both English and ASL were used in the Baird home, and not all of his work is about deafness. His painting called *Ski Shop* shows the reflection of a row of skis in a store window. "I am no longer interested in whether I am a Deaf artist or an artist who happens to be deaf," says Baird. "But what makes me an artist; that really matters."[36]

Baird's work about the deaf experience often incorporates sign language. The expressive hands in his paintings are usually making a sign for the meaning of the work. The first painting I saw of Baird's, which is still one of my favorites, is a self-portrait. It doesn't show his face, but just his upper torso, with art supplies, such as brushes and colored pencils floating all around him in the air. His white shirt has paint stains and his hands are signing. I knew immediately that this is an artist telling us about himself and his work. Later I found out that he is signing the word *art*. In addition to being a visual artist, Baird was also an actor with the National Theatre of the Deaf. "Each craft," he explains, "gives the other more strength."[37]

HARRY R. WILLIAMS

In the deaf community, Harry R. Williams (American, 1948–1991) is legendary.[38] His beautiful symbolic paintings are executed with color and precision reminiscent of Salvador Dalí. Williams, who was born hearing to hearing parents, became deaf at eighteen months after being given the antibiotic streptomycin for tonsillitis. He had two hearing siblings and two deaf ones. At the age of four, Williams started drawing as a way to communicate with his parents and stayed with art for the rest of his life. Williams had only one solo show. It was in 1990 at the International Deaf Cultural Arts Academy in Stockholm, and he sold everything in the exhibit. Sadly, Williams died of AIDS in April of 1991. He was only forty-two.

Although he couldn't hear, Williams was fascinated with music and often showed a violin in his paintings. It is usually a violin without strings, because Sonnenstrahl says that Williams as a deaf person saw himself that way. In one painting, *LA Inner Vision*, Williams shows a violin suspended over Los Angeles at night, with the city lights sparkling below. Instead of having strings, the violin contains an image of a sunrise over blue ocean waves and a sandy beach. The painting tells us that visual beauty for the deaf takes the place of sound for the hearing. "My eyes are my ears," says Williams. "Colors," he explains, "are music to the eyes."[39]

Williams calls himself a "symbolist" painter, and in one of his last paintings, *Coffin Door II*, he uses symbols to reveal his thoughts on life and death.[40] By reading the painting from left to right like a book, we see both the painting's meaning and the artist's courage. It is a surrealist scene with gentle blue ocean waves. In the background on the left is a floating rectangle containing a view of Los Angeles that is connected to the shore by an empty rowboat. Williams is telling us that he has left his hometown of Los Angeles and taken the boat to shore. In the center foreground is a large door shaped like a coffin that is modeled on a similar door at Gallaudet University, where Williams obtained his B.F.A. Near the top of the coffin door we see his hand. He is approaching death. But rising out of the ocean in the background on the right is an antique white marble Greek sculpture that is still intact and framed against dark cypress trees that symbolize the

Isle of the Dead. Through his art Williams says that death is not an end but the doorway to a timeless place. He is on the threshold of a new state of being.

Communication and the Deaf

Sassouni, Silver, Thornley, Baird, and Williams are all graduates of schools established to educate the deaf. Deaf education, which began in eighteenth-century France and came to America in the nineteenth century, taught reading, writing, and sign language.[41] Some students also learned to speak. Now verbal communication for the deaf is helped by the invention of cochlear implants, which are small electronic devices implanted underneath the skin behind the ear.[42] Designed to give a degree of hearing to the deaf, they make spoken language easier to learn and are becoming increasingly popular.[43] At present more than seventy thousand people have these implantable devices. There is currently a debate about deafness and communication, with more and more people choosing cochlear implants and the spoken word, while others prefer to express themselves by signing.

Before sign language was standardized to American Sign Language (ASL) in nineteenth-century America, deaf individuals used a variety of different signs they developed in their families. This type of communication is called home sign, and it is much simpler and more limited than ASL. It can also differ greatly from family to family, so that a deaf person home-signing in one family may not understand another family's signs. ASL provides a standard language that many people can share. Each country has its own variety of sign language: in Japan it is JSL (Japanese Sign Language) and in France it is FSL (French Sign Language). Just as people can learn a foreign language, individuals who sign according to one country can learn the sign language of another culture.

JOHN LEWIS CLARKE

Someone who could converse in two sign languages was John Lewis Clarke (American, 1881–1970).[44] As a Blackfoot Native American, he already knew Indian sign language and then learned ASL through his education in schools for the deaf. Clarke was born hearing to hearing parents but became deaf after scarlet fever at the age of three. When he ceased to hear, Clarke also ceased to speak. His Blackfoot name, Cutapuis, means "he who talks not." Clarke, who was the grandson of a Blackfoot chief, also had one grandparent of European descent, his paternal grandfather, Malcolm Clarke.

Clarke began sculpting in childhood with clay from the riverbanks near his Montana home. It was a way to communicate to his parents about all the animals he saw. Throughout his life, Clarke continued to portray animals, and although he could paint and draw, wood sculpture was his favorite medium. He refined his talent for wood carving in schools for the deaf and also studied drawing at the Art Institute of Chicago. After carving altars for churches in a Milwaukee factory, Clarke returned home to the Blackfeet Indian Reservation in East Glacier Park, Montana. He set up a studio there where would he live and work for the next fifty-seven years.

Roaming the Montana countryside in his Jeep, Clarke sought wood for his sculptures. He was able to see the potential animal inside a piece of wood, with the bumps in the wood becoming its ears and paws. Known as the "Bowie Knife Sculptor," he loved animals and knew them so well that his art captures their essence as well as their likeness. Wood-carvers from around the world came to visit him and study his techniques.[45] Clarke exhibited widely and won prizes;

his works were bought by President Warren Harding and John D. Rockefeller. In the last years of his life, as cataracts obscured his vision, Clarke refused to stop working. He continued to carve animals through his sense of touch.

Prejudice and Deafness

With all of his accomplishments and his obvious intelligence, Clarke was still called a "deaf and dumb Indian."[46] This is not only cruel, it is inaccurate. I knew when I was very young and heard the phrase "deaf and dumb" that people who were unable to hear or speak were being unfairly criticized. It was obvious they had intelligence, thoughts, and emotions but did not express themselves through the spoken word like the majority of the population. If I realized this in childhood, many others must have realized it as well. It is a phrase rarely heard today, but why did people use it and what made them stop?

Oliver Sacks, in his book about deafness called *Seeing Voices*, notes that for centuries a lack of speech was equated with a lack of intelligence.[47] He says this prejudice comes from the recognition that human intelligence does not develop to its fullest extent without the acquisition of language, whether it is spoken, written, or signed. But the prejudice toward deaf people continued even when they were fluent in the richly expressive ASL. Saks shows that the prejudice was stopped by the deaf themselves, through the 1988 uprising at Gallaudet College (now Gallaudet University) that demanded a deaf president to head the school. The deaf won their fight to have a deaf president head Gallaudet, and as one young woman student said, "The words 'deaf and dumb' will be destroyed forever; instead there'll be 'deaf and able.' "[48]

RUSSELL CHILDERS

Another artist with hearing difficulties is Russell Childers (American, b. 1915).[49] When he was ten years old, Childers was committed to Fairview State Home for the Feebleminded, two miles southeast of Salem, Oregon. His mother begged the judge not to send her child away, but his teacher at school said the boy was incorrigible. He was also subject to "fits." Several years later his mother died, but Childers remained institutionalized at Fairview for thirty-nine years, labeled retarded, deaf, and incapable of speech. When his case was reviewed in the 1960s, it was discovered that Childers was not deaf, but hard of hearing, and he could speak. He was transferred to an adult foster home, where for the first time in his life he was given hearing aids and speech therapy. He also learned to read and write. Because Childers was diagnosed with autism, it is likely that the "fits" he had as a boy were not epilepsy but the rages of a hearing-impaired autistic child. The writer Bob Keefer, who interviewed Childers in 1992, noted that the artist was sometimes in his own world, and his speech could be difficult to understand. "But," says Keefer, "he communicates superbly through his work."[50]

During the years he spent at Fairview, Childers began to sculpt. It may have started during World War II, when he saw a picture of a wood-carver in *Life* magazine. The image made such a great impression on him that he found some pieces of wood and without any instruction began to carve. Soon sculpture became a focus in his life. After his transfer to an adult foster home, his sculpture began to be noticed, first by the staff at the home and then by the art world. Childers had exhibitions, and his work was bought by private collectors and by a museum. Although he always called art his "hobby," he never stopped making sculpture. In his seventies, with a back bent from years at the workbench and glaucoma blinding him so that he walked with a white cane, Childers continued to carve by feeling the wood instead of seeing it.

His wooden sculptures cover a wide range of subject matter, from feeding dolphins to life at Fairview and childhood with his mother and family. He worked mostly from memory. But with the photographic memory of an autistic savant, Childers could re-create details as delicate as shoelaces and lacy crocheted caps. Michael Whitenack, who was the director of Visual Arts Resources in Eugene, Oregon, gave the artist a great compliment: "If your house was burning down, and you could grab only one thing, it would be the Russell Childers sculpture."51

Creativity and Cancer

In the next chapter, we will see how artists, despite enormous distress and through continued effort, find a way to change themselves and their art in response to another transforming illness: cancer.

Part 4

The Challenges of Adulthood

Chapter 12

Cancer and Creativity

Is not disease the rule of existence? . . .
Now, at midsummer, find me a perfect leaf
or fruit. —*Henry David Thoreau*

ancer—it is still the most dreaded diagnosis. Yet more than 10 million people are alive today after having had cancer, and the number is growing. Approximately one out of every two men and one out of every three women have a risk of developing this illness.[1] Treatments to combat cancer can be extremely harsh, and as someone who has had the disease, I think this is one of the reasons it is so frightening. The artists in this chapter speak about the prejudice toward people with cancer and how it makes a hard time more difficult. In the past, cancer was often terminal, but with improved medicine and expanding alternative health care, more people are able to survive. Some require long-term treatment while others recover completely. Whatever the outcome, the seriousness of the initial diagnosis brings us face-to-face with mortality. Such a confrontation can lead to introspection and self-examination and be a path to creativity and greater strength.

For all of the artists in this chapter, cancer is a transforming illness that affects both their work and their lives. When we change, our work also changes. Art not only mirrors personal growth but can also deepen and accelerate the process, as it did for Vincent Desiderio.

VINCENT DESIDERIO

"Now I can paint better," says Vincent Desiderio (American, b. 1955), referring to his renewed strength after cancer, "because I paint with greater enthusiasm."[2] "They got rid of it," he explains, "but it was an agonizing time. The chemo is terrible and so is the radiation." Although he had both together for more than half a year, Desiderio never said "Why me?" Instead, he says, "Why not me? Why should it be someone else who gets this?" In the end the experience made him stronger.

It began in 2001 with a swollen lymph node in his neck that did not go away. It wasn't terribly uncomfortable, but when Desiderio noticed a slight dizziness he went to a doctor to have it checked. He was commended for coming in early: people often delay seeking help until they have much larger swellings, because they are in denial about their lymph nodes growing. The biopsy discovered a very aggressive type of nasal pharyngeal cancer usually found in people from Southeast Asia. Desiderio had never even traveled there. He also found out that Babe Ruth died of this cancer before effective treatment was available. The lymph node could not be removed because it had wrapped around blood vessels in his neck, creating a dangerous risk of heavy bleeding. Fortunately his doctor located the source of the cancer in Desiderio's nose. As a result, the original site could be targeted directly with radiation. Because of this discovery, his illness had a positive outcome.

"First, it terrified me that it had to happen," admits Desiderio. "When I was recovering I felt shell-shocked." Now he feels courageous, with renewed strength and a better sense of himself. Although illness, chemo, and radiation forced Desiderio to put his work on hold for almost a year, afterward he finished an entire group of paintings. His perfectly drawn figurative canvases can be enormous, sometimes twenty-four feet long, but the work went so well that his show was a great success. Desiderio believes that illness cuts away the screen of complacency in life that obscures our inner potential. "One of the great things about how I feel now," he says, "is that I don't require validation from outside." His strength is within. "You can't worry about the past or the future," insists Desiderio. "You have to live each day; you have to live in the present. When you do that, things work out so much better."

Breast Cancer

One of the most common cancers is breast cancer. Each year in America, more than two hundred thousand women will have this illness.[3] This means that one in seven women either has breast cancer now or will develop it during her lifetime. Three artists in this chapter had breast cancer: Nancy Fried, Anne Thulin, and Martha Jane Bradford. Each woman has had a different disease experience and produces different kinds of work, yet for all of them, the illness was transformational.

NANCY FRIED

Nancy Fried (American, b. 1946) had cancer four times from 1986 to 1990.[4] It changed her art, it changed her life, and it changed the lives of others. A mammogram and a biopsy revealed abnormalities in Fried's right breast in November 1986. An operation in early December found two distinct kinds of breast cancer: a malignant tumor and a calcification from a separate invasive cancer of the breast ducts. Fried had a mastectomy but no chemotherapy or radiation. Then, in the summer of 1987, doctors removed an ovarian tumor that turned out to be benign, but the operation also discovered a rare type of malignancy, cancer of the appendix. Three years later, in April 1990, Fried had breast cancer for the third time. It was in her left breast, and she had a lumpectomy followed by seven weeks of daily radiation. According to test results, none of the cancers was the result of metastasis. After having four separate primary cancers in four years, she has continued to be well.

Fried's experience with breast cancer in 1986 was so distressing that she began to express her trauma through art as a way to cope. Her art had always been autobiographical, and now she translated her anguish into work. Fried began to make sculptures of herself with one breast. These beautiful works of art are smaller-than-life-size statues made of glazed terra-cotta. It is soft clay that is fired in a ceramic oven called a kiln, covered with a glaze, and then fired again. The statues often just focus on her torso. One, called *Mourning*, shows a figure with one breast holding a severed breast in her hand. Fried said the sculpture shows her going through a process of loss because the two breasts are kissing good-bye. The cancer that inspired these sculptures made Nancy Fried famous. It was difficult for her to move her right arm after the mastectomy, but she believes, "You are the most centered when you are working."

When Berta Walker of the Graham Modern gallery in New York saw the work about breast cancer in Fried's studio in 1987, she canceled an already planned exhibit to give Fried a show. "This won't sell," thought Walker, "but it needs to be seen."[5] The exhibition was an enormous success. Fried received excellent reviews and sold almost everything, including two pieces to the Metropolitan Museum of Art. Fried's illness continued to inspire her work. When she got severe burns during radiation treatment for her 1990 lumpectomy, she sculpted a breast with flames around it, showing her physical and emotional distress. Fried, who says her art is not only about loss but also about regeneration, accepts herself completely as a one-breasted woman. "It is unusual," admits Fried, "but I am an artist and that is also unusual, and besides it lets me hug my daughter more closely." Because of her one breast, people recognize her, ask her if she is Nancy Fried, and then say how much they like her art.

It also means a great deal to Fried that her work has helped others. "By making something private public," she says, "you find you aren't the only one."

As her work became known, people told her how much it helps them. A young woman born with only one breast says that she stopped wearing bras with built-in prostheses. A woman who had a double mastectomy admits that neither she nor her husband looked at her naked after the operation. She used to be so proud of her body but had started to take Valium because it was too difficult to acknowledge she was having a hard time. After seeing Fried's sculptures, she began therapy as a way to uncover her emotions and fully accept herself. A young man born with only one testicle also finds strength in Fried's art. He no longer thinks it is necessary to pad his clothes. Fried, who believes in going forward with life, says, "Don't say 'why me,' but 'why not me'—it happens."

Reacting to Illness through Art

Both Nancy Fried and Anne Thulin are sculptors who had breast cancer. Fried is a figurative artist; Thulin's art is abstract and conceptual. Each woman found a distinct way to express her experience of illness through art and benefited greatly from her own kind of creativity. All forms of art are pathways to speak about life, and people express their experiences in unique ways. These various modes of expression add to the richness of our culture, just as our differences as individuals add to the richness of our world.

ANNE THULIN

In the spring of 2001 Anne Thulin (Swedish, b. 1953), who lives and works in New York and Stockholm, felt a lump in her breast.[6] After a mammogram and a biopsy found cancer, Thulin, who was living in New York at the time, went back to Sweden because her insurance that paid for the mammogram and biopsy in New York would not cover an operation there. A lumpectomy performed in Sweden to remove the tumor found that several lymph nodes were also affected. While she was being scheduled for chemotherapy and radiation, Thulin was offered a choice of two types of chemotherapy: a weak course that did not cause hair loss and stronger, more thorough treatment that resulted in both hair loss and menopause. Thulin chose the stronger one because she wanted to survive.

Sometimes her blood levels dropped so low that the chemotherapy had to be delayed, but Thulin persevered and finished the regimen. Believing the mind helps the body, she visualized the chemo as healing and nourishing. During her treatments Thulin tried to be as relaxed as possible so the medicine could reach all her cells. She also listened to music. Hearing the same music today brings immediate nausea, but at the time it was a great help to her.

When Thulin returned to New York after chemotherapy and radiation, she felt exhausted but went back to her studio. After six months of struggling to make art like her previous work, she knew it was time to forget about old ideas and create something completely new. After this realization, Thulin thought about the days in Sweden when she was lying in bed during chemotherapy. She remembers thinking, "Here I am not moving but my body is moving because I am breathing." In response to this experience, Thulin began to create large inflatable sculptures that are filled with air as the body is filled with breath.

They have a soft, strong presence and some of them even contract and expand. Because of this, the sculptures seem to breathe and be alive like the artist herself.

Now Thulin has greater faith in herself and her creative ability. If one idea doesn't work, she knows that "something else will come up." Thulin's life has also changed. "I am more aware of my time," she explains, "because I don't have as much energy as I had before." Thulin is also very careful about nutrition. "I am more humble and gentle with myself," she says, "and more aware of what is important for me."

The Importance of Self-Care

Taking care of ourselves is a part of life that becomes even more important during illness and recovery. Some people have friends or family who will care for them but not everyone does. Even for those who do, as adults we must also look after ourselves. When we are well, there is a tendency to take health for granted, but sickness can highlight our needs. Both Anne Thulin and Martha Jane Bradford discovered the importance of self-care and the acceptance of limits as a way to stay well.

MARTHA JANE BRADFORD

Martha Jane Bradford (American, b. 1946) had breast cancer and a recurrence, but it enhanced her creativity and changed her life.[7] In late 1995 Bradford discovered a lump on her breast that felt sore. A mammogram and biopsy in January 1996 found cancer. After her first lumpectomy, doctors discovered the tumor did not have clean margins. A second, more invasive lumpectomy was successful. It was followed by chemotherapy and radiation. Then two years later a routine mammogram found a local recurrence. Because she went for frequent checkups the recurrence was found early. Bradford had a mastectomy but no chemotherapy or radiation and since 1998 she has remained well.

After chemotherapy and radiation in 1996, Bradford had so little energy that she was unable to work. Finally, through perseverance, she started making very small pieces because they were easier to do. Then in 1997 she had a breakthrough. Martha Bradford invented a new way to make digital fine art. Before she was sick, Bradford experimented with creating art on the computer but returned to painting because it was her primary means of expression. Now unable to make large paintings and forced to work small, she turned to the computer once more. Bradford found that it allowed her to work small, which was physically necessary, but the result could be large, which was artistically satisfying. She calls her new technique digital drawing.

Instead of making small works by drawing with pencil or pastels on paper, Bradford uses an electronic stylus and draws on a nine-by-twelve-inch electronic palette that transmits digital signals to her computer. On her website she gives clear, illustrated instructions for anyone who would like to learn how to use her method.[8] Although the images are small while the artist works on them, they can be printed out to the size of large paintings. Bradford creates beautifully drawn landscapes and houses, but her digital technique is adaptable for other styles of art as well. "Nobody works on this scale or level of detail," she says, "and I came to it as the result of being sick."

Bradford is now able to paint again but also continues to create digital art. And since having been ill she makes it a point to exercise. Cancer has given Bradford insight into herself and others. "Don't blame yourself for getting sick," she says, "and if you are tired, reduce the scale of your work and simplify the process. Be gentle with yourself. You're fighting for your life."

Bradford is also very open about prejudice toward people with cancer. She has a caring husband, but there were other women in her breast cancer support group who were not as fortunate—their husbands left them after the initial diagnosis. Bradford also points out the irrational fear some people have that cancer is contagious. She heard a woman warn someone, "Don't touch that; it was Great-aunt Myrtle's and she died of cancer." Prejudice makes people who have had cancer feel like outcasts. Unfortunately, I speak from experience.

Prejudice and the Fear of "Catching" Cancer

The physical aspects of illness are upsetting, but emotional pain makes a hard time worse. One of our greatest stresses is a feeling of isolation. There is a degree of physical isolation in every illness, the aloneness of being sick in bed or being alone during the time of recovery. But there is also emotional isolation caused by prejudice from people who fear the sick. It limits interpersonal contact and sends a dehumanizing message to the sick person that he or she is something to avoid. Regrettably, people with cancer are subjected to this type of behavior.

Cancer is not contagious, but some people are so afraid of "catching" it that they avoid anyone who they suspect is ill. When I was in chemotherapy, I ran into an old friend I hadn't seen for years. Usually he gave me a hug hello, but this time he didn't even want to shake my hand. Looking at his face, I could tell he saw me as a pariah, a feared contaminated object, not even a person, and something that should be avoided at all cost. I remember looking at him and thinking, "This man is crazy. How on earth does he think he can catch ovarian cancer? It's not contagious, and he doesn't even have ovaries."

Compassion and Unconscious Fear

Although the experience was very upsetting for me, I later thought about his fears with compassion. Cancer had claimed both of his parents, and he was profoundly afraid he would die of it, too. That a friend his age had been sick was further proof of his vulnerability. I had become the incarnation of his fear. But his fear was not conscious, and that is why it had such a powerful hold on him. What is conscious can be faced and surmounted; what is unconscious can overwhelm us in an instant. In an ideal world, people would be conscious of their fears, but this is not our current reality. It is not always possible to make someone who is prejudiced aware of the roots of his or her fear, even though it would be a better world if this happened.

We cannot control others; we can only hope to control ourselves. Therefore, a more practical approach would be to become conscious of another person's prejudice toward us and see it as his or her problem and not our own. At the root of every prejudice is fear. To realize this and to acknowledge a person's fear, no matter how irrational it may seem, is the beginning of compassion. Compassion toward people disarms any prejudice they may feel toward us. Through compassion, we acknowledge the whole person and see prejudice as just a minor part of the total human being. One of the ways compassion strengthens us is by creating immunity to irrational prejudice and its unwanted pain. Because compassion is a type of unconditional love and profound acceptance for another being, it opens a path for the other person to let go of fears, release any prejudice, and transform.

Lung Cancer

More than any other illness, lung cancer has unnecessarily made millions sick worldwide. I call lung cancer unnecessary because it is associated with smoking, an unnecessary habit. Smoking has sickened and killed too many good people, and artists are no exception. According to the American Cancer Society, approximately 100 million people died in the twentieth century from tobacco use, and if current smoking habits persist, we can expect 1 billion people to die in the twenty-first century.[9] Both Jacob Lawrence and Elizabeth Murray smoked and developed lung cancer, but they battled their illness with work.

Jacob Lawrence

Success came early to Jacob Armstead Lawrence (American, 1917–2000), and it stayed with him throughout a long and productive life.[10] In his twenties he became famous for *The Migration Series*, a group of sixty paintings that form an epic narrative about the journey of African Americans from the South to the North in search of better jobs and a better life. Lawrence's family took part in the migration, so he was painting not only a country's history but his own as well. An artist who often made works as part of a series, Lawrence was a storyteller through his art.[11] He also created a narrative series of paintings on the African American abolitionist Harriet Tubman and on Toussaint-Louverture, the leader of the slave revolt in Haiti. His work shows us why it is so important to have artists from many different backgrounds. While each one expresses an individual culture—African American, Native American, Asian, Middle Eastern, or European—together they convey the diversity of our world.

Lawrence, who became a professor of art at the University of Washington in Seattle, dedicated a large part of his life to education. When New York City public schools were not teaching African American history, Lawrence visited the students with his paintings. "I've always been interested in history, but they never taught Negro history in the public schools," he said in 1940.[12] "I don't see how a history of the United States can be written honestly without including the Negro."

In the late summer of 1998 Lawrence, who had been a smoker, was diagnosed with lung cancer.[13] He underwent chemotherapy and radiation. An intense worker all of his life, Lawrence countered his diagnosis with a barrage of activity. He refused to let illness stop him. He finished a series of paintings on the theme of builders and another on the theme of games. He was working on a series with a university theme until a few weeks before his death in June 2000. In addition to painting and despite an ongoing illness, Lawrence had multiple exhibitions of his work, and he received numerous awards for his achievement. He wanted to remain as active as long as possible. Michael Kimmelman, an art critic for the *New York Times,* spent some time with Lawrence and his wife of fifty-nine years, the painter Gwendolyn Knight Lawrence, at the Metropolitan Museum of Art.[14] Kimmelman said that although Lawrence's wife pushed her husband's wheelchair, he tried to sit in it as little as possible.

In December 1999, six months before his death, Lawrence and his wife established the Jacob and Gwendolyn Lawrence Foundation, a nonprofit organization that promotes the creation, study, and exhibition of art, and helps children from low-income families. In addition to work about the African American experience, Lawrence also made paintings about racial harmony and his hope for world peace. Throughout his work he insisted on the integrity of artistic expression. "My belief is that it is most important for an artist to develop an approach and philosophy about life," said Lawrence. "[I]f he has developed this philosophy, he does not put paint on canvas, he puts himself on canvas."[15]

ELIZABETH MURRAY

Elizabeth Murray (American, b. 1940) is known for her lively paintings that combine abstract shapes with images of everyday life such as
coffee cups, cats, and musical notes.[16] These colorful works are created from many small canvases of different shapes that combine to
form a vibrant whole. Murray starts her large, complicated pieces
with a drawing, and after the canvases are constructed for her, she
paints them. Murray says she doesn't know what will eventually appear in her work. But she believes that "when something makes me
laugh, I know I've got it right."[17]

Murray was working on one of these large pieces in March 2005
when tests found she had lung cancer that had metastasized to the
brain. She had surgery, radiation, and chemotherapy. After coming
home from the hospital, Murray couldn't work for two months. Then
she began to paint again. "I feel such a huge relief," she said. "I can
still do it."[18]

At first it was very difficult. Murray cannot reach the top of her
large paintings while standing on the floor. To paint the upper part of
a canvas, she works on a rolling platform that is accessed by a three-
step ladder. "I was really tottering in there," she reveals. "I could
barely climb the ladder."[19] Murray is an excellent colorist, but after
brain surgery she had difficulty finding the color she wanted to work
with even if she had just used that color and put it down. Determined
to paint, she took the brush or color that was immediately available
and adjusted her efforts later. A large work called *The Sun and the Moon*
that she did after surgery and during chemotherapy is one of the best
paintings of her life.

Smoking was undoubtedly a cause of Murray's lung cancer, but I
believe something else may have aggravated her illness—the toxic dust
and fumes from 9/11. Murray lives and works on Duane Street, just

six blocks north of where the World Trade Center once stood.[20] When the Twin Towers came down, the dust literally poured through her windows. Immediately after 9/11, many people were unaware of the dangers posed by inhaling the dust and fumes. More than a thousand firefighters were affected because of their exposure, workers who cleaned up the site have health problems,[21] and studies have found breathing difficulties in people living near Ground Zero.[22] It is possible that the environmental hazards of this tragic event impacted Murray's health as well.

Despite her ordeal, Murray continues to paint. In the fall of 2005 the Museum of Modern Art in New York presented a retrospective of her work; she is only the fourth woman to be awarded this honor. Chemotherapy has taken away her hair, but Murray still has her wonderful smile, and her husband, the poet Bob Holman, has shaved his head in solidarity. "No matter what happens," says Murray, "I am glad to be going through this. You get insights, epiphanies. You have new knowledge that you cannot ever get away from." But then she continues, "I want to stay alive for my kids and my husband. But I just could not stay alive if I couldn't work."[23]

Medical Treatment as the Subject of Art

Some artists survive their bouts with cancer; others do not. Yet in the face of a dire diagnosis, artists will fight illness with creativity. As a result, they change and their work changes. Even when the artists do not survive, their work still triumphs. It becomes more powerful as a result of their struggle, which is sometimes depicted in their art. Both Hannah Wilke and Robert Arneson show themselves undergoing chemotherapy in their work. Most people would not think of chemotherapy as a subject matter for fine art, but these artists demonstrate how powerful its imagery can be. Chemotherapy is a very difficult experience, yet both of them show it in an extremely profound way. Through the intensity of their struggle they communicate personal hardships as a universal experience.

HANNAH WILKE

Hannah Wilke (American, 1940–1993) worked in a wide range of mediums: photography, performance art, video, collage, and sculptures made of latex and even bubble gum.[24] But it was the latex that may have contributed to her lymphoma years later. When I first saw Wilke's work in the 1970s at the Whitney Museum, I could smell the latex the sculpture was made of before I turned the corner and saw the piece. Having been poisoned by an insecticide a few years earlier, I remember thinking, "Working with this material could be dangerous to a person's health." I don't know what kind of latex Wilke used, so I cannot make any definite statement about its effect, and Monona Rossol, the head of ACTS (Arts, Crafts, and Theater Safety), says that smell is not an accurate measure of toxicity.[25] But Rossol also says that if a person works with a cancer-causing material, an illness may not show up for five years and can in some cases take twenty years or more to manifest.

Wilke made the latex sculptures toward the beginning of her career. Later she concentrated on photography. Early photographs showing Wilke as her own model are more glamorous than profound. But after a diagnosis of lymphoma, her imagery took on new depth. She is still the model in her work, but now we see a part of life that is usually hidden in secret sorrow. Taken in the last two years before her death, these photographs of Wilke during chemotherapy and a bone marrow transplant were the subject of her posthumous show called "Intra Venus," a wordplay on the name of a goddess and a medical treatment. They are Wilke's final pieces and by far the best work of her life.

Our society's emphasis on slenderness and beauty makes it harder to accept yourself when the side effects of chemotherapy and a bone marrow transplant have taken these things away from you. But Wilke shows herself after losing all her hair, bloated from weight gain, her skin discolored, and with bandages and tubes making a patchwork of her body. Through her art she says that cancer and its difficult treatments are facts of modern life. The bravery and honesty of these last images don't portray superficial beauty, but the depth of beauty found through emotion and struggle. Wilke also wrote about the prejudice toward those who are sick. "People are afraid to love people who are ill," she explained. "We start distancing from them before we lose them; we lose them and we lose ourselves."[26]

Self-Portraits to Universality

Robert Arneson's work, like that of Hannah Wilke, is mainly self-portraits. For both artists, an individual experience with cancer inspired images that speak to everyone. The self-portraits created during a struggle with illness and the anguish of chemotherapy become statements of the human condition. Again, what was once personal is now universal.

ROBERT ARNESON

Robert Arneson (American, 1930–1992) originally wanted to be a cartoonist, so when he changed to sculpture, painting, and drawing, he still worked with a sense of humor.[27] In an early 1965 ceramic sculpture of his head and shoulders, Arneson shows marbles spilling out of a jagged crack running through the center of the piece. He calls it *Portrait of the Artist Losing His Marbles*. Usually portraying himself in his art, Arneson said, "I choose myself as subject matter because I can take liberties with my own face that I can't with another model."[28]

In February 1975 Arneson noticed blood in his urine and after immediate surgery he was diagnosed with bladder cancer. It has been suggested that art materials may have caused the illness. This is possible because cadmium pigments and benzidine dyes in art supplies are carcinogens,[29] but Arneson's degree of exposure to them has not been studied. Smoking, however, is a known cause of bladder cancer, and Arneson was a smoker.

For the seventeen years he battled cancer, it was a major transforming illness. Seeking both conventional and alternative medical care, he had more than thirty-five operations. Yet Arneson believed the illness gave him a greater sense of purpose and a quieter lifestyle. His work also changed, reflecting the response to an ongoing struggle. When he was well enough to return to art after his first operation, Arneson made a self-portrait ceramic sculpture called *Man with Unnecessary Burden*. It shows him grimacing about a large rock on top of his head, which is symbolic of his illness. But he also reveals a determination to battle cancer in *The Fighter*, a 1982 drawing of himself as a prizefighter wearing boxing gloves with his fists raised and ready. Arneson's suffering sensitized him to the suffering of others, and in the 1980s he began making sculpture about the ravages of war and the threat of nuclear annihilation. In these serious pieces, such as his 1983 work *Ground Zero*, showing a blackened skull on a rough black cross, the faces are no longer his but generalized to represent everyone. Arneson's awareness of his own mortality translated into a concern for all humankind.

During the last twelve years of his life, Arneson turned increasingly to creating sculpture in bronze. While ceramics may break, bronze pieces can last for millennia. In the face of deteriorating physical health, Arneson may have been hoping to survive through his art. Among the most powerful of these late bronzes are works about the ravages of cancer and chemotherapy, such as *Chemo I* and *Chemo II*, which portray a disintegrating head and shoulders. Made in 1992, which was the start of his chemotherapy and the last year of his life, these portrait busts are mounted on pedestals covered with the names of his chemotherapy medications and their side effects. Arneson also made a drawing of himself throwing up during chemo. While this may be surprising subject matter in fine art for some, it is a compelling image for others who have experienced the extreme nausea of chemotherapy. I look at it and I remember.

Anyone who has ever experienced extreme distress can relate to depictions of late-stage illness. They strike a very deep chord in us, reaching a place isolated through poor health, cut off because of terrible pain and discomfort. And in reaching that place, art tells us we are not alone; we are not the only one who is suffering, who has suffered, who will suffer. By expressing the human condition, art reveals the strength of our basic interconnection.

Problems with Hands, Arms, Legs, and Feet

In the next chapter we see how artists' creativity intensifies and their lives change for the better when they triumph over problems with arms, hands, legs, and feet. It brings them to a completely new stage of their creative process.

Chapter 13

Difficulty with Hands, Arms, Legs, and Feet

Courage is resistance to fear, mastery of
fear—not absence of fear. —*Mark Twain*

How many times have you cut a finger or sprained an ankle and become angry because the injury limited your activity? What if instead of healing, your hand or foot was permanently impaired? What would you do? Most of the artists in this chapter have problems not only with their arms and hands but also with their legs and feet, yet they all transcend what appear to be limits and succeed in creating excellent art. Six of them work while sitting in a wheelchair and all of them must change their creative process and produce art in a different way in order to stay productive. But it makes them stronger.

Ambidexterity

Even though we know that making art involves the brain and the eye, we generally think of it as working with our hands. Most of us are either right-handed or left-handed, but some people are ambidextrous and equally comfortable using either hand. Cornelius Ketel (Dutch, 1548–1616) could not only paint with both hands but also with both feet.[1] Although Ketel was ambidextrous, he painted primarily with his right hand. Martin Wong and Pierre-Auguste Renoir were also ambidextrous and painted primarily with their right hands. It would be interesting to know whether their right hands were dominant or whether it is easier for ambidextrous people to use their right hands in a mostly right-handed society.

MARTIN WONG

Martin Wong (American, 1946–1999) was completely ambidextrous. I remember seeing a video of him working on a large painting showing the San Francisco Chinatown where he grew up.[2] To my surprise, Wong was painting with both hands simultaneously. Each hand held a brush with a different color paint and was making different kinds of brushstrokes on different parts of the canvas. Toward the end of his life, when advanced AIDS prevented Wong from creating large-scale works, he changed to small canvases with still-life images. Taking a group of cactus plants that he bought at a flower market, Wong featured one plant per canvas. Highlighted against dark backgrounds, they glisten like jewels.

PIERRE-AUGUSTE RENOIR

Pierre-Auguste Renoir (French, 1841–1919) was also ambidextrous. When he had a bicycle accident in 1880 and broke his right arm, he wrote in a letter to a friend that it was not a problem.[3] He was painting with his left hand and said he was making more progress. In 1897, after refracturing his right arm in another bicycle accident, Renoir again painted with his left hand. The French artist Camille Pissarro (1830–1903) admired his new work: "Didn't Renoir, when he broke his right arm, do some ravishing paintings with his left hand?"[4] Renoir's perseverance held him in good stead when he kept working in spite of another problem, severe rheumatoid arthritis.

Arthritis

One of the most common ailments in the world today, arthritis is a leading cause of disability. The word *arthritis* means an inflammation of the joints, a condition that can produce pain, stiffness, and reduced mobility. According to the Centers for Disease Control and Prevention (CDC), arthritic conditions currently affect 43 million people in the United States.[5] Of that number, 7 million have their lives significantly limited by the disease. The two most common kinds of arthritis are osteoarthritis, the milder form of the illness that can come with age and wear, and rheumatoid arthritis, which is more debilitating.[6] A chronic inflammatory autoimmune disease, rheumatoid arthritis can twist the body and distort the joints with rheumatoid nodules. Yet artists like Renoir have continued to work despite its crippling effects.

RENOIR AND ARTHRITIS

Renoir noticed the first symptoms of arthritis in December 1897.[7] It was after he had broken his arm for the second time in the summer of that year and now he had pain in his right shoulder. In an effort to keep his hands and his body healthy, Renoir began to exercise by juggling balls and playing games like shuttlecock and billiards. Despite his efforts, the following December brought a more severe attack and after that the arthritis progressed. His pain worsened and Renoir became increasingly debilitated. First he walked with one cane, then two canes, then crutches, and eventually he used a wheelchair. Rheumatoid arthritis also affected his hands. Stiffening the joints, it turned the thumbs in toward his palms and bent his fingers toward his wrists. "Visitors who were unprepared for this," said his son Jean Renoir, "could not take their eyes off his deformity."[8] But Renoir refused to stop painting; he sat in his wheelchair and worked. Remarking on his father's perseverance, Jean Renoir said, "The more intolerable his suffering became, the more he painted."[9]

According to Jean Renoir, his father did not strap brushes to his hands, because his inflamed skin could not bear to touch the wooden handle of the brush. Instead, small, soft cloth pouches were placed in his palms and tied around the backs of his hands with strips of gauze. Then a brush was inserted in the cloth holder. Renoir wrapped his twisted fingers around the brush handle and painted by moving his arms, not his hands. Henri Matisse, who visited Renoir during the late stages of his illness, said, "His finger-joints were swollen and horribly disfigured, yet now he painted his best works!"[10]

The Fight to Stay Creative

Artists fight to stay creative for as long as they can. It is so important for them that they will work in spite of late-stage illness and with no art supplies at all. This happened to Li Kung-lin, who took strength in the act of making art, even though he created images that only he could see.

LI KUNG-LIN

Li Kung-lin (Chinese, ca. 1041–1106), also known as Li Lung-mien, was a government official for thirty years, a scholar, and one of the leading painters of the Northern Sung dynasty.[11] His style of art shows gracefully outlined images accentuated with delicate washes, and in his younger years he made paintings of horses. Artists know that to re-create a subject in art, you must study it first. To achieve great naturalism and spirit in his art, Li Kung-lin spent so many hours studying horses at the imperial stables that a monk warned him he might be reincarnated as a horse in his next life. Although he painted a great variety of subjects, Li Kung-lin is most famous for the religious images he did in his later years. But as he aged, the artist's hands were severely affected by arthritis. Finally unable to hold a brush, Li Kung-lin still retained such a passion for art that he continued drawing by pressing lines on his bedsheets with his crippled hands.

Juvenile Rheumatoid Arthritis

Both Li Kung-lin and Renoir had arthritis that started in adulthood; juvenile rheumatoid arthritis (JRA) begins in childhood. The cause of this autoimmune disease is unknown, but there is a genetic susceptibility and also possibly environmental triggers such as a virus.[12] Although 50 to 75 percent of affected children outgrow JRA, the folk artist Maude Lewis had this condition for the rest of her life.

MAUD LEWIS

Maud Lewis (Canadian, 1903–1970) lived her entire life in Digby County, within an hour's drive from the place where she was born.[13] "I don't go nowheres," she said. "I'm contented here."[14] Creating art despite severe and crippling juvenile rheumatoid arthritis, Lewis became the Grandma Moses of Canada. The exact onset of her illness is unknown. In a photo of her at four, she looks like a healthy child, but a photograph taken a few years later shows obvious signs of JRA. The illness has already pulled her chin in toward her neck, giving her a pronounced overbite, and she is hiding her affected hands. There is pain associated with juvenile rheumatoid arthritis, and even though Lewis is nicely dressed, she looks stressed and unhappy.

Although she was a bright child, Lewis never completed her education. The other children ridiculed her so severely that the twenty-minute walk from school would reduce her to tears. Instead, Lewis, who was very shy, stayed home with her mother, who gave her art lessons, and together they made greeting cards. She felt safe there away from the world and happy making art. This isolation and early creativity influenced Lewis's later work as a folk artist. She not only learned to paint and draw but also was able to spend the necessary time alone for creative activity.

From the garden of her house, Lewis could see the train tracks. She used to wave at the trains and sometimes the engineers would toot their whistles back. From a distance her deformities were not visible, and it was a way for her to make contact with the world. When a child isolates herself, as Maud Lewis did, it may not indicate that she wants to be alone but that she needs to be alone because social interactions are too painful.

As the disease progressed, Lewis became dwarfed and crippled. It stopped her growth, and throughout her life she remained the size of a child. Her shoulders became unnaturally sloped, her back hunched and twisted, and rheumatoid nodules deformed her hands, affecting her right hand more than the left. Lewis worked by using her left hand to prop up her right arm so that she could continue to paint right-handed. Because of her unusual appearance, Maud Lewis suffered prejudice for the rest of her life. Her biographer Lance Woolaver, who also lives in Digby, says that as a child he thought of Lewis as the witch from "Hansel and Gretel" and that he would hide in a ditch if he saw her coming up the road. It was only later as an adult that he appreciated the beauty of her art and realized she was a wonderful person.

Maud Lewis's work shows nothing of her hardships or the pain of arthritis. Instead, she portrays a sunny world of oxen and flowers, bluebirds, cats, and butterflies. These are memories from the Nova Scotia countryside of her childhood and sparked by her imagination. "I don't copy much," said Lewis. "I guess my work up."[15] Born Maud Dowling, she was married at thirty-four to Everett Lewis, a fish peddler. They lived together in his little ten-by-twelve-foot one-room house with a sleeping loft but no plumbing or electricity. During the first few years of married life, they drove around in Everett's car, Lewis selling her greeting cards and her husband selling fish. But as the arthritis progressed, she was no longer well enough to ride in the car. She stayed home painting and advertised her art with a painted sign outside their house.

In addition to paintings, Lewis decorated dustpans, seashells, and almost every surface of the little house inside and out, even drawing flowers on the windowpanes. In spite of a life of semi-isolation, she became known through her work. People who bought her art told others about her. Books were written about Lewis, and she was featured in newspapers and magazines, and seen on television. Her painted works, including the little decorated house, are now part of the permanent collection of the Art Gallery of Nova Scotia. Explaining how she accomplished all of this with a painful and debilitating illness, Lewis said, "As long as I've got a brush in front of me, I'm all right."[16]

Creativity, Stress Reduction, and Subject Matter

Maud Lewis appears to be telling us that during creative activity she feels better despite the ongoing symptoms of juvenile rheumatoid arthritis. Because our minds can generally concentrate on only one thing at a time, focusing on art will distract us from pain. As the psychologist Mihaly Csikszentmihalyi says, "People who know how to transform stress into an enjoyable challenge, spend very little time thinking about themselves."[17]

There are also other benefits of creativity. The psychologist Paul Camic, who works with people suffering from chronic physical pain, finds that creative activity not only diminishes the perception of pain but also lowers depression and increases self-esteem.[18] Creativity, which is enjoyable, may produce a response in our body similar to laughter. Norman Cousins originated the study of laughter as beneficial,[19] and now Lee Berk and a team of researchers at Loma Linda University in California find that laughter releases endorphins (our natural painkillers), reduces stress hormones, lowers blood pressure, and even boosts our immune system.[20]

Another way creativity alleviates stress is through the subject matter in a work of art. Maud Lewis painted cheerful images of nature and country life that delighted her and the people who saw them. But images of distress also reduce anxiety. Artists can find emotional release by expressing their anguish in art. Other people who see the work may identify with the subject matter and find relief as well.

Working with the Preferred Hand

In making art, most people prefer to use one hand over the other. Although Ketel, Wong, and Renoir were ambidextrous, the majority of us are not. Like Maud Lewis, who was right-handed, Maria Izquierdo, Nell Blaine, John Callahan (see chapter 14), Horace Pippin (see chapter 15), Chuck Close (see chapter 14), and Ernie Pepion (see chapter 18) are right-handed artists whose illness affects their right hand. Yet also like Lewis, they struggle to work with their right hand by propping it up with the left to paint and/or wearing a brace to give the dominant hand more support. Hendrick Goltzius preferred to use his severely burned right hand over his less injured left (see chapter 5). But why would artists go to such lengths to work this way?

First, handedness is largely genetic. We usually do not decide to be right- or left-handed, we are born this way. Choosing to override the dominant hand takes great effort. It is easier, whenever possible, to work in the way most familiar to us. This is relaxing and allows the mind to concentrate more fully on the task before us. For a person with impaired mobility, using the accustomed hand can also restore a sense of wholeness and diminish the feeling of loss that may come with illness. By adulthood we have built up a lifetime of skill in the dominant hand, and for right-handed artists, this is usually the hand more capable of the fine motor control necessary to make delicate lines and shapes.

Left-handed artists may have a different experience. In the past, left-handed people like Michelangelo were forced to use their right hand to adhere to strict social conventions that disparaged the use of the left. Even today, social pressures encourage left-handed people to use their right hand for certain activities. Because of this, left-handed people may have an easier time switching dominant hands. Ginny Ruffner (see chapter 15), a left-handed artist whose left hand was paralyzed in a car accident, finds that using her right hand to draw is not that difficult because she had used it all her life for activities such as eating and sports. It also has all the fine motor skill she had in her left. But for most right-handed people, the dominant hand is very much preferred, and artists like Maria Izquierdo are determined to use it for as long as they can.

MARIA IZQUIERDO

In February 1948 Maria Izquierdo (Mexican, 1902–1955) suffered her first embolism. It left her paralyzed on her right side for eight months. From that moment until her death from the fourth embolism more than six years later on December 2, 1955, Izquierdo struggled to keep creative. At first her friends rallied around, organizing auctions and charity drives to sell her work, but as the years went by they abandoned her. Still Izquierdo painted. Her daughter, Aurora, described Izquierdo's method of working: "She never worked with her left hand. She placed her paintbrushes in her right hand, which she supported with her left arm."[21] Working long hours with her knees covered by a blanket, Izquierdo kept producing art.

Working with Both Hands

Even though artists will often struggle to use their dominant hand, sometimes illness limits its availability. When this happened to Nell Blaine after polio, she worked out a new system for herself. Using both hands to paint, she had each hand do a different kind of work.

NELL BLAINE

Nell Blaine (American, 1922–1996), who turned to art as a sick child (see chapter 4), had a second transforming illness at the age of thirty-seven.[22] While on a trip to the Greek island of Mykonos, Blaine contracted bulbar spinal polio. By the time a seaplane arrived to take her to a hospital in Athens, her breathing was so difficult that she was starting to turn blue. In Athens, Blaine had a tracheotomy and was put in an iron lung. After the acute crisis phase of the illness, she was sent to an American military hospital in Germany and from there to the polio unit at Mount Sinai Hospital in New York. Eventually Blaine was able to breathe on her own, but for the rest of her life, she remained mostly paralyzed and in a wheelchair. She could move her head and neck and her left arm and hand, but there was only a very small amount of movement in her right hand, and the right thumb was paralyzed. Still, Blaine wanted to use her right hand.

A surgeon who operated on the hands of musicians performed surgery on Blaine's right hand. He took a muscle from one of her fingers and crossed it over to allow Blaine to use her thumb so she could hold a brush. With limited movement in her right hand and more capacity in her left, Blaine developed a new way of painting that used both hands. She did oil paintings with her left hand and small watercolors with her right. "My right arm doesn't lift," she explained, "so when I'm working in watercolor I have to wet the brush with the paint with my left hand and pass it over to my right."[23] She also supported her right arm with her left hand. Marticia Sawin, Blaine's biographer, described the difference in the artist's work when she was using her right or left hand. The right hand made many small, graceful calligraphic strokes, while the left hand worked in a manner that produced strong surface planes and the feeling of volume.

Blaine sat at an easel whose legs were far enough apart so that her wheelchair could fit in between. Sometimes she traveled or painted out of doors with the help of friends, but she also brought the outdoors in. She did this by ordering beautiful flowers that became the subjects of her still-life paintings and by making many studies of the views from her windows. Yet each version of the view was original. "The challenge," she explained, "is to see freshly each time."[24] In addition to paintings and drawings, Blaine also did etchings, and works from her shows were often sold before the show opened. "I do what I can do," she said, "and feel I have expressed my whole self."[25]

Changing Hands

Artists will fight to use the hand they used before, but sometimes it is no longer possible. When the right side is paralyzed by a stroke and the preferred hand cannot move at all, the artist must change hands to keep working, as Katherine Sherwood (see chapter 3) and Alexander Helwig Wyant did. But painting left-handed sometimes improves an artist's work.

ALEXANDER HELWIG WYANT

Alexander Helwig Wyant (American, 1836–1892) showed a gift for drawing when he was a boy, but his talent was not encouraged.[26] He was apprenticed to a harness maker and afterward became a sign painter. But he still longed to make fine art. When Wyant was twenty-one, he saw an art exhibition in Cincinnati with landscape paintings by George Inness (American, 1825–1894). Wyant was so impressed with Inness's work that he traveled from Ohio to New York to meet the artist. Inness became Wyant's mentor and friend and encouraged the young man to paint. After studying in America and Europe, Wyant opened his own studio in New York and became a successful landscape painter.

As nineteenth-century America was expanding west, Wyant joined a government-sponsored expedition to New Mexico and Arizona. He wanted to paint scenes of the newly opening lands and also hoped the trip would restore his failing health. But it did the opposite. During the severe exposure and hardships of the journey, he had a stroke and was sent home by train. Back in New York with a paralyzed right arm, Wyant taught himself to paint left-handed. As the years went by, the paralysis extended to his entire right side and affected his walking, but Wyant continued to paint. His early work, which was carefully drawn, had begun to get looser and more painterly before the stroke.

Using his left hand accelerated this trend. His landscapes became impressionistic—bolder and more atmospheric, with contrasting areas of light and dark that give them power. Wyant is best known for the paintings he created using his left hand.

Aids to Assist the Creative Process

In order to keep working, artists will use devices to help a creative process challenged by physical needs. To paint despite arms that were affected by illness, Boris Kustodiev had an attachment put on his easel so that he could reach it more easily while sitting in a wheelchair. In photographs of the artist working, it appears to be a flexible metal extension ending in a small clamp that held the canvas and tilted it closer to him as he painted.

BORIS MIKHAILOVICH KUSTODIEV

Despite long-term problems with his arms and legs, Boris Mikhailovich Kustodiev (Russian, 1878–1927) was extremely prolific.[27] One of the most popular artists of his day, Kustodiev was a painter, a sculptor, an illustrator, a graphic artist, and a theater designer despite suffering from two severe diseases of the spine. In 1909 he began to have pains in his arm and neck that did not go away. "My arm is causing me great pain," he said in 1910, "but work I must because those commissioned pieces have to be finished."[28]

His attitude toward work was so strong that when he went to Leysin in Switzerland for treatment, he painted when he was a patient at the clinic there. Working while undergoing medical treatment was a pattern he continued for the rest of his life. The Swiss doctors diagnosed tuberculosis of the spine, and for the next two years Kustodiev had to wear a brace from his waist to his chin that was removed at night. Throughout his life Kustodiev focused on his art rather than his illness. "I should be lost," he said, "if it were not for my hopes for the future with ever more work."[29]

His right arm became increasingly painful, and in 1913 doctors found a malignant tumor on his spine. It was the first of his three cancer operations. Walking was also becoming more difficult for him, even with crutches or two canes, and in 1916, after a second operation to remove another tumor, Kustodiev's lower body was paralyzed. He began working from a wheelchair, using an easel with a metal attachment that held the canvas and tilted it closer in to him so that his brush could easily reach the painting. Then, using the flexible metal arms, he returned the canvas to its original position so he could view it. This lessened the strain on his right arm, because he did not have to reach as far. The composer Dmitri Shostakovich, who admired the ease with which Kustodiev managed his wheelchair and painted, said, "I watched in awe as he worked."[30]

During his eighteen years of illness, despite severe pain and a third cancer operation in 1923, Kustodiev not only increased his output but also expanded his creative process. While continuing to paint brightly colored images of Russian life and sensitive portraits, he began to make porcelain sculpture, illustrate books and periodicals, and create graphic work, such as linoleum prints (these are like wood-block prints but done with blocks of linoleum). Kustodiev also became a major designer for the Russian theater. When the famous Russian opera singer Feodor Ivanovich Chaliapin saw Kustodiev rolling towards him in his wheelchair, he was struck by the artist's advanced illness, yet he marveled that the physical difficulties did not overwhelm him. This is because Kustodiev was not focused on his illness but excited by the theater design he was planning to do. "He impressed me by his moral energy," said Chaliapin. "There was not the slightest trace of sadness in his face. His eyes sparkled with the joy of living."[31]

Legs and Feet Used in Creating Art

We often think that hands rather than feet are important for making art, but for a ceramic artist in the nineteenth century, legs and feet were necessary for the creative process. Many ceramic vessels, such as jars and pitchers, are made on a spinning platform called a potter's wheel. The artist places a mound of clay in the center of this platform and shapes it by hand as it rotates. In our age, most commercial pottery wheels are electrified, so the platform spins on its own, but in the past artists kept the platform turning by kicking another wheel attached to its base. This is why a nonelectric pottery wheel is called a kick wheel. An artist with only one leg would not be able to stand or steady himself and also kick the wheel. But after losing his leg, Dave Drake still found a way to work and create the largest ceramic vessels of his life.

DAVE DRAKE

The ceramic artist and poet David Drake (American, 1800–ca. 1870), known as Dave, was born in slavery.[32] He lived in Edgefield, South Carolina, where he worked in the pottery businesses of the Drake, Miles, and Landrum families. There he made pitchers, jugs, and the large ceramic jars that were used for food storage before refrigeration. Some of his huge vessels held forty gallons. Considered utilitarian objects in their day, we now recognize them with their beautiful shapes and rich earth tones as works of art. Not only was Dave the first African American ceramic artist to sign his pieces, but he also wrote poetry on them. On July 4, 1859, Dave made a large jar inscribed with the following verse: "The fourth of July is surely come/to blow the fife and beat the drum."[33]

It is possible that this seemingly patriotic poem has multiple interpretations.[34] John A. Burrison of Georgia State University believes

Independence Day might symbolize Dave's wish for freedom, and beating a drum could refer to South Carolina's law forbidding slaves to practice drumming. Burrison thinks another poem also contains hidden political protest. He says the bears in Dave's poem "The sun, moon, and—stars/in the west are plenty of—bears" may refer to the constellations Ursa Major and Ursa Minor, called the Big and Little Dippers. They were known as the "drinking gourd" and used as a guide for runaway slaves traveling north on the Underground Railroad.

Dave's poetry and bravery are even more remarkable because slaves were supposed to be kept illiterate in South Carolina. There were laws forbidding their education, and they could be killed for reading, writing, or educating other slaves. Aaron De Groft of Florida State University thinks that in spite of this prohibition, Dave may have been secretly teaching other slaves to read through exposure to his poetry.[35] Slaves who were not supposed to be taught learned to read by hearing words repeated again and again while looking at letters. De Groft points out that this secret teaching may have been done by house slaves, some of whom could read, and by sympathetic white people. Although the learning had to be secret, Dave's pottery, which was used in so many facets of daily life, would be a readily available way to expose other slaves to the written word.

It is likely that Dave learned to read and write from one of his owners, Dr. Abner Landrum, who was liberal and pro-Union. Although Edgefield was a stronghold of slavery, Dave may have become literate while he worked as a typesetter for Landrum's newspaper, the *Edgefield Hive.* To honor Abner Landrum's death in April 1859, Dave wrote a memorial verse to him on one of his large jars: "When Noble Dr. Landrum is dead/May Guardian Angels visit his bed."[36]

But not all of Dave's owners were kind. As a slave he was treated like a commodity, bought and sold multiple times, yet always remaining in the Edgefield district as a valuable master potter. In 1833 he is listed as being sold along with a woman called Lydia (also known as Lidy) and her two children. They were possibly his wife and family. In 1842 Lidy and the children were sold and taken away to Louisiana.

Jill Beute Koverman, a curator at the McKissick Museum of the University of South Carolina, says there was a period of seventeen years, from 1840 to 1857, when Dave stopped writing poetry on his ceramics and sometimes even stopped signing or dating his works. She thinks that he was in danger during this time, especially from 1846 to 1848, when he belonged to B. F. Landrum, who was abusive. Koverman notes the death of a slave named Anne, who hung herself in B. F. Landrum's pottery after she had been whipped. Dave may also have been oppressed and fearful for his safety. As Orville Vernon Burton of the University of Illinois says, "It was violence that kept slavery operative."[37]

Koverman believes it was sometime during the seventeen years without poetry that Dave lost his leg. She cites accounts that say he got drunk and lay down on the railroad tracks. Whether Dave lay down on the tracks purposefully or fell down because of drinking shows the despair to which he was driven. But with an indomitable will, he found a way to keep going. Realizing that with only one leg he was no longer able to turn a kick wheel and stand, he had Harry Simkins, a slave with disabled arms, kick the wheel for him.

Starting in 1857 his poetry returns, his writing larger, and in 1859 Dave makes the tallest ceramic jars of his life, measuring twenty-nine inches in height. On November 9, 1860, he inscribes on a piece, "A noble jar for pork or beef/then carry it a round to the Indian chief."[38] But in his poems we also see how much Dave misses his family and longs for civil rights. "I wonder where is all my relations," he writes. "Friendship to all—and every nation."[39]

Quadriplegia and Creativity

Quadriplegia is a loss of function in all four limbs. But despite this extensive paralysis, one of the most famous painters in the world is quadriplegic, and so is one of the leading cartoonists. With improved medical care, the incidence of quadriplegia is increasing in our society, and it is not surprising that some of these people are artists. Three of the individuals in the next chapter were artists before they became quadriplegic; the others turned to art only after they lost the use of their arms and legs.

Chapter 14

Working with Quadriplegia and Beyond

*The only difference between a stepping
stone and a stumbling block is the way
you approach it.* —*Proverb*

For most of us who have two functioning arms and legs, losing the use of just one extremity is a distress, but to lose the use of all four and become quadriplegic is an enormous challenge. Yet when such a challenge benefits creativity, it leads us to redefine our concept of loss.

CHUCK CLOSE

Chuck Close (American, b. 1940) is one of the most famous artists in the world today and he is also quadriplegic.[1] When he was forty-seven, a blood clot congested his anterior spinal artery at C-3, the third cervical vertebra, leaving him almost completely paralyzed from the neck down. Although Close already had an international reputation, he thought he would never paint again. But having learning difficulties early in life (see chapter 8) gave him the strength to face what he calls the "event" in adulthood. John Guare, who wrote a book about the artist's experience with quadriplegia, *Chuck Close: Life and Work 1988-1995*, asked him why he doesn't call it a catastrophe. Close answered that *catastrophe* is a loaded word and an event is just what happens. He is right, because thinking about life in catastrophic terms is more emotionally limiting than any physical event could be. Close also has a great sense of humor. When asked how he views people who walk, the artist replies with a smile, "Oh, we call you the temporarily abled."[2]

After the event Chuck Close returned to work. Following extended physical therapy and with some limited movement in his arms and legs, he invented a new way to paint. Unable to move his fingers, he picks up a brush by pressing it between both hands. Then, turning it sideways, Close places it between his teeth. Clenching the brush in his teeth, he leans forward and pushes it into a slot on a Velcro strap that is part of a brace he wears on his right hand and wrist. In addition to the brace, he further supports his right hand with his left to paint. And because his right hand cannot move, he uses his upper arm to control the movement of the brush.

Sitting in his wheelchair, braces on his legs and wrist, brush securely in its holder, Close works on canvases that can be as large as nine feet tall. All of his art consists of portrait heads. Each portrait is composed of a grid made of many small squares that look like individual abstract paintings up close but combine into a face when viewed from a distance. Close paints one square at a time until the finished work is a dazzling whole.

Previously he filled in these squares by airbrushing layers of paint or with dots of color, but now he loads each square with small abstract designs. It is a technique he invented in the hospital art therapy room, where he made small paintings filled with colorful shapes such as circles, diamonds, and lozenges. These small abstract works were manageable with limited arm movement. At first Close worried about not being able to create the enormous canvases that made him famous but then he realized that the small paintings could combine into a larger whole. Close still composes all his portraits from a grid of many small squares, but now the squares are filled with abstract shapes of color that unite to create a face and make his art even stronger. An intense worker, Close paints whether he is happy, sad, or inspired or not. "If you wait for inspiration," he insists, "you'll never get anything done."[3]

In the first part of his career Close worked only in black and white. Then about two years before the blood clot, he started using the primary colors of red, yellow, and blue. But as the artist sat in what he described as a grim, gray hospital room he rethought the role of color in his work and expanded his palette. Close is now one of the greatest colorists of his generation. Color may also be important to him because of what happened during his first week in the hospital. In an effort to reduce the swelling in his spine, Close was given heavy doses of steroids, and as a result, he hallucinated for days. Calling these horrifying experiences "daymares" because they occurred while he was awake, Close says he felt as if he were on his hospital bed careening through one huge, terrifying black-and-white room after another, always afraid he would crash into a wall. Everything was completely colorless in this quaking, unstable world. Focusing on color in his art counteracted the black-and-white daymares and became a way for him to take his life back.

Before his paralysis, Close worked while sitting in a chair attached to a platform he built on the prongs of a forklift. This way he could rise up and down as he painted large canvases in his New York studio. Now the artist works in a barnlike building on Long Island, where he has an opening in his studio floor so that his paintings can be lifted up and down and tilted on a mechanical easel while he sits in his wheelchair painting. Close's art is changing, too.[4] The squares of color have become more prominent, dissolving the face into the canvas and making the image more abstract. There is a psychological transformation as well. The experience of illness and recovery has given his portraits an emotional presence. His faces that were once studies in information now engage the viewer with a depth of humanity. Close remains a determined and steady worker. "Every day," he states, "when I roll out of my studio and look over my shoulder, I say, 'That's what I did today.'"[5]

JOHN CALLAHAN

John Callahan (American, b. 1951) was not an artist before his auto accident at twenty-one, but after he became quadriplegic he turned his life around.[6] Callahan had been severely alcoholic, drifting from job to job, smoking three packs of cigarettes a day, and despite being intelligent, funny, and talented, he had no idea about what to make of himself. Then the accident that left him paralyzed from the neck down opened up a new career and a new life. After years of intensive therapy, both physical and psychological, Callahan re-created himself. He stopped smoking and drinking, joined AA, went to college, got his degree, and found out who his birth parents were (he was adopted). He also writes books and makes animated films and has become a nationally syndicated cartoonist.

Callahan showed a talent for drawing in childhood, but he felt that art was somehow never enough. It was only years later when he combined images with words and humor that his true gift came forward. One day, when he was thirty and a college senior, he drew a really funny cartoon. "Then I drew another and another," he recalls. Originally Callahan planned to become a teacher, social worker, or lawyer, but now he realized cartooning was his path. "Suddenly," he states, "I knew this was what I did."[7] Having regained some function in his arms and hands, Callahan found a way of working that he still uses today. Sitting in his motorized wheelchair with a tablet on his lap, he holds a pen in his right hand, which he braces with his left. "I have to keep pressure on my fingers," he explains, "to keep them closed around the pen. My drawing comes from the shoulders, not just the arms and wrists."[8]

In his cartoons about the difficulties of life, Callahan finds comedy where other people see tragedy. Because of this he often gets angry letters, which he cheerfully publishes in his books. His angry letters appear to be from able-bodied people who don't realize that the artist is challenged and can see humor in his own experience. Callahan has written about his personal journey in two autobiographical works: *Don't Worry, He Won't Get Far on Foot* and *Will the Real John Callahan Please Stand Up?* Speaking about his work, Callahan says, "I get a sense of fulfillment that keeps me going."[9] He is also an inspiration to other people with challenges like Kate Ansell, who reviewed one of his films at the 5th Disability Film Festival in London. "The day I found out that John Callahan was disabled," she writes, "I practically wept with joy. Finally, I had found my role model."[10]

Special Challenges and Holographic Talent

Cindi Bernhardt and Brom Wikstrom are also quadriplegic and work while sitting in a wheelchair. With more limited hand and arm movement than Close or Callahan, they paint by holding a brush in their mouths. Both artists are active in international associations that help challenged artists: VSA arts (formerly Very Special Arts) and the Association of Mouth and Foot Painting Artists (AMFPA). VSA arts is a nonprofit organization affiliated with the John F. Kennedy Center for the Performing Arts in Washington, D.C. Founded by Ambassador Jean Kennedy Smith in 1974, it helps individuals with disabilities create and enjoy art. The Association of Mouth and Foot Painting Artists is not a charity but a for-profit association owned by the artists that generates an income for them from the sale of their work. In 2005 AMFPA published a book written by Marc Alexander called *Artists Above All: Art Celebrating the Conquest of Misfortune*, with color reproductions of the work and insightful biographies of the artists. The members of this association cannot use their hands due to accident, illness, or birth defect and paint by holding a brush either in their mouths or with their feet.

Many people fear that if their hands are lost, their talent is gone. They believe talent is localized in one part of the body. But challenged artists show us this is not true by painting with brushes held in their mouths. Although creative ideas begin in our mind, their physical expression is not limited to our hands. Instead, talent appears to be spread throughout our body the same way an image is diffused throughout a piece of holographic film. Holograms, which seem to leap out three-dimensionally from a flat holographic film plate, are very different from photographs. Cutting away a piece of a photograph removes part of its image. Not so with a hologram. Because the complete image is embedded in every part of the film, removing part of the holographic film still leaves the full image. Likewise, losing your hands does not remove your talent. Your ability is still there, ready to be expressed by another part of the body.

According to the neurosurgeon Karl Pribram, the reason abilities seem to be holographically encoded in the body is because memories are stored holographically in the brain.[11] He finds that memories for specific skills are not located in one place but appear to be diffused throughout the brain, forming a type of interference pattern similar to the interference patterns in a piece of holographic film. This gives the brain greater flexibility, allowing us to shift learned abilities to different parts of the body when needed. Our skills are not limited to our hands.

Using another part of the body to do a task that was previously done with the hands is like changing the course of water to flow elsewhere. It is the same water, as it is the same talent, but its stream is redirected for use in another place. Just as building a dam in one part of a river blocks the water's flow at that point but channels it somewhere else, eliminating the use of your arms and hands redirects the flow of talent. We see this in Cindi Bernhardt. Sitting in a wheelchair and holding a brush in her mouth, she paints without the use of her hands.

CINDI BERNHARDT

When Cindi Bernhardt (American, b. 1963) was a college freshman, she was doing gymnastics in a place where gymnastics was not allowed.[12] While practicing back handsprings in a room with a low window, she accidentally went out backward through the window and fell two stories to the ground. Her neck was broken at the fifth cervical vertebra, and the next thing she remembers is waking up in the hospital completely quadriplegic at eighteen. Unable to use her hands or legs, Bernhardt, who once expressed herself through gymnastics and dance, began a completely new career. "Art," declares Bernhardt, "became my new way of dancing."[13] Although she had never previously painted, since the accident Bernhardt has become a professional artist. "I discovered I had a creative ability," she says, "which I never knew I had before."[14]

It was in the hospital rehabilitation program that she first began to make art. After learning to sign her name by holding a pen in her mouth, Bernhardt used the pen to do her first drawings. Then she tried charcoal and pastels that were placed in special holders so she could grip them in her mouth. She also worked in oil paints and acrylics, but her favorite medium is watercolor.

Now an accomplished mouth painter, Bernhardt uses a paintbrush placed in an extender, which is a soft plastic tube such as dental tubing. This enlarges the reach of her brush and also protects her mouth.

Bernhardt moves her head to make big brushstrokes, but she paints fine detail by manipulating the brush with her teeth. Bernhardt states that if anything ever happens to her jaw or mouth, she will still be able to paint by using a halo, which is a headband that holds a brush at the artist's forehead. "There is never an end," she insists. "There will always be a way to express oneself through creativity."[15]

When the tragedy of 9/11 struck, Bernhardt was so distressed that she made a painting of a weeping American eagle. Originally created to express her personal feelings, it was printed in the *New York Times* to honor the victims and rescue workers. After her accident, Bernhardt went back to school, earning associate degrees in child development and mental health. In addition to working with at-risk children, she is also a motivational speaker who gives public presentations. "I believe that acceptance is one of the most important parts in recovery," insists Bernhardt. It's not giving up and you don't have to like it, she says, "but you accept it and this gives you the freedom to move on."[16]

BROM WIKSTROM

When he was a young man growing up in Seattle, Brom Wikstrom (American, b. 1953) would take short trips around the country visiting different places and working as a commercial artist.[17] At twenty-one he was employed by a sign company in New Orleans and decided to go for a swim. It was a hot afternoon, but when he dove into the muddy Mississippi Wikstrom miscalculated its depth. "A sharp smack of darkness flashed through me," he recalls, "as I crashed headlong into five inches of water."[18] The dive broke his neck at the fifth and sixth vertebrae, leaving him paralyzed from the shoulders down. His friend, who was also at the beach, pulled him out of the water. Wikstrom was taken to a hospital, where he developed such severe infections that he was offered the last rites. Although he was religious, Wikstrom refused them. "I was not ready to give up," he says, "and admit that I might die."[19] After seven weeks he was transferred from New Orleans to the University of Washington Hospital in Seattle to begin a long process of recovery.

With physical therapy and a special metal brace on his forearm, Wikstrom managed to bring his fingers together enough so that he could hold a fork to eat and turn pages in a book, but he couldn't make art. Realizing that he had full function in his neck and shoulders, Wikstrom started to paint by holding a brush in his mouth. At first he was very discouraged by what he made, but he persevered. Then he had a surprise visitor who changed his life.

Wikstrom had casually mentioned his admiration for the work of Jacob Lawrence (see chapter 12), who was a professor at the University of Washington. "Professor Lawrence came after lunch one day," says Wikstrom, "his warm smile lighting up the room."[20] Lawrence looked at the work Wikstrom was doing in the hospital and strongly encouraged him. Having his art taken so seriously reinforced his determination. "My life was not over," he realized, "but had taken a drastic turn and art would help me to make the most of it."[21]

Before the accident Wikstrom created black-and-white pencil drawings, but somehow having a paintbrush in his mouth made him extremely aware of colors. "I developed a sense of color," he says, "that I did not have before."[22] Today his beautifully colored works are a combination of realism and cubism. For Wikstrom, these works of art are "landmarks of my development as a painter and as a person."[23] In addition to painting, he also gives art sessions at Children's Hospital in Seattle, using creativity as nonverbal therapy with children. He took courses in art therapy to "share what I could with patients who in many cases were much more disabled than I. It was a singular pleasure to feel worthwhile again."[24] Wikstrom is also a role model for the children. They see him as someone who despite physical difficulties is creative and happy. Wikstrom is now married, and he and his wife enjoy traveling. "I encourage you to do the best with your life," he advises, "and remember to never give up on your dreams."[25]

Creativity Beyond Quadriplegia

What condition could be beyond quadriplegia? It is total body paralysis: breathing with a ventilator, no movement possible except for the eyes. Yet despite this locked-in syndrome, Peggy Chun continues to make art using her eye movements and brain waves. Chun shows us that creativity is less a product of our physical body than an expression of our will and intention.

PEGGY CHUN

The colorful paintings of Peggy Chun (American, b. 1946) reflect both the beauty of Hawaii and her interests in life.[26] Her art is primarily in watercolor, and the great variety of work on her website is organized by subject matter for easy access. There are scenes of life on the Hawaiian Islands, images from her Midwestern roots (Chun was born in Oklahoma), paintings of her three cats and other animals (she paints their adventures and their daydreams), humorous works of whimsy, and art about Christmas (her favorite holiday). Chun also has sections featuring work done with her left hand, by holding a brush in her teeth, and with her eyes as she continues to be creative despite an ongoing illness.

In 2002 Chun was diagnosed with amyotrophic lateral sclerosis (ALS), also called Lou Gehrig's disease, an illness that took the lives of her mother, her grandfather, and her twin sister, Bobbie, who was also a painter. In ALS motor neurons progressively degenerate, leaving paralysis in their wake. Motor neurons are nerve cells that extend from the brain to the spinal cord and then to the muscles in the body.

They control our voluntary movement, and as they are damaged in ALS, the body becomes increasingly paralyzed, usually leaving only eye movement and intelligence intact. This total body paralysis is called the locked-in syndrome, and as the disease progressed, Chun needed a ventilator to breathe, but she kept working.

On her website, Chun writes about the way ALS affects her work, both in biographical essays and in the short paragraphs that often accompany and give added depth to the individual pieces of art. She tells us that as ALS affected her right hand, she changed to her left to keep making art. Like other right-handed artists who switched to using the left hand, she noticed that her style became looser. Her left hand failed seven months later, and Chun painted by holding a brush in her teeth until her jaw became too weak to continue.

Now completely paralyzed and on a ventilator, she makes digital art with a computer by having electronic sensors track the movement of her eyes. Chun not only separates the work done in different ways on her website but also signs them differently by showing the technique: an "LH" near her signature for art done with the left hand, a "T" for teeth, and an "E" for eyes. She was a realist painter before but now makes abstract work on the computer. For her new digital art, Chun uses the ERICA system of Eye Response Technologies. It enables her to make colorful compositions and also provides a digital voice for communication despite paralyzed vocal cords. "Form and color are my playground!" exclaims Chun, and her new work is gorgeous.[27] "ERICA allows me to paint with a simple eye gaze on the computer screen," she says. "I can paint in bed!"

Chun has embarked on a new artistic adventure—painting with brain waves. In addition to the ERICA system for eye-movement-created art, she is also using the OTIS hardware system with Brain Art software to make art on a computer using thoughts alone. OTIS is a non-invasive, wearable brain-imaging system that uses small infrared sensors placed on the head to detect brain activity. It is a product of Archinoetics, a Hawaii-based technology company that also designs Brain Art, the software program connecting Chun's brain activity to the computer. By controlling her thoughts, Chun can choose colors, create patterns, and adjust the speed at which she works. Through practice, she has become expert in creating a new digital art that includes her recent abstract painting, *The Singing Brain*. No wonder she is called the "Unstoppable Peggy Chun."

Chun's continued creativity is helped by a loving community of friends. Realizing that her health insurance would not cover complete round-the-clock needs, they organized themselves into a group they call "Peg's Legs" to provide supplemental care. They learned how to do this from Sheila Warnock's book, *Share the Care: How to Organize a Group to Care for Someone Who Is Seriously Ill.* "My body is shut down," says Chun, "but with Peg's Legs I'm whole." Like the artist, her friends in Peg's Legs also experience transformation. As Chun evolves through her illness and her art, her friends evolve through their acts of compassion, and she has dedicated artwork to them. "After all," says Chun, "you don't paint with your hands, you paint with your heart."

Creativity and Injuries

In the next chapter we will see how accidents, hazards, and injuries affect the lives of artists. These unexpected events can turn a life around in seconds. But using creativity as strength, artists overcome trauma to change themselves and their work.

Chapter 15

Accidents, Hazards, Injuries, and Art

A ship in port is safe, but that is not what
ships are built for. —*Benazir Bhutto*

L ife is unpredictable, which makes it interesting—and difficult. While unforeseen events can bring us both benefits and
hardships, sometimes the hardships are benefits in disguise.
We can never fully predict or control life's surprises, but when they
happen what we can control is our response to them. In this chapter,
artists turn hardships into benefits by using adversity as an opportunity for growth. They respond to unexpected trauma with creativity
and strength. It keeps them going and they make wonderful art.

The Dangers of Art

Making art can be dangerous. Dramatic accidents at work can take a
life in seconds. Joan Brown (American, 1938–1990) was installing
one of her sculptures in India when the floor above her collapsed,
killing her and her assistant.[1] Pedro Alderete (Canadian, born in
Cuba, 1961–2005) died when he was trapped between a hydraulic
platform and a warehouse door while finishing a large public mural.[2]

Besides facing dangers at work, the artists in this chapter suffer accidents in life—car accidents, farm accidents, war wounds, and injuries caused by heavy machinery. There are additional perils, so silent at first that they seem to be unnoticed. Exposure to solvents and other toxic materials are the quiet but deadly health hazards that bring major disabilities and sometimes death.

For excellent information on health hazards in the visual arts and how to protect yourself, I strongly recommend *The Artist's Complete Health and Safety Guide*, by Monona Rossol, a chemist and industrial hygienist.[3] She discusses art materials for all mediums: what is safe, what is unsafe, and how to stay healthy while being creative.

Lip Pointing/Tipping Brushes

We now know that all precautions should be taken not to ingest paint or other art materials, but in the past some artists were actually told to "lip point" or "tip" their brushes. This meant putting the brush (pigment and all) into the mouth so that it could be moistened by saliva while the lips pressed the brush hairs into a point. It is a terrible practice, and with poisonous pigments it can be lethal. When coal-tar dyes, which are now known to be carcinogens, were developed in the nineteenth century, they were used in the Japanese kimono painting industry. Artists painting with these dyes and lip pointing their brushes developed very high rates of bladder cancer.[4]

Tipping brushes was also deadly for the Radium Girls, who worked at the U.S. Radium Corporation in Orange, New Jersey.[5] One of these women, Grace Flyer, brought their problems to public attention. When Flyer started working in 1917, she was a recent high school graduate. Painting numbers on watches, clocks, and machine dials with a mixture of radium powder, glue, and water that glowed in the dark seemed like an easy, well-paid job. But in the 1920s Flyer became sick and other women started to die. Although the company tried to slander the five women who sued them by saying they had syphilis rather than radiation poisoning, the Radium Girls won their case. Their monetary compensation was small and all of the women died, but they brought health hazards into public awareness and changed the standards of an industry.

Silent Hazards: Toxic Materials

In more recent times, resins, plastics, lead pigments, and solvents have compromised the health and taken the lives of artists. Some of these materials have expanded the type of art that can be created and in that way they have enriched our culture, but the cost for certain individuals has been enormous. Seemingly unnoticeable at first, these toxins can build up in the body to the point of causing illness and even death. Duane Hanson, Jay DeFeo, and Tesia Blackburn all had their health compromised by art materials.

DUANE HANSON

The sculptures of Duane Hanson (American, 1925–1996) look so lifelike that people crowd around them in admiration.[6] "People like to people-watch," said Hanson, ". . . and they seem to approach my figures as people they know."[7] We really do know them because we see the people in Hanson's sculptures everywhere. His sculpture called *Old Couple on a Bench* shows a tired older couple in leisure clothes sitting down; *Queenie* depicts a woman in a work uniform pushing an industrial cart loaded with cleaning supplies; *Old Man Dozing* is a sculpture of a man who has fallen asleep in a chair; while *Woman with a Laundry Basket* portrays a woman in a housedress, her hair in curlers, holding a basket of laundry with a box of detergent at her feet. Hanson achieved the lifelike quality of his work by using real individuals as models, "dressing" the sculptures in clothes the people would wear, and using objects from daily life. The art is made from casts of their bodies and faces, which the artist finished by hand and then painted by showing every wrinkle, every discoloration, and every varicose vein. The sculptures are brought to perfection by the imperfections of everyday people. They capture our interest not through idealism but through the strength of their reality.

Hanson's early sculpture was made of polyester resin, a substance now known to cause cancer. He started working with resins in 1959 and in 1971 he was diagnosed with non-Hodgkin's lymphoma. The illness reoccurred in 1975 and then again in 1995, causing his death, in January 1996. Realizing the resins had given him cancer and wanting to work with a less toxic material, the artist turned to polyvinyl acetate, a safer substance. But in order to make his sculpture, Hanson heated the polyvinyl acetate to 220 degrees Fahrenheit, increasing its minor hazards substantially.[8] In the last year of his life, Hanson started to work in bronze, which he painted to look as real as his earlier work. His sculpture *Man on a Lawnmower* is made of bronze. Like Robert Arneson (see chapter 12), who turned to bronze when he had terminal cancer, Hanson may also have wanted to create work that would outlast him as long as possible.

One of the reasons Hanson's sculptures are so effective is that he genuinely cared for the people in his work. "I have deep feelings and affection for blue-collar workers," he revealed. "I can show the harsh realities of life through them, the cement on a man's hands, the paint spattered on his clothes."[9] "I express my feelings of empathy and sympathy for the subjects I portray," he said, "through their weariness and despair."[10] Hanson was a compassionate person, but extended chemotherapy with its fatigue and distress may have made him even more receptive to the plight of others. There is sadness in Hanson's people, but they are also humorous and reflect the complexity of our society. "I'm not duplicating life," he explained. "I'm making a statement about human values."[11]

JAY DEFEO

From 1958 to 1966, Jay DeFeo (American, 1929–1989) worked on *The Rose*, her most famous painting.[12] She painted it and repainted it again and again; it was the focus of her life and it is beautiful. The white pattern emanating from its center point looks like rays of light spreading out over paint so thick it resembles lava from the eruption of some great volcano. The small, slender artist worked on a ladder to paint the canvas, which measures approximately eleven feet high by seven and a half feet wide. When complete, *The Rose* weighed over a ton, and DeFeo called it a "marriage of painting and sculpture."[13]

In creating *The Rose*, DeFeo used white lead pigment, which is a known health hazard. Her husband at the time, the painter Wally Hedrick, said, "Her hands would be covered with white lead. It killed her."[14] Lead contamination was definitely one of the causes of DeFeo's gum disease and tooth loss and may also have contributed to the lung cancer that ended her life in 1989. But smoking is another cause of gum disease and a major cause of lung cancer. DeFeo smoked two to three packs of cigarettes a day and also drank heavily during the time she worked on *The Rose*.

As the artist's gum disease advanced, her teeth fell out. She lost single teeth and she also lost a dental bridge of four teeth that was composed of two of her natural teeth and two artificial teeth. DeFeo used these teeth as subjects for photographs and paintings, calling them "my model: out of my own head."[15] The paintings *Crescent Bridge I* and *Crescent Bridge II*, made from 1970 to 1972, show the dental bridge with its two artificial teeth connected to two natural teeth that still have their long roots. Although the paintings transform an ordinary object into extraordinary works of art, I still wish the artist had not injured herself to the point of illness.

After being exhibited in museums, *The Rose* went to the San Francisco Art Institute in 1969. When it started to show some signs of deterioration, the painting was placed under protective covering and out of public view. Realizing the work's importance, David Ross, director of the Whitney Museum in New York, acquired *The Rose* in 1995 for the museum's permanent collection and had it restored. "If I did nothing else as director of the Whitney," states Ross, "but bring that painting back, then I'm happy."[16]

TESIA BLACKBURN

Many of DeFeo's college and graduate students were profoundly affected by her death and changed their painting practices. Tesia Blackburn (American, b. 1954), who did not study with DeFeo but admired her work, also saw the artist's death as a warning.[17] "Her passing left me dumbstruck," says Blackburn, realizing that she, too, was in danger from her art materials.[18] In the past there was less awareness about health problems resulting from exposure to turpentine and mineral spirits, the solvents that are used in oil painting. Some people who limit their contact with these solvents can paint with oils throughout their life, but others, especially students and young artists, are not as careful. "It was a badge of honor, painting and eating and drinking and sleeping all in the same room," explains Blackburn. "When we slept it was six feet from the easel with a can of open turpentine on the floor." Blackburn painted long hours, had several paintings with turpentine washes going at once in her apartment, and didn't wash her hands carefully enough when it was time to eat. Eventually the exposure made her sick.

"The bloody noses in the morning, the dizziness, nausea, and headaches, it all finally got to me," she admits. She also had bouts of double vision and says, "The cuticles on my hands were always split and bleeding no matter how much I attended to them. I didn't realize it at the time, but I was poisoning myself with oil-based paint." Monona Rossol agrees that all of Blackburn's symptoms are consistent with exposure to the solvents used with oil paint. She explains that wearing rubber gloves would not be helpful either, because these solvents dissolve latex; in fact, that is how rubber cement is made: by dissolving rubber latex in a solvent. This was also Blackburn's experience: "I never wore rubber gloves to paint, because they would just 'melt' away."

When Jay DeFeo died, Blackburn knew she had to change her life. "I remember crying," she says, "the day I got rid of my oil paint." She taught herself to work with acrylics instead and became an expert. Blackburn lectures widely and teaches courses to show others how to use this less toxic medium. Many people have thanked her for making them aware of their occupational hazards, and her own health has returned. "I'm not nauseated anymore," she reveals. "I don't have headaches and my vision is completely clear."

Farm Accidents

In addition to the hazards specific in making art, there are accidents in every workplace which affect artists and nonartists alike. Frank Day was a migrant farm worker when he had a disabling accident that turned him to art. It gave him an opportunity for creativity that poor people rarely have. I wonder how many other very talented individuals are currently working in orchards, factories, or mines, whose gifts if they had the opportunity to express them could enrich our world.

FRANK DAY

During the last sixteen years of his life, Frank Leverall Day (American, 1902–1976), a Konkow Maidu from the foothills of the Sierra Nevada Mountains in California, made more than two hundred paintings of Native American ceremonies, customs, and traditions.[19] "If I do not do this," he said, "all things will be forgotten."[20] Day's mother died when he was two, and he was raised by his father, Billy Day, a tribal leader. But in accordance with federal regulations regarding the education of Native American children in the early twentieth century, Day was taken away to an Indian boarding school to learn European American culture. He stayed there from age six to fourteen. When he was ten years old and home on a visit, Day asked his father to teach him about his Maidu heritage. His father agreed but told him to take off his school jacket. Day took the jacket off and burned it. He knew as a Maidu that he must do this. "I had to sacrifice something," he said, "to receive instruction from my father."[21]

After his father died in 1922, Day traveled around the country visiting different Native American tribes. While observing their culture, he supported himself through odd jobs. Returning to California in the early 1930s, Day became a lumberman and a migrant agricultural worker until 1959, when a serious farm accident left him with two broken knees. Day's long convalescence in the hospital became a turning point in his life. He began to make art during rehabilitation and also met Florence Stubblefield, a nurse at the hospital. She became his second wife and strongly encouraged his creativity.

Frank Day, a self-taught artist, is a storyteller through images. In brightly colored oils on canvas, using his experience and imagination, Day preserves the life and traditions of the Maidu. Although he also made paintings about history and his personal life, most of Day's work centers on Maidu culture. He depicts their everyday life before contact with white people and also portrays Maidu rituals and legends. In addition to painting, Day worked with anthropologists. He spoke about his tribe, preserving a record on tape of their customs and songs. No longer able to dance himself, Day choreographed others doing traditional Maidu dances. "One of the reasons I'm doing this [is] to make things clear," he explained, "that one day it may be used for a good purpose."[22]

Accidents with Heavy Machinery

Useful in daily work and fundamental to our mechanized, industrialized society, heavy machinery is also inherently dangerous, and accidents with it can permanently change a person's existence. But when accidents occur, as happened to Mark di Suvero, confronting the trauma with creativity can enhance the level of art.

MARK DI SUVERO

In 1960 the sculptor Mark di Suvero (American, b. 1933 in China) was preparing for his first one-person show in New York and supporting himself by doing odd jobs.[23] One of these jobs was transporting pieces of lumber on top of an elevator. But on March 26, 1960, the elevator kept rising and wouldn't stop—crushing and pinning di Suvero at the top of the shaft and breaking his back. The doctors doubted he would ever walk again or have the strength to make sculpture. But the artist was determined to get better and work. Di Suvero was in a wheelchair for the next two years, but by 1965 he was able to walk again, using crutches.

The sculpture di Suvero made after the accident changed his art. Sitting in his wheelchair near a low workbench and wearing an asbestos apron, he began to weld metal. The small pieces he created working in this way became the forerunners of the huge metal sculptures for which he became famous. The accident also appears to have influenced another aspect of di Suvero's art. Having been partially paralyzed and very much wanting to move again, he started making sculptures with moving parts that can be pushed, rocked, or used as seats. He says his sculpture "... has an element of motion or pivoting which invites the viewer to physically participate."[24] Di Suvero creates his enormous abstract sculptures by hoisting steel girders and huge pieces of metal into place using a crane. Some of his works are as tall as small buildings. His art, which is often painted, suggests the large, active brushstrokes of abstract expressionism. "My sculpture," he explains, "is painting in three dimensions."[25]

Traffic Accidents

Car crashes are the leading cause of unintentional death and disability in our technological society. Someone in the United States is injured in an auto accident every fourteen seconds. It can happen whether you are the driver, like Ginny Ruffner, or the passenger, like Howardena Pindell.

HOWARDENA PINDELL

In September 1979 Howardena Pindell (American, b. 1943) had just started her new job as a professor of art in the State University of New York at Stony Brook. She was riding to work in a car driven by Donald Kuspit, the chairman of the department.[26] Pindell was a passenger in the backseat and Margaret Sheffield, an art critic, was the passenger in front. They were fifteen minutes away from school and Kuspit was slowing down for a light, when suddenly from across the road a woman on pain medication drove through the median strip and hit their car on the driver's side. All three of them were injured. Pindell, trapped in the backseat and unconscious, was rescued by the police.

Suffering a concussion and misaligned hips, she remembers waking up in the ambulance with terrible pain. After she used orthopedic shoes, her leg lengths eventually straightened out, but her lower back and general strength remain affected. The concussion produced temporary memory loss and permanently altered Pindell's perception. At first she was unable to read, and although that side effect passed, she still cannot always see all the objects in her visual field. "It was really horrible," she says, "but it could have been much worse."[27]

"My work changed drastically . . . after I was injured," states Pindell.[28] Before the accident she made abstract paintings in muted tones, but in 1980 she started the *Autobiography* series of self-portraits in vibrant colors. Her colors intensified, explains Pindell, because "everything seemed heightened by my awareness of life and death. I could have been killed."[29] The fragility she felt after the accident made her conscious of the possibility that she could have been burned alive while trapped in the car. Having spent time in India, the artist thought of widows who in the past were burned alive after their husbands died.

Pindell, who addresses racism, feminism, and social justice in her work, connected their domestic slavery to the slavery in her African American heritage and put an image of a slave ship in some of her paintings. Its dramatic white form, which also looks like a coffin, may refer to the many slaves who died imprisoned in the holds of ships and to the artist's fear about being trapped in the car. Pindell's problems with perception can sometimes make it difficult for her to find an object that she may be looking for. But the brain injury also allows her to hyperfocus and concentrate on small repetitive tasks that might bore another person. The artist uses this ability to focus on repetition by creating a variety of patterns in her work that give her paintings added richness.

Heart failure in 2002 sent Pindell to the hospital, and she is now on medication. "I get discouraged from not having physical strength," she admits. "I have to force myself to exercise."[30] Pindell fell down two long flights of stairs in the subway station near her home in 2004, and the injuries she sustained developed into arthritis. "I am very lucky," she says, "that even though I use a cane, I still get around."[31] Pindell does more than get around; she paints, writes on art and racism, and teaches at a university, where she is head of the master of fine arts program.

GINNY RUFFNER

Strength and humor pulled Ginny Ruffner (American, b. 1952) through a nearly fatal car accident.[32] "I'm a lemonade from lemons kind of person,"[33] she explains. Internationally known for her glass sculpture, Ruffner describes her convalescence as "five weeks in a coma, five months in the hospital, and five years in a wheelchair"[34] from an experience she calls the "wreck." On December 22, 1991, Ruffner was driving on Interstate 77 in North Carolina when a young, uninsured woman, racing down a ramp on her right, cut across both lanes of the road. To avoid the car, Ruffner went faster and then lost control, crossing the median, hitting a dip, and careening into on-coming traffic. She had a head-on collision with one car before being hit again by another.

In her New York Times article "Starting from Scratch," Ellen Pall says that Ruffner suffered a diffuse type of brain injury called a shearing injury. It happens when someone moving fast, such as a per-son in a car, suddenly turns and slows down. This can cause the bod-ies of the nerve cells and their axons, which are the long structures leading out from them, to pull away from each other, stretching and sometimes permanently damaging the axons. In addition, impacts can throw the brain against the bones of the skull, creating further injury.

When the doctors in the hospital said they didn't think Ruffner would live, her mother firmly told them, "Ginny grew up in a family of optimists."[35] And as Ruffner says, "I'm way too stubborn to leave yet."[36] But the struggle was immense. After the accident, she was paralyzed on her left side, including her drawing hand. She couldn't walk, had spasms and double vision, and, most difficult of all, she had no memory of herself or her art.

Through physical and mental exercises, Ruffner began to regain her life. Her mind that was so strangely empty after the accident became lively once more. Family and friends brought her pictures of the art she had created, sparking memories of her past work, and she began to draw using her right hand. When her hand had tremors, she used an ankle weight on her wrist to steady it. "I knew I would make art again. That I had no doubt about," insists Ruffner. "I think that probably was what brought me back."[37]

Ruffner, who is also driving again, walks with a cane and says about her slow speech, "I don't consider myself handicapped. I just talk funny."[38] She creates art now by making drawings and supervising assistants who build the finished work. And Ruffner's art has expanded. In addition to glass, she also works in metal and has designed a pop-up book to accompany her recent traveling exhibition called "The Flowering Tornado." Two pages in the book illustrate the way she overcomes obstacles. On one page, a profile contains a frame limiting its space with words that limit life, such as *never, bad, can't,* and *dumb.* It is a mindset she wants to avoid. Another page shows her strength and determination. A spiral form springs out of a bed of flowers surrounded by phrases such as "avoid the trap of fear"; "imagination with courage"; and "put your will into action." As Ruffner says, "You can view every situation as 'Oh poor me,' or 'What a great opportunity.'"[39]

War Injuries

I sincerely believe that one day war will end, but, sadly, that time of peace has not yet come, and our human history has been marked by combat. Accidents, illness, and death are among the tragedies of warfare, and when artists are soldiers they share these experiences. Some artists, like Pierre-Auguste Renoir (French, 1841–1919), are exempted from service because of a number they draw in the draft; others, like Jean-Frédéric Bazille (French, 1841–1870), die in battle. Still others are wounded, and these war injuries can become a transforming illness.

World War I

During World War I, which was supposed to be the war to end all wars, illness and injuries were constant companions to the misery of life in the trenches. Horace Pippin and Josef Sudek both lost the use of an arm at the front; Fernand Léger was gassed.

HORACE PIPPIN

Horace Pippin (American, 1888–1946), who enlisted to serve in World War I, became a corporal in the 369th Colored Infantry Regiment.[40] His African American unit was the first from the United States to reach the Rhine River and received citations from the French government. While Pippin was fighting in France, a German bullet pierced his right shoulder, severely injuring his right arm. For his service and his wounds, Pippin received the Croix de Guerre from France and the Purple Heart from the United States. Speaking about his partially paralyzed right arm, Pippin explained, "I could not use it for anything."[41] No longer able to do the heavy manual labor he did before the war, Pippin delivered clothes for his wife, who was a laundress, took odd jobs that he could manage with his injury, and began to make art in his spare time. Making art, said Pippin, "brought me back to my old self."[42]

He started by decorating discarded cigar boxes with charcoal and then began making larger scenes that he burned onto wood panels with a hot iron poker. At first Pippin viewed creativity as therapy for his injured right arm; eventually it would become his career. In 1928, at the age of forty, he created his first oil painting, *The End of War: Starting Home.* After his war experiences, Pippin painted recollections from his life, scenes from American history, still lifes, and images from the Bible. In order to paint, Pippin, who was right-handed, propped up his disabled right arm with his left hand, so that his right hand could hold a brush. Seven years after he made his first painting, Pippin began to receive recognition, eventually becoming one of the most famous African American artists of his time. "When I was a boy I loved to make pictures," said Pippin, "but it was World War I that brought out all the art in me."[43]

JOSEF SUDEK

In 1915 Josef Sudek (Czechoslovakian, 1896–1976) was drafted for World War I and sent to fight on the Italian front.[44] Almost a year later, and just before he was to go on leave, a grenade explosion wounded his right arm. At first it did not seem serious, but an infection set in, then gangrene, and doctors eventually had to amputate the arm at his shoulder. "For years I was going from hospital to hospital," said Sudek, "and had to give up my bookbinding trade."[45] Having done some photography before, he decided to become a photographer instead. The images Sudek took of the other patients in his three years at different army hospitals are his first serious works.

One of the doctors at the veterans' home was impressed with Sudek's determination and arranged for a scholarship at the Prague School for Graphic Arts. Combining his disability pension with work as a commercial photographer, Sudek managed to set up a small studio, earn a living, and also create fine art. When he wasn't working in the studio, he would photograph the streets of Prague, the countryside, and the injured men at the veterans' home. Determined to do the best work possible, Sudek used a large-format camera that stood on a tripod and needed film holders and other equipment. Despite having only one arm and being a small man, he carried this heavy load everywhere. When one hand wasn't enough to adjust the settings, Sudek would hold the camera in his lap, steady it with his left arm, and change the dials with his teeth. He also developed and printed all the images himself with one hand. With an ability to capture the atmospheric power of timeless moments in a quiet world, Sudek is considered to be one of the leading photographers of the twentieth century.

FERNAND LÉGER

Joseph Fernand Henri Léger (1881–1955) was a promising young painter when he was drafted during World War I.[46] Calling it "this life and death struggle into which we were plunged,"[47] Léger fought in the trenches of the Argonne and Verdun. As a soldier and a stretcher bearer, he saw the wounded and the dying, casualties of the violent battles at the western front. Then, in September 1916, Léger was gassed at Verdun.

Dispersed from an exploding shell, mustard gas is a horrible weapon that blisters the skin and can cause blindness and severe lung damage.[48] It could penetrate all the masks and protective materials available to soldiers in World War I, but it could not penetrate metal. In the midst of war, Léger spoke of his admiration for a white metal cannon gleaming in the sunlight and appearing unharmed in comparison to the wounded soldiers. The strength of metal would inspire the strength of his new work. Having been severely wounded himself, he began to portray images that looked invincible.

During a long convalescence in a series of hospitals, Léger conceived a new art, and his painting *The Card Players* (also called *Soldiers Playing Cards*) began this new style. Created in Paris during a sick leave in December 1917, it shows a group of soldiers who are not flesh and blood but constructed of shining metal parts like the gleaming white battlefield cannon. He had painted geometric forms before the war, but now his forms were metallic. For Léger, mechanical metal forms conveyed "a feeling of strength and power."[49] They filled his art for the rest of his life. Even when the people in his paintings are flesh colored, their bodies seem to be made of tubular steel, giving his work a strong modern look. The art historian Werner Schmalenbach calls Léger one of the few outstanding classically modern artists: "There were no more than ten—and he was one of them."[50]

World War II

Josef Beuys and Sam Francis were fighter pilots who fought on opposites sides of the war. Severely injured when their planes crashed, they became artists as a result of their experiences. I don't know if Beuys and Francis ever met each other, but both of them studied medicine before the war, then switched to art. Both also worked for peace eventually and strongly supported environmental causes.

JOSEF BEUYS

One of the best known—and probably the most controversial—incidents in the life of Joseph Beuys (German, 1921–1986) is his plane crash in the Crimea during World War II.[51] Left unconscious, he was rescued by Tartars, a nomadic people native to the area. In one version of the story, Beuys said he was in the wreckage for days before the Tartars found him. They wrapped him in fat and felt for insulation and took him to their tent before bringing him to a German field hospital. Possibly Beuys was transported through the snow in a type of sled. In another version, he wasn't wrapped but recalled the felt tents of the Tartars and the fat in the smell of their food.

Some art historians dismiss the incident as complete fantasy, but in his essay about the incident, "Crash Course: Remarks on a Beuys Story," Peter Nesbit finds the crash actually happened on March 16, 1944, and that Beuys was delivered a day later to a German field hospital. He may have thought he spent days in the wreckage and then days with the Tartars because time dilates when we are sick or distressed: moments can seem like hours and hours can feel like days. The experience had a profound influence on Beuys. Before being drafted, he studied medicine; afterward he studied sculpture. Beuys used fat, felt, and sleds throughout his art. Referring to his rescue, they become symbols for healing. The artist also wore a flying vest as part of his public image, which he related to the crash.

In sculpture, videos, photography, and performance pieces, Beuys turned his personal survival into a desire for planetary survival. Although he was a pacifist and a member of the Green Party, Beuys made a work of art, *How to Explain Pictures to a Dead Hare*, that I find very negative. In this 1965 performance piece, he walked around an art gallery explaining the pictures to the hare. Beuys is not the only person to use dead animals in his art, a practice that is both cruel and unnecessary. A more positive work is his conceptual piece for planting seven thousand trees. Believing that creativity is an integral part of life, he insisted that "everybody is an artist."[52]

SAM FRANCIS

During World War II, Samuel Lewis Francis (American, 1923–1994) enlisted to become a fighter pilot.[53] While he was on a 1944 training flight over the Arizona desert, an emergency landing changed his life. His spine was severely compressed in the crash, and when the doctors examined him they found a previously undetected case of spinal tuberculosis. Bedridden in army hospitals for three years and forced to lie on his stomach in a full body cast, Francis started to paint using watercolors he was given in the hospital. What started as therapy became the focus of his life. The painter David Park encouraged Francis to keep painting and arranged a visit to the California Palace of the Legion of Honor. Francis, who had never been to an art museum, was overwhelmed, especially by an El Greco painting. "It knocked me out," he exclaimed. "I probably would have died if it had not been for painting. The picture by El Greco changed my life."[54]

The creativity and perseverance Francis developed as an injured young man became a source of strength in later crises. When he was treated for tuberculosis of the kidney in 1969, Francis again painted in the hospital. Unable to do large works in oil, he made drawings and watercolors. Toward the end of his life, when prostate cancer put him in a wheelchair and he had lost the use of his right arm in a fall, the artist painted left-handed while sitting in a wheelchair.

In the 1960s Francis joined the peace movement, and when he became enormously successful with his art he turned the profits into benefit for others. He cofounded an alternative energy company to develop wind power for use; started a publishing company to print books on psychology, philosophy, and the arts; and opened the Sam Francis Medical Research Center, which specializes in infectious and environmental diseases. Francis was also a poet, and in his writing we can see his attitude toward life and illness: "Time is the swiftest of all things . . . darkness covers light." But then he writes, "Light fills darkness."[55]

Michelangelo and the Response to Illness

In the next chapter we see how Michelangelo, one of the greatest artists in the Western tradition, responded to illness. Physical difficulties affected him in childhood, during his work on the Sistine Chapel, and through old age to the end of his life. Not only talent but enormous perseverance in the face of pain brings us Michelangelo's art, which has both enhanced and changed our culture.

Part 5

Creativity and the Response to Illness

Chapter 16

Michelangelo's Problems and Perseverance

*The spirit of a man will sustain his
infirmity. —Proverbs 18:14*

A sculptor, a painter, an architect, and a poet, Michelangelo
Buonarroti (Michelangelo di Lodovico Buonarroti Simoni,
Italian, 1475–1564) was one of the great geniuses of the
Italian Renaissance and a prodigiously hard worker.[1] His response to
illness was creativity, and his response to good health was the same. As
a result, he worked when he was sick and he worked when he was well,
leaving us magnificent art that influenced the course of Western culture. Michelangelo was so admired during his lifetime that he was
called Il Divino (the Divine One) and yet he was almost prevented
from becoming an artist at all.

The Buonarroti family had once been prominent, but when
Michelangelo was young, they were living in diminished circumstances.
Still, his pretentious father, Ludovico, did not want his son to become
a laborer (an artist) who worked with his hands. Ludovico was so out-
raged by this possibility that he would hit his son when he caught him
drawing. But Michelangelo persevered, creating art in secret and with

such dedication that his father finally relented. At thirteen he was apprenticed to the Florentine painter Domenico Ghirlandaio (Italian, 1449–1494) to begin his professional training. A year later Lorenzo the Magnificent of Florence started a school for sculpture headed by Bertoldo di Giovanni (Italian, ca. 1420–1491). When he was looking for excellent students, Ghirlandaio recommended Michelangelo. At fourteen Michelangelo began his studies, and when he was fifteen Lorenzo the Magnificent took him into his house to be raised with his own children. As a result, he not only learned sculpture but also had a humanist education, which was founded on classical philosophy and art combined with the theology and ideas of the Renaissance. This education would be the basis of Michelangelo's imagery for the rest of his life.

He was born in the small mountain town of Caprese while his father was its temporary mayor, and at the end of Ludovico's term the Buonarrotis returned to their native Florence. Shortly afterward, the infant Michelangelo was sent away from his mother to be wet-nursed by a woman in Settignano, a village near Florence. She was the daughter of a stonecutter who was also married to a stonecutter. With its many quarries, the region was home to both sculptors and stonemasons. Later, the artist spoke of this experience: "I also sucked in with my nurse's milk the chisels and hammers with which I make my figures."[2]

A Broken Nose and the Desire for Beauty

Although the artist makes something positive out of being sent away from his mother for years during childhood, it was still an emotional stress. Nathan Leites, in his psychological study *Art and Life, Aspects of Michelangelo*, believes this experience of abandonment and others that followed, such as the death of Michelangelo's mother when he was six, profoundly affected the artist's life and work.[3] Abandonment can produce depression, lead to emotional isolation, and result in a poor self-image, all of which took a toll on Michelangelo's emotional life, despite his enormous professional success. These negative feelings were further aggravated when he had his nose broken as a teenager. Yet the incident that caused him such anguish may have enhanced an aspect of his art.

When he was about fourteen, Michelangelo was severely injured in an argument with Pietro Torrigiano (Italian, 1472–1528), a fellow art student. But there are two versions of the story. The art historian Giorgio Vasari said that Torrigiano was jealous of Michelangelo's talent and hit him in envy, while Torrigiano insisted that Michelangelo had a bad habit of deriding other students' work and made disparaging remarks to him. In both versions of the story Torrigiano is aggressive and smashes his fist into Michelangelo's face, breaking his nose.[4] Michelangelo may also have been knocked unconscious; according to his biographer Ascanio Condivi, he "was carried home as if dead."[5]

Later Torrigiano would brag about the incident: "Clenching my fist, [I] gave him such a punch on the nose that I felt the bone and cartilage crush like a biscuit. So that fellow will carry my signature till he dies."[6] It was true; Michelangelo's nose remained flattened for the rest of his life. Torrigiano, who was banished from Florence for this violence, became a mercenary soldier. Later he worked as a sculptor in northern Europe and eventually died in the dungeons of the Spanish Inquisition.[7]

Michelangelo, who loved beauty, felt marked for life. This was in the Renaissance, before reconstructive surgery, and nothing could be done to repair the damage. We become aware of his feelings about his appearance in the poetry he writes as an adult. His poems praise the beauty of other people but say, "I see myself so ugly,"[8] and "My face has the shape that causes fright."[9] Looking at paintings of him, we see that even though his nose was flattened, Michelangelo was not ugly. He was of medium height, well built, with broad shoulders, hazel eyes, and dark hair. It is likely that an unhappy childhood and a lack of classical beauty laid the foundation for his poor self-image,[10] but the trauma of having his nose broken magnified his distress enormously.

Having an intense desire for beauty and believing he did not possess it may have made Michelangelo more intent on creating the beautiful in his art. The psychologist William G. Niederland says the desire to compensate for what we believe is a personal deformity can inspire great efforts to repair it.[11] Michelangelo was not able to alter his face, but he could make ideal beauty a hallmark of his work. His magnificent figures that we admire today are what the artist admired and wanted to be himself. According to Vasari, Michelangelo destroyed many preparatory sketches for his work so that no one could see all of his efforts and think he was less than perfect. But this perfectionism was directed solely toward his art and not at all to his physical appearance. While lavishing enormous care on his work, going to stone quarries to choose the best marble, and spending years creating a sculpture, he neglected himself.

Throughout his life, Michelangelo felt profoundly unattractive and treated himself poorly. His self-hatred manifested in habits such as not changing his clothes, even to go to bed. When he was young, he slept in his work clothes, and when he got older, he didn't even take off his boots. Although he insisted that this practice saved time dressing for work the next day, it showed poor regard for his welfare and the results were harmful. Michelangelo wore buskins, which are leather boots that reach halfway to the knee. He would wear these leather buskins next to the bare skin of his legs for months at a time, keeping them on all day and all night. When he finally removed them, his skin came off with the leather.

The Sistine Chapel and Changing Art

Michelangelo's great talent was recognized early, and he received important commissions. The marble sculpture of the *Pieta* with Mary holding the dead Jesus on her lap, his statue of *David*, and the *Doni Tondo*, a painting of the Holy Family, were all made in his twenties to early thirties. Michelangelo's work was so admired that Pope Julius II gave him an enormous commission, but it was one that the artist tried desperately to refuse. In February 1508, when the pope insisted that he paint the ceiling of the Sistine Chapel, the artist protested that he was a sculptor, not a painter. But Julius was adamant.[12] Michelangelo finally signed the contract in May for a project that was difficult from beginning to end.

The chapel is enormous. Measuring 128 feet long by 45 feet wide, its vaulted ceiling is over 65 feet off the ground, almost the height of a seven-story building. To reach the ceiling, Michelangelo built a large scaffold that he climbed to work. The commission called for a fresco, which is the application of paint onto a section of freshly plastered wall or ceiling. Initially the artist hired assistants to help him, but when he saw their work he fired them all and did everything himself. The original contract called for twelve figures, but the completed fresco contains more than three hundred. Michelangelo was thirty-three when he started the ceiling at the entrance to the room and thirty-seven when he finished it at the far end near the altar wall. From 1508 to 1512, the reluctant artist was forced to do a job he detested—one that would become his greatest masterpiece.

While he worked on the Sistine Chapel, his art transformed. The early work contains classical images in a High Renaissance style, but as the project continued, his figures start to twist and bend. Two of Michelangelo's first biblical figures, the prophets Zechariah and Joel near the entrance, are painted in Renaissance poses, calmly sitting and reading. But the prophet Jonah, a later figure close to the altar wall, is much larger. With his head thrown backward and eyes looking up, he is almost twisting out of his chair. One of the earliest figures from antiquity that Michelangelo paints is the Delphic Sibyl, shown sitting quietly and holding a scroll. The body of the Libyan Sibyl, which was painted later, is completely turned around in a position that strains the limits of anatomy. We also see progressively twisting positions in the decorative nudes that Michelangelo included as part of the composition. The two nudes above Joel face each other, while the nudes near Jonah are bending and turning out of their seats.

But why did these changes take place? Art historians differ in their theories.[13] Howard Hibbard believes that after assessing his work on the first part of the ceiling Michelangelo wanted more forceful imagery. He suggests that when the scaffold was taken down and moved so Michelangelo could work on the second part, the artist was able to view and judge his work from ground level. This is certainly true because the images in the later part of the ceiling are larger and more easily seen from far away. Frederick Hartt agrees but notices that the figures already start to change while the artist is working on the first part of the ceiling. Hartt also believes Michelangelo's later figures may be in response to the military heroism of Pope Julius II and the possibility of a unified Italy. This is doubtful because Michelangelo saw himself as a citizen of Florence and had a difficult relationship with the pope. Julius II refused to pay him on time and struck Michelangelo with his staff during an argument. He also pushed the artist to work faster, threatening, "You want me to have you thrown off the scaffolding."[14]

Difficult Working Conditions

There is another theory why the figures on the Sistine Chapel ceiling transform. In an excellent paper Peter Bencivenga wrote when he was my student at the New School University in New York, he associates the increasingly twisting bodies in the painting with Michelangelo's own twisting and straining body as he worked on the more than 5,800-square-foot ceiling. Standing for hours at the top of the scaffold, Michelangelo would bend backward, look up, and twist his body to paint. The artist was so unhappy working on the Sistine Chapel that he drew a caricature of himself painting and also expressed his misery in a poem: "I've got myself a goiter from this strain. . . . My belly's pushed by force beneath my chin. My beard toward Heaven, I feel the back of my brain . . . In front of me my skin is being stretched while it folds up behind and forms a knot. I am bending like a Syrian bow."[15]

Bencivenga believes that Michelangelo's own twisting and bending body not only unconsciously influenced the figures he created in the Sistine Chapel but that these twisting and bending figures in turn influenced the artist's later work. He points out that the sculptures Michelangelo made before he painted the Sistine Chapel ceiling, such as *David*, are in graceful, comfortable Renaissance poses. But after the Sistine Chapel his figures, such as the nudes he creates for the Medici tombs and his statues of struggling slaves, twist and turn. These dynamic sculptures were so admired that they helped to bring forth a new style called Mannerism. If Bencivenga is correct, physical strain may have been one of the factors that turned the Sistine Chapel ceiling into a pivotal work for Michelangelo and for the history of Western art.

There were additional stresses in painting the ceiling. Michelangelo's face was constantly covered with paint drippings and his eyesight was affected. Continually looking up for extended periods of time, he had difficulty readjusting to normal vision. Michelangelo's eyes were so badly affected for months after he finished the project that he could not see well if he was looking down. The artist could only read letters or view drawings if he held them up over his head while tilting backward, his position when painting the ceiling. Vasari was surprised that Michelangelo's eyes recovered at all. After Vasari painted ceilings in the Palace of the Duke of Cosimo his vision was permanently damaged.[16]

A Portrait with Evidence of Gout

Two medical doctors, Garabed Eknoyan and Carlos Espinel, have further information about Michelangelo's physical condition during the time he painted the Sistine Chapel. Although the doctors worked separately and published their results three months apart in different medical journals, both of them discuss Michelangelo's urinary tract problems and find evidence of gout. In an article he wrote for *Lancet*, Dr. Carlos Espinel, a specialist in blood-pressure disorders and a professor at Georgetown University, finds evidence for gout in a portrait of Michelangelo done by Raphael (Raffaello Santi or Sanzio, Italian, 1483–1520).[17] The portrait is part of *The School of Athens*, a large fresco that Pope Julius II commissioned for a wall of the Stanza della Segnatura, a room in the Papal Apartments at the Vatican. Raphael was working on this painting while Michelangelo was working on the ceiling of the Sistine Chapel. Sitting on the stairs in the foreground of Raphael's fresco, which portrays the scholars of ancient Greece, is a figure thought to represent the philosopher Heraclitus but believed to be modeled on Michelangelo.

When Espinel looked at the face he could see a resemblance to Michelangelo, but when he looked at the figure's knee he saw evidence of gout. Unlike the knees on other figures in the painting, which appear normal, the knee on the portrait of Michelangelo is diseased. Espinel identifies the clusters of hard-looking lumps underneath the skin as gouty tophi, which are called gonagra when they are visible on the knee. Michelangelo was known to have urinary tract problems and eventually suffered from gravel and kidney stones. Espinel says that the presence of both tophi and kidney stones in an adult male supports a diagnosis of gout. Produced by an excess of uric acid, which can settle in the joints, gout may be caused by plumbism, also called lead poisoning. In Michelangelo's time wine was made in lead containers, and Espinel says that the artist might also have been exposed to lead in his paints.

Although Espinel does not relate Michelangelo's gout to his art, it may have relevance to his work. Like other forms of arthritis, gout can be extremely painful. If this is the case, then Michelangelo's discomfort while painting the Sistine Chapel would have been even more extreme. This may give further support to Bencivenga's idea that the artist's physical distress influences the images he creates. Michelangelo wrote about his discomfort in letters to his family. "I am unhappy and not in too good health staying here," he wrote in 1509,[18] and in 1512, near the end of the project, Michelangelo revealed, "I suffer the greatest toil and discomfort."[19]

Looking at the Raphael portrait of Michelangelo, we see a brooding figure depicting a man known to have been depressed for much of his life. In addition to psychological factors, I believe there is another reason for Michelangelo's well-known depression—the presence of a painful chronic illness. It is depressing to be in pain and even more depressing to be in pain for years, as was apparently the case with Michelangelo.

Urinary Tract Problems, Kidney Stones, and Gout

Writing in the journal *Kidney International*, Dr. Garabed Eknoyan, a professor at Baylor College of Medicine, finds that Michelangelo suffered from long-term urinary tract problems and gout.[20] He also thinks these conditions have great relevance to the artist's work. A specialist in kidney disorders and the history of nephrology (kidney disease), Eknoyan cites evidence of the artist's illness in the imagery of the Sistine Chapel ceiling.

By 1548, Michelangelo suffered from gravel in his urine, kidney stones, dysuria (painful, burning, or difficult urination), and the inability to urinate. Eknoyan thinks these problems that may eventually have led to kidney failure in the artist's old age appeared much earlier in his life. He believes that Michelangelo developed kidney stones when he was relatively young and that the artist suffered from them while he was working on the Sistine Chapel. Eknoyan explains that most people get only one kidney stone and it never recurs, but Michelangelo's poetry shows that he passed many stones. People with multiple stones tend to have the condition at an early age, and while there is no way to know the exact onset of Michelangelo's illness, the artist began complaining of poor health in 1500, when he was twenty-five. Kidney stones are not only painful, but people with this condition also tend to get infections such as cystitis (a urinary tract infection) and pyelonephritis (a kidney infection). In letters to his father and brother from 1500 through 1512, Michelangelo relates recurrent episodes of poor health that Eknoyan believes may indicate the presence of repeated infections.

Eknoyan also thinks that Michelangelo's kidney problems may have been related to his gout. It is known that the artist suffered from severe gout as an older man, but he may have had the condition prior to working on the Sistine Chapel. The tophi or bumps on Michelangelo's knee look like they had been growing for some time before becoming as obvious and prominent as they appear in the 1511 Raphael portrait. According to Eknoyan, the presence of kidney stones and gout would further predispose the artist to urinary tract infections and bladder infections. He believes the presence of these painful conditions may be reflected in the images of a kidney that Michelangelo incorporates into the ceiling of the Sistine Chapel.

Images of a Kidney

The first reference to a kidney, according to Eknoyan, is in the garments of God shown in the third panel of the ceiling from the altar wall. Illustrating Genesis 1:9–11, the image is called *Separation of Land from Water*.[21] As God divides the landmasses from the oceans, the kidneys separate solids from the liquids in the body. This painting of God flying with his arms raised over the waters below is made even more dramatic by his outer garment, a large swirling mantle, and an inner garment, the tunic that wraps around his lower body. Eknoyan finds that these two pieces of clothing correspond to the structure of a bisected right kidney. The dark red outer garment not only is in the shape of a kidney but also matches the color of the parenchyma, which is the inner part of the organ. He explains that although God has a red mantle in the two preceding panels, it is not the dark red seen here. The tunic wrapped around God's lower body suggests the renal pelvis, a tubular structure in the center of the kidney. Even the folds of God's mantle, where it is pulled together at the lower left, reflect anatomy, says Eknoyan: they are in the shape of the ureter, the renal artery, and the renal vein as they enter and leave the kidney. An excellent anatomist, Michelangelo was familiar with the structure and function of the kidney. He had dissected human bodies since he was a teenager and had even thought of publishing a book on anatomy.

A second reference to kidneys and the pain of renal illness is in the figure of a very distressed-looking male nude sitting in one of the corners of *Separation of Land from Water*. Although other nudes in the painting twist and turn, Eknoyan explains that the position of this figure is characteristic of people with kidney pain: its arched body shows the costovertebral junction where the kidney is found. People with severe kidney pain arch their backs this way in an effort to immobilize their kidneys and to be able to put their hands on the source of pain. Eknoyan also notices that the figure grasps two kidney-shaped pillows on either side.

As an artist, Michelangelo was familiar with the Renaissance phrase "Every painter paints himself,"[22] and Eknoyan believes that this arching figure with the frightened face is the artist, either fearing his next episode of kidney illness or experiencing the actual distress of a kidney stone. Michelangelo may be expressing his suffering, just as Henri Matisse expressed the pain of his gallstones through a figure that he never acknowledged to be a self-portrait (see chapter 1).

Michelangelo was a religious man, and connecting a kidney with God may be seen as a desire for divine intervention to relieve his pain and restore his health. In the fresco, God is looking down and to the left with his arms upraised, and the object of his attention appears to be the arching nude holding the kidney-shaped pillows. If the nude represents Michelangelo, then the garments of God that resemble a kidney may be his desire for divine healing expressed through imagery as a visual prayer.

Were these references to the kidney included unconsciously or on purpose? Eknoyan thinks it was a conscious choice, but I believe it was unconscious. So much of art is the expression of unconscious creative processes. Even the most carefully planned pieces contain references that the artist never consciously intended, yet they are there for others to uncover. I find that in my own work what I know I am thinking and what I don't realize I am thinking both find their way into the finished painting. Whether Michelangelo encoded these anatomical references on purpose or accidentally may never be known, but the fact that they are there to be discovered by others shows the depth and richness of his art.[23]

An Injury and Acute Illness

Twenty-four years later Michelangelo again worked on the Sistine Chapel, but this time he was commissioned to paint the enormous altar wall at the far end of the room that measured forty-eight feet high by forty-four feet wide. He had begun the preparatory drawings in 1535. As before, the artist tried to refuse the project but was forced to accept it, and from 1536 to 1541 he worked on the huge fresco. Michelangelo was sixty-one when he started and sixty-six when he finished, and it, too, is a masterpiece. Illustrating the Last Judgment, it shows Jesus separating the blessed ascending to Heaven from the evil who are condemned to Hell. Mary and the saints are in exalted positions near Jesus, and at the bottom of the painting are the dead, rising from their graves to be judged.

Because of the enormous size of the fresco, Michelangelo again worked on a scaffold, but he was older now and it was more difficult. One day he had a bad fall and severely injured his leg. In anger and pain, and refusing any treatment, the artist made his way home alone. There was a Florentine doctor living in Rome at the time who was a great admirer of Michelangelo. His name was Baccio Rontini, and when he heard of the artist's injury he set out to find him. After knocking on the door of Michelangelo's house and receiving no answer, Rontini managed to climb into the building. By going from room to room, he finally located the artist, who was in a terrible state. Rontini stayed with Michelangelo until he was well. After recovering completely, the artist returned to painting on the scaffold. Working continuously, he completed the *Last Judgment* a few months later, and when Pope Paul III was invited to see it, he fell to his knees in awe.

The artist had two episodes of acute illness so serious that he appeared to be near death both times. The type of illness is not known, but Michelangelo was very sick in the summer of 1544 and then again in December 1545. During both confinements the artist was cared for at the Strozzi Palace in Florence. In gratitude Michelangelo gave Roberto Strozzi, the owner of the palace, two of his statues: the *Rebellious Slave* and the *Dying Slave*. Michelangelo had given works of art and other objects away throughout his life. Although he purchased land for his family, the artist was not interested in material possessions for himself. "However rich I may have been," he said, "I have always lived like a poor man."[24] Michelangelo preferred a simple, spare existence, and when he worked as an architect on the rebuilding of St. Peter's in Rome, he refused to be paid. For him it was an act of devotion.

Gout and Insomnia

In later years the artist's symptoms of gout became increasingly severe. Writing to his brother Lionardo in 1555, Michelangelo described the condition as "the cruelest pain I've had in one foot, which has prevented me from going out and has been a nuisance to me in a number of ways. They say it's a kind of gout."[25] The artist's fingers were also affected. Eknoyan believes it was most likely gout but that it could also have been rheumatoid arthritis. In 1563 Michelangelo apologized for not answering his brother's letter sooner. "I cannot use my hands to write," he explained, "therefore, from now on I'll get others to write and I'll sign." But even as early as 1557, Michelangelo revealed that "writing is very irksome to me." Although unable to write, he sculpted until the end of his life. Eknoyan says this was possible because holding a chisel and hammer in the palms of his hands was easier for Michelangelo than grasping a pen with his fingers. Even so, it must have been painful, yet the artist persevered. "The way we react to pain and illness today," says Eknoyan, "is totally different from how things were then. Then it was taken as part of life."[26]

Michelangelo also suffered from insomnia but he used it for creativity. The artist did not sleep much and often when he couldn't sleep he would get up and work. He was able to work on those dark nights before electricity because of a hat of thick paper that he made for himself. In the center of the hat over his head was a lighted candle made of goat tallow that illuminated wherever he looked and freed his hands to hold the hammer and chisel.

Speaking of this compulsion to work, Vasari said, "The spirit and genius of Michelangelo could not rest without doing something," because the artist believed "the exercise of the hammer kept him healthy in body."[27] In an age when the average life expectancy was about thirty-five, Michelangelo lived to be almost eighty-nine. In spite of having been a sickly child and suffering from chronic illness, he died less than three weeks before his eighty-ninth birthday and continued to sculpt until six days before his death. Working whenever and for as long as he could, Michelangelo persevered despite years of pain and left us one of the great legacies in the history of art.

The Relationship Between Creativity, Illness, and Identity

Work was a great part of Michelangelo's identity, but creativity connects with our identity in many ways. For certain artists, illness and creativity bring out their ethnic heritage. Others find their identity and creativity expand as they also become writers. Some individuals are controlled by their idea of what constitutes an identity, while others discover previously hidden talents when dementia interrupts their capacity for language.

Chapter 17

Creativity, Illness, and Identity

Illness was no doubt the final cause of the
whole urge to create. By creating, I could
recover; by creating I became healthy.
—Heinrich Heine

How many of us really know who we are and all the deep sources from which our creativity springs? Part of our identity and our abilities may be hidden away like treasures at the bottom of the sea until we are forced to find them. Most of us swim on the surface of life until a storm of illness impels us to dive within and discover new sources of inspiration and strength— yet they were there waiting for us all the time. Some artists discover this inspiration through their ethnic identity. Others expand their identity as creative individuals by making different kinds of art or by changing from visual art to writing. Sometimes an artist can focus on negative aspects of an identity to the detriment of health. Still other people with declining mental abilities reveal new aspects of their identity by uncovering talents that were hidden until dementia allowed them to shine through.

Art and Ethnic Identity

Even though we are all basically the same, our small differences create the rich ethnic diversity of our world. These cultural traditions have been the source of human art for millennia. Some artists like Itchiku Kubota and Robert Yarde already worked in their heritage but found a new way to express themselves, while Henry Ossawa Tanner and Greystone Abbott discovered their ethnic roots through creativity. Kubota's art is in the ancient lineage of the Japanese kimono, while Tanner and Yarde find creative strength in the culture of African Americans, and Greystone Abbott expresses the imagery of Native America. But all of them made an artistic transition during illness.

ITCHIKU KUBOTA

When Itchiku Kubota (Japanese, b. 1917) was fourteen, he apprenticed himself to learn kimono painting using the method of *yūzen* dyeing.[1] "I felt," he says, "as if I had been called to the trade of kimono dyeing and made up my mind to study *yūzen*."[2] This classic way of painting on kimonos and dyeing the fabric originated around 1700. It is a type of resist-dyeing process, where certain areas of the kimono are painted with glue to avoid coloration while the surrounding fabric absorbs the dye.[3] These places can be painted or dyed separately later. After working intensely for a kimono company, Kubota collapsed from exhaustion at nineteen. This physical crisis became a turning point, and he opened a studio of his own. One year later he saw a piece of fabric that would change his life.

A small four-hundred-year-old strip of cloth in a museum became his revelation. Its colors were faded and the painting and embroidery were damaged, but he was struck by the beauty of its *tsuijigahana* style of dyeing. This is also a resist-dye process. But rather than being covered with glue, areas of the fabric are tied off in an extremely complicated form of tie-dyeing that is combined with painting and embroidery. Although *tsuijigahana* had not been done for hundreds of years, Kubota says, "I vowed to devote my life to bringing its beauty alive again." He learned all he could about the ancient technique and was so determined to succeed that despite being drafted into World War II and spending six years as a Russian prisoner of war in a Siberian labor camp, and then having his work rejected by galleries, Kubota persevered. He made *yūzen* kimonos during the day to support his family and practiced *tsuijigahana* at night.

After the textile expert Tomoyuki Yamanobe suggested that Kubota combine the styles of *yūzen* and *tsuijigahana*, the artist had his first exhibition at the age of sixty. But a year later, on the day of his second exhibition, Kubota became ill with acute hepatitis. "For the next two months," he recalls, "I struggled against death. While in the hospital I thought over all I had done and decided to turn to developing my own style."[4] He reinterpreted *tsuijigahana* with modern fabrics and colors, creating a new form of art. Kubota's work is influenced not only by classic Japanese designs but also by French Impressionism and views of nature. Kubota became enormously successful; his kimonos are shown all over the world. But he says about his work after having hepatitis, "This was the time of deepest import in my life as an artist."[5]

HENRY OSSAWA TANNER

Henry Ossawa Tanner (American, 1859–1937) was about thirteen when he saw a man painting landscapes in a park near his home.[6] The young boy was so impressed that he immediately wanted to become an artist. The next day, with fifteen cents from his parents, he bought himself art supplies. "I went straight down to the spot where I had seen the artist the day before," he remembered. Then he started to paint.[7] After bringing his artwork home that evening, Tanner admitted he was "well content with my first effort." Although his parents approved of painting as a pastime, they did not regard it as a career. Unlike his father, who was a minister and later a bishop in the African Methodist Episcopal (AME) Church, Tanner did not want a religious vocation, so his parents secured a position for him in a flour business owned by family friends. In order to paint, Tanner got up at dawn to catch the morning light before he left at seven to sell flour. When the strain of working and painting made him sick within a year, his parents relented and let him become an artist.

After studying at the Philadelphia Academy of Art, Tanner moved to France, the center of the nineteenth-century art world. During his second year in Paris, he contracted typhoid fever. When Tanner returned home to Philadelphia to recuperate with his family, his art began to change. As a classically trained painter, he produced beautiful landscapes and images of people, but back in America he confronted his heritage. The art historian Darrel Sewell believes that Tanner's ethnic awareness came from his participation in the Congress on Africa, an 1893 African American convention that was part of the World's Columbian Exhibition in Chicago. He began painting scenes of African American life. *The Banjo Lesson* shows an older man teaching a young boy to play the instrument, and in *The Thankful Poor*, people pray before their simple meal. These paintings are among his most famous works.

Returning to Paris, Tanner continued to express his heritage as the son of an AME bishop by painting scenes from the Bible. He was very successful in both America and France, becoming a full member of the National Academy in New York and a chevalier of the Legion of Honor in Paris. In her biography of Tanner, Marcia Mathews relates how the artist died as an old man, peacefully in his sleep, "with the paint still fresh on his last canvas."[8]

RICHARD YARDE

Richard Yarde (American, b. 1939) was known for his images of African American heroes and jazz culture when a severe illness changed his life.[9] One of the medications he had been taking for high blood pressure damaged his kidneys, and in 1991 Yarde almost died of kidney failure. Left with symptoms resembling a stroke, he could hardly walk, his speech was slurred, and he had no feeling in his hands. When the doctors told him to stay home, rest, and watch TV, "I was emotionally shattered," says Yarde. "I thought they were basically waiting for me to die."[10]

Instead, he was determined to survive. After a year of rehabilitation, Yarde regained his speech and was able to move again but still had problems with high blood pressure and medication. Although he returned to painting and to teaching at the University of Massachusetts, he slept hooked up to a dialysis machine until his kidney transplant operation in 1998. Yarde became deeply spiritual while he was sick. He repeatedly recited the twenty-third psalm as a source of strength and received healing from a charismatic priest, Father Ralph DiOrio of Worcester, Massachusetts. This opened a new world for him and it influenced his new art. After his experience of healing hands, images of hands become prominent in Yarde's new work. "I was literally trying to heal myself," he explains, "through my process of working and imagery."[11]

Yarde's new art is about healing and is based on the circle and the square as universal symbols. The square is the shape of his large-scale watercolors and the circle is formed by an image of Ringshout, a dance performed by African American slaves for healing, spiritual transformation, and community solidarity. In Yarde's work the dancers are symbolized by their shoes as they move counterclockwise in a circle. Forbidden to have instruments, the slaves clapped their hands and stomped their feet to create the rhythm of the ritual. By making the shoes very modern, Yarde has taken this historical ceremony into the present. He also uses the circular Ringshout pattern to show other images related to health. Instead of the shoes there are circles containing X-rays, ultrasounds, DNA patterns, Braille writing, and acupuncture. Yarde says that he wants his art to "have roots in African American culture and . . . connect to all cultures."[12]

GREYSTONE ELIZABETH ABBOTT

When Greystone Elizabeth Abbott (American, b. 1959)[13] was growing up, she "always knew something was wrong."[14] But she didn't know what it was, and although Abbott was a bright child she did poorly in school. It was not until her sister, a clinical psychologist at the Menninger Clinic, had her tested as an adult that Abbott found out she was severely dyslexic. Her reading problems due to dyslexia are made worse by scotopic sensitivity syndrome, also called Irlen syndrome after the psychologist Helen Irlen, who identified its symptoms.[15] People with this visual-perceptual problem show extreme sensitivity to bright lights, such as sunlight, fluorescent lights, and the glare of white paper. They also have trouble with light and dark contrasts; black type may seem to jump around on a white page. Using colored filters or wearing tinted glasses prescribed by a professional can help this condition. An optometrist trained to treat scotopic sensitivity syndrome made Abbott two pairs of specially tinted glasses, one for reading and one for the computer. But if she reads without them, the letters jump around.

In 1994 Abbott enrolled in college. It was before she knew the names of her difficulties or had tinted glasses, but she believed that by going slowly, she could succeed. Taking one or two courses per term, she maintained a 4.0 average. In 2000, when Greystone needed only eight more credits for her associate's degree, a woman in the disabilities center of the school insisted that she take a math course. Abbott told her she was unable to complete this course because of her learning difficulties and submitted the results from her tests at Menninger. But the woman maintained that no one with a 4.0 average could have learning problems. Stalemated and unable to graduate, Abbott decided to take some time off from school and enrolled in a pottery class. She was so excellent that it became her career. Abbott also became an expert in ceramic glazes. She experimented with glazes to discover new techniques, just as she had persevered with learning disorders to find her own way to learn. "Don't tell me it can't be done," insists Abbott. "I'll figure it out."[16]

After gaining technical proficiency, Abbott wanted a personal voice for her art and found it through her Cherokee Choctaw heritage. "It's like I came home," she reveals.[17] Inspired by a deepening awareness of her tradition, she chose the Four Chiefs as the first image to appear on her ceramics. It shows four Native American chiefs in colorful robes sitting together with a peace pipe. The next image she used—the Clan Sisters, four women in Native American dress with long hair—became her trademark; Abbott's reverence for nature also comes from Native American culture. It is "respecting all living things," she states, and "taking care of the earth."[18]

Painting with Physical Difficulties

Identity in creativity can take many forms. Some artists identify with the size of their work or the amount they produce as a sense of pride. When we are ill, identifying with the size of art we formerly produced or our previous work pace can limit creativity and injure our health. We should listen when physical difficulties tell us to take it easier and identify with the quality rather than the size or quantity of our work. Adjusting her work schedule to accommodate a heart condition kept Alice Neel active into her eighties.

ALICE NEEL

"My life was saved in 1980," insisted Alice Neel (American, 1900–1984),[19] "when I had a pacemaker put in."[20] Although heart problems slowed her work schedule, the English art critic Cherry Smyth believes Neel's later output is her best. Known for her incisive portraits that capture the essence of people rather than their beauty, Neel called each person a new and unique universe. Although the artist portrayed their features accurately, she was really looking into them rather than just looking at them. Neel said she so strongly identified with the individuals she painted that when they went home after a sitting, she felt as if part of herself had left as well. Portraiture was her way of conveying the truth about life. "I told the truth as I perceived it," said Neel, "and . . . did the best and most honest art of which I was capable."[21]

After years of emotional and financial hardships, Neel had a show at the Whitney Museum of American Art at the age of seventy-four. Creativity was central to her life, and although the artist slowed her schedule, she did paint a bit more than the doctor-prescribed hours. "I'm supposed to paint only two hours a day," she admitted at eighty-three, "but I usually work longer. After all, I wouldn't be living if it weren't for art!"[22] Neel, who worked until six weeks before her death from colon cancer at eighty-four, insisted, "The thing that always made me happiest in the world was to paint a good picture."[23]

Painting and Writing

There are times during poor health when painting is no longer possible. Karen Koenig (see chapter I), Margaret Bourke-White (see chapter 3), and Cecilia Beaux (see chapter 3) all focused on writing during illness. None of them limited their identity to being strictly visual artists. Instead, they saw themselves as creative people, which is a larger, more encompassing, fluid identity. Writing became another way of fully expressing themselves. For Emily Carr, who also began to write because of poor health, it opened up a new world.

EMILY CARR

"At sixty-four my heart gave out," recalled Emily Carr (Canadian, 1871–1945), "but I was able to paint and I learned to write."[24] For the rest of her life she would paint when possible and she would write when she couldn't paint.[25] The movement and color of her landscapes capture the essence of nature as a living entity, and Carr is one of her country's most esteemed artists. She loved animals and was also an early advocate of Native America, or First Nations as it is called in Canada. "Indian people and their art touched me deeply," said Carr.[26]

In 1898 at the Ucluelet Indian Reserve on Vancouver Island, she was given the name of "Klee Wyck," which translates as "laughing one." Years later, in 1941, *Klee Wyck* would become the title of her first book. Recounting her experiences with the First Nations, it was an immediate success and won the Governor General's award in Canada, which is equivalent to the Pulitzer Prize in the United States. Carr published this book when she was nearly seventy, and it is the first of seven. She started writing it in the hospital after her second heart attack in 1939. "It was *Klee Wyck*," she explained, "that gave my sick heart courage enough to get better."[27]

From 1937 to her death in 1945, she had four heart attacks, two strokes, congestive heart failure, arthritis in her hip and knees, partial deafness, three stays in a nursing home, and repeated hospitalizations, and used a wheelchair. Determined to stay creative, Carr had a typewriter by her bed at the nursing home. In 1942, after a third heart attack, she published *The Book of Small*, anecdotes from her childhood, which was chosen as Canadian Book of the Year. Then in 1944 came *The House of All Sorts*, about her experiences as a landlady (she was highly argumentative and disliked her tenants). Just before her death from a fourth heart attack in 1945, Carr finished *Growing Pains*, her autobiography. It was published posthumously in 1946. Later, in 1953, her short stories were gathered into two books, *Pause: A Sketchbook* and *The Heart of a Peacock*. Then in 1966 her journals were published as *Hundreds and Thousands*.

For Carr, writing was not only a means of self-expression but a way to counter insomnia. "As I cannot sleep," she said, "I may as well write."[28] After years of obscurity, success came late to Emily Carr but it stayed. It was not until her sixties that her art was widely shown and her books began to be published. But her paintings are greatly admired today and all of her writing is still in print.

Multiple Identities

Carr saw herself as both a writer and a painter. People with multiple talents can feel as if they have multiple identities. Albrecht Dürer was a visual artist, a scientist, and a writer who saw himself as a member of all three of these professions. In the final stage of illness, unable to paint, Dürer wrote his most celebrated book on anatomy.

ALBRECHT DÜRER

Albrecht Dürer (German, 1471–1528) was a naturalist as well as an artist, and when he heard that a whale far larger than had ever been seen before was beached on the coast of Zeeland in the Netherlands, he felt impelled to go there.[29] It was early December 1520, and he was almost lost at sea on the hazardous journey. By the time he finally reached the marshy coast of Zeeland, a tide had carried the great whale back into the ocean. Returning with a serious illness, Dürer later described the symptoms in his diary: "A violent fever seized me, with great weakness, nausea, and headache. And before, when I was in Zeeland, a wondrous sickness came over me, such as I have never heard of from any man and this sickness remains with me."[30]

Along with the onset of his symptoms, the diary also contains frequent entries for doctors and medicines. Dürer most likely contracted malaria, the disease that would be a cause of his death seven years later. Although malaria is generally associated with the tropics, it was once endemic in the Netherlands.[31] Carried by the *Anopheles atroparvus* mosquito, it is a type of malaria found in temperate zones. Less deadly than the tropical illness, it usually becomes a chronic disease that progressively weakens the body.

For the next seven years, Dürer suffered precarious health, and from 1524 to 1525 he produced only engravings. Although the artist was as well known for his woodcuts and engravings as he was for his paintings, they are also smaller and easier to manage for a person who is sick. Dürer produced a smaller quantity of work during illness, but his art continued to evolve. His drawing style becomes looser and his painting appears more three-dimensional with strong shadows creating drama and form. Then, in 1526, six years after the onset of the illness and one year before his death, Dürer completed *The Four Apostles*, a large two-panel oil painting that is considered to be his greatest work.

Dürer was also a writer, and during his illness he started to publish books: *The Teaching of Measurement with Rule and Compass* in 1525 and *The Theory of Fortification* in 1527. In the last year of his life, too weak to paint, Dürer turned completely to writing. His final book, *On Human Proportion*, was finished in 1528. The artist, who died in April 1528, did not live to see its publication in October of that year. But it remains his most important written work and is still in print today. Dürer was a kind person who often gave his art away as gifts. He also believed in religious tolerance and admired the work of Martin Luther, who was then very active in Germany. At Dürer's death, Martin Luther returned the admiration, saying, "It is natural and right to weep for so excellent a man."[32]

The Unhealthy Aspects of an Identity

Having a sense of identity is a fundamental strength, an anchor in the storms of life. Often this identity comes to us through work. After Vincent van Gogh failed at his previous careers of art dealer, schoolteacher, bookseller, student of theology, and evangelical pastor, his new career and identity as an artist became extremely important. But he misinterpreted certain aspects of the artist's identity, which caused him severe problems. Believing that poor health aids creativity, van Gogh did not take care of himself, and his short dramatic life was filled with wonderful art but little concern for his own well-being. "The more I am spent, ill, a broken pitcher," he wrote to his brother Theo, "by so much more am I an artist—a creative artist."[33] Van Gogh had both physical and emotional problems—but what was his underlying illness?

VINCENT VAN GOGH

There are many theories about the ongoing difficulties of Vincent Willem van Gogh (Dutch, 1853–1890), but the most convincing one is that he had acute intermittent porphyria (AIP).[34] Although it is likely that the artist also had emotional problems,[35] AIP seems to be the underlying condition that accounts for many of his different symptoms.[36] The idea was proposed in articles by Loretta Loftus, a professor of medicine at the University of Missouri–Kansas City School of Medicine, and Wilfred N. Arnold, a professor of biochemistry and molecular biology at the University of Kansas Medical Center, and then published in a book by Arnold, *Vincent van Gogh: Chemicals, Crises, and Creativity*. Acute intermittent porphyria is a metabolic disorder in which the body produces a toxic increase of the precursors of porphyrin that can cause periodic attacks of varying length and severity. (Porphyrins, which are pigments, form part of many substances in the body such as hemoglobin that transport oxygen in the blood.) Symptoms may include gastrointestinal distress, auditory and visual hallucinations, seizures,[37] confusion, problems with urination, sexual impotence, constipation, fever, and incapacitating depression, all of which van Gogh experienced. Yet he was lucid and creative between the episodes, recovering quickly after the attacks.

Philip Sandblom, a surgeon and an expert on creativity and disease, agrees with the diagnosis of AIP and says that van Gogh's "artistic powers were not diminished. On the contrary, between the attacks he engaged in exuberant artistic activity. It is to this period that we owe an impressive number of brilliant paintings."[38] Sandblom also points out that van Gogh knew he was ill and tried combating his sickness with creativity. "I fight with all my strength to master my art," insisted van Gogh, "and tell myself that success would be the best lightning rod for my disease."[39] The illness developed in 1880, which was also when he decided to become an artist,[40] and over the years his output increased as the condition worsened. This sounds like a classic transforming illness, but what went wrong? The answer lies in van Gogh's poor health habits and his addictions.

Attacks of AIP can be brought on by fasting, alcohol, smoking, and drugs, which were all part of van Gogh's lifestyle. Supported by his brother Theo, van Gogh used the money to buy the best art materials he could rather than spend it on clothes or food. Artists often curtail their living expenses in order to buy art supplies, but van Gogh went further. Both starvation and smoking can precipitate attacks of AIP. Van Gogh starved himself and smoked to quell his hunger cravings, saying that "then one does not feel an empty stomach so much."[41] The artist was so addicted to nicotine that Arnold says he was never without a pipe and even smoked on his deathbed. Van Gogh was also addicted to caffeine and drinking. "I kept myself going," he admitted, "on coffee and alcohol."[42]

He not only drank excessively but he also drank absinthe.[43] Absinthe is a liqueur containing the toxic compound thujone and several related chemicals called terpenes. Arnold believes it aggravated van Gogh's illness and created a pica in him for terpenes. A pica is an abnormal craving for unnatural "foods." Van Gogh developed a pica for the terpenes of pinene and camphor. Pinene is an ingredient of turpentine, and van Gogh was known to drink turpentine and also to eat his paints. To combat his insomnia the artist took huge doses of camphor. "The combination of overexposure to camphor, absinthe abuse, and fasting or malnutrition would be injurious for anyone," states Arnold, "but devastating for someone with AIP."[44]

AIP is a hereditary illness. Loftus and Arnold have found evidence suggesting that it, rather than syphilis, caused the death of Theo and that van Gogh's sister Willemina and brother Cornelius may also have been affected. The remaining two sisters, Elizabeth and Anna, showed no signs of the disease that most likely precipitated the suicide of their brother Vincent. Van Gogh's art is enormously popular, and I think it is because we respond not only to its great beauty but to the passion and intention of the artist. "I have walked on this earth for thirty years," he said, "and out of gratitude I want to leave some souvenir." His work fulfills this intention and his wish, "How can I be useful, of what service can I be?"[45]

Creativity and the Layers of Identity:
Frontotemporal Dementia

There are many aspects to our identity: those we are aware of and use every day and others that remain hidden until a circumstance such as illness allows them to come forward. Sometimes a new aspect can emerge as a talent. Dr. Bruce L. Miller, a neurologist and the director of the Memory and Aging Center of the University of California at San Francisco, has discovered that certain people with frontotemporal dementia (FTD), a degenerative neurological disease, can show enhanced talent in visual art while their ability to speak lessens.[46] FTD usually affects the left side of the brain, causing problems with language and behavior. But because it spares the right side of the brain, artistic talent may become more accessible. "The last place one would expect to find any aptitude flourishing, let alone emerging," explains Miller, "is in the brain of someone slowly wasting away with dementia, but the evidence is pretty dramatic."[47]

Most people with FTD have very diminished capacities, but there are some individuals with this condition who are intensely driven to create. And the compulsion that leads them to make art also improves the quality of their work. They become perfectionists who will repeatedly create the same image until they get it right. These individuals produce very structured compositions showing an excellent sense of color and design, giving their work a strong graphic quality. Unlike Alzheimer's dementia, which has a later onset and destroys the ability to create complex art, frontotemporal dementia, which can appear between the ages of thirty-five and seventy, may not only start a person drawing but can also enhance the talent of someone who is already an artist. Two of Miller's patients, Jancy Chang and Anne Theresa Adams, are artists whose work improved after the onset of FTD, while for another patient, Victor Wightman, visual creativity was an entirely new experience.

VICTOR WIGHTMAN

Victor Wightman (American, 1951–2004), a lawyer and union organizer, was an outgoing, athletic man who showed a noticeable change by the age of fifty. Speech and writing became increasingly difficult for him, and while Wightman had no previous interest in visual art, his family discovered that he had painted colorful images on his bedroom wall and all over the walls and ceiling of his bathroom. When tests revealed frontotemporal dementia and ALS (amyotrophic lateral sclerosis, also called Lou Gehrig's disease), Wightman became Dr. Miller's patient. As the disease progressed, and he could no longer read music or play the piano, his art continued to flourish, showing excellent color and design. Using acrylic paints, Wightman preferred painting on three-dimensional objects rather than paper. To encourage his creativity, his family bought him items from thrift shops. The colorful geometric designs he painted on a pair of small wooden deer bring them to life as works of art. Continuing to paint even when ALS made it difficult for him to move his fingers, he changed from his right hand to his left to keep going. In the last two years and three months of his life, Victor Wightman created more than four hundred works of art.

JANCY CHANG

Jancy Chang (American, born in China, 1946–2004) was an artist and an art teacher whose problems with language affected her work. She was in her forties when grading papers, composing lesson plans, and remembering the names of her students became increasingly difficult. But the language deficits that forced her retirement from teaching at fifty-two also enabled an explosion of creativity. "The more she lost her social and language abilities," says Miller, "the wilder and freer her art became."[48] Chang was a talented artist capable of working in a variety of styles. She made classical Chinese paintings, abstract works similar to Jackson Pollock's, and realistic images like those of Andrew Wyeth. But with the onset of FTD, she created a new style fusing Eastern and Western art. The work is intensely colored, with well-structured compositions and a beautiful use of patterns. Her image of Sumo wrestlers in purples, reds, and blues is extremely dramatic. As the dementia progressed, Chang's work became less realistic but still retained its color and strong presence. When Chang died in 2004, Miller traveled to Santa Cruz, California, and spoke at her funeral. He says that her family displayed all of Chang's art there to honor her memory.

ANNE THERESA ADAMS

Anne Theresa Adams (Canadian, b. 1940), who has been interested in art since childhood, is a scientist as well as an artist. With a Ph.D. in cell biology from the University of British Columbia, she did research and taught at a university. Formerly very articulate, Adams began having problems with language in the late 1990s, and in 2002 she was diagnosed with a type of FTD called primary progressive aphasia (PPA). Adams's early works are well drawn and realistic, but it appears that the benefits of FTD are present before the symptoms of the disease become very apparent: by 1993 the colors become brighter, the compositions are more structured, and patterns play an increasingly important role. I mentioned this to Miller and he agrees. Adams not only paints scenes as strong, graphic images, but she produces work with extreme detail, such as her still life of small stones that look very real and her images of invertebrates in circle designs. Adams also paints unusual subject matter. She translates a mathematical formula into visual art, makes a geometric design about her migraine headache, and analyzes Ravel's *Bolero* by painting her favorite treble and bass notes for each bar of music. These abilities are so extreme that Miller sees them as a type of acquired savant syndrome. Losing certain areas of brain tissue to FTD allows other parts of the brain to come forward, transforming a person from a generalist into a specialist like a savant. Adams's debilitating illness reveals the capacity of the human mind.

Helping Others through Illness

In the next chapter, artists use their illness to help others. They become public figures who battle prejudice to show the world the difficulties and the triumphs of artists with challenged health. As role models, they are vehicles of empowerment who make the world a better place.

Chapter 18

Using Illness to Benefit Others

*Courage conquers all things; it even gives
strength to the body.* —*Ovid*

Helping others makes the world better—and it helps us, too. Research shows that acts of kindness called altruism can bring us joy, benefit our health, and increase our life span.[1] Studies of altruistic people find that helping others gives them a sense of well-being similar to what they experience with exercise. Called a "helper's high," it is associated with the release of endorphins, our natural opiates. This sense of well-being after doing good work has acted like a painkiller for some people, easing the difficulties of their illness. But these benefits happen only if we act altruistically because we want to, not if we are forced to or if we deplete ourselves.

People who are altruists see their own well-being as connected with the well-being of others. They share the benefits of their lives so that other people can benefit as well. This desire to help can arise from many causes, and one of them is the experience of suffering. Suffering hardens the heart of some people, but it leads to compassion for others, like the artists in this chapter. Having been sick, they are no strangers to suffering and want to alleviate it for themselves and for others. They do this by making their illness public. It takes courage to be a public role model but that is what each of these artists has become. Speaking out about illness through their art and their words, they reduce its stigma and provide an example for others to follow.

Cancer: Public Awareness through Art

In 1999 Hollis Sigler estimated that twenty thousand people had seen the group of paintings and drawings she called *Breast Cancer Journal*—and the number is higher by now. "People were moved and grateful for the work,"[2] she said, as the art created by one person became meaningful to many. Communication ends isolation, and creativity that springs from our inner feelings can break the wall of separation that illness builds. By viewing art that reaches us, we realize we are not alone, and identifying with the subject matter enhances our response. According to the psychologist Sylvano Arieti, creativity is one of the most important ways we evolve as human beings, and psychological growth can happen not only in the artist but in everyone affected by the art.[3]

HOLLIS SIGLER

At four o'clock on a July afternoon, thirty-seven-year-old Hollis Sigler (American, 1948–2001) found a lump in her right breast.[4] The size of a pea, it turned out to be malignant, and when her breast was removed, doctors discovered the cancer had spread to three lymph nodes. It was 1985, and after an operation and chemotherapy Sigler became another quiet member of what she called the silent epidemic of breast cancer, an illness no one discussed. Five years later she had what seemed like a local recurrence, and then in 1991 the cancer spread to her bones. With stage four breast cancer and realizing that silence both isolated and victimized her, Sigler decided to act. "An epidemic was raging," she insisted, "but no one talked about it."[5] By attacking the wall of silence with art, *Breast Cancer Journal* became her outcry.

Starting with twelve works, *Breast Cancer Journal* grew to more than one hundred. While confronting a life-threatening illness, Sigler expressed her hopes and fears through imaginative scenes in which dresses, houses, and furniture symbolize the human presence. She created these works as quickly as possible to convey her feelings at the moment. "Perfection does not concern me," said Sigler, "the message does."[6] On the picture frames surrounding her colorful images, she writes quotations and information about the disease. When the work was shown at the National Museum of Women in the Arts in Washington, the exhibit's opening was packed. Experts on breast cancer gave speeches and so did Hollis Sigler. The show was presented in October 1993 during National Breast Cancer Awareness Month and coordinated with a petition drive by the National Breast Cancer Coalition to increase federal funding. When the petition, containing 2.3 million signatures, was delivered to the White House, Sigler, as one of the representatives, got to shake President Clinton's hand.

As a result of the petition, Congress raised the budget for breast cancer research from $95 million to $400 million. Sigler's activism prolonged her life. "The increase in funding research over the last decade has resulted in the kinds of drugs I am taking right now," said the artist in 1999.[7] Starting in Washington, *Breast Cancer Journal* traveled to museums, hospitals, and galleries around the country for years. Sixty of the images were also gathered into a book, *Hollis Sigler's Breast Cancer Journal*, with an essay by the artist. Sigler died of breast cancer in 2001, but not before she became one of the voices that brought a silent epidemic into public awareness. "Crisis," said Sigler, "seems to bring out different parts of ourselves we do not always know we possess."[8]

Art Can End Self-Pity and Isolation

When we see art about another person's experience with illness, it can help to relieve the feelings of "Why me?" that poor health can bring. Realizing that others have endured the difficulties we now face gives us the strength to endure them, too. Pain is isolating, but making and viewing art can ease the hurt. These images can be so compelling that one of Dan Savage's paintings about having cancer was stolen from an auction.

DAN SAVAGE

When he was twenty years old and a student at Lancaster University, Dan Savage (English, b. 1982) felt a small lump in his right testicle.[9] His doctor was almost certain it was nothing, but tests revealed that the lump was a teratoma, the tumor of an aggressive testicular cancer. The most common malignancy in young men, testicular cancer has a high rate of cure with early detection. Savage had a professor who survived testicular cancer and always told his students to check themselves. Savage, who did this conscientiously, went to the doctor the same day he found the lump. Referring to his cancer, surgery, and chemotherapy, the artist says, "I accepted it and used it for inspiration."[10]

Savage documented the illness and treatment by drawing every day, despite his condition. When his right hand was hooked up to an IV, he drew with his left. These drawings eased his stress and also became the basis for thirteen highly articulate works in charcoal and paint called *A Walk in the Park*. The title comes from an unthinking remark by one of his doctors who said that because Savage was young and strong, the chemotherapy would be nothing, just like a walk in the park. Of course it was not. Done in black, white, and blood red, Savage's images show him in obvious pain, bending in nausea, losing his hair, attached to medical devices, and praying. After chemotherapy, he remained well and now has his own business designing architectural glass.

Like Lance Armstrong, who had testicular cancer and does enormous good throughout the world, Dan Savage became a public presence. After making a speech to the hospital's medical personnel, he gave a presentation at the annual conference of the Teenage Cancer Trust and donated one of his artworks to their charity auction, which was when it was stolen. Savage, who has also been on television and radio, believes testicular cancer should not be an embarrassing subject. He also emphasizes the importance of early detection in this illness on the rise in young men. "By talking about it all," says Savage, "I show there is life after cancer."[11]

AIDS

PUBLIC PRESENCE, SOCIAL ACTION, AND PHILANTHROPY

Illness may be isolating, but we can combat its isolation with action. One of the ways we take action is by admitting we have the disease and then working publicly to eradicate it. This takes bravery, especially if there is a social stigma associated with the disease, and one of the most heavily stigmatized conditions is AIDS. Keith Haring had AIDS, but he never denied he was ill. Instead, he made posters to combat the spread of HIV infection and set up a philanthropic foundation to carry on his work after he died.

KEITH HARING

Keith Haring (American, 1958–1990) was a generous man.[12] Even as a child he would treat people to ice cream at the local store in Kutztown, Pennsylvania, and as an adult he gave away many works of art as gifts. His friend Julia Gruen said that Haring would spend the month of December creating art to give as Christmas presents. Haring's work has a bold graphic style that turns cartoon images into fine art. Starting as a graffiti artist in the subway, he eventually gained world fame and great commercial success. One of his projects, a mural for the Princess Grace Maternity Hospital in Monaco, greatly pleased Princess Caroline. "When I look at it," she said, "it makes me happy—it's just bursting with life."[13]

When Haring painted the mural in 1989, he had already been diagnosed with AIDS the year before. AIDS severely impacted the gay community in the 1980s, and Haring lost many of his friends. Although the artist thought he would get the illness, when he found out it was still a shock. But "you can't despair," he insisted, "because if you do, you just give up and you stop."[14] With a strong interest in social causes, Haring made posters for AIDS awareness and against apartheid, nuclear weapons, and drugs. To ensure that his work would continue, the artist set up a foundation in 1989.

The Keith Haring Foundation continues his commitment to helping both children and AIDS organizations. Some of the charities it supports are UNICEF; the Children's Village; the Special Olympics; Best Buddies; amFAR, which works to stop the global AIDS epidemic; the Gay Men's Health Crisis in its fight against AIDS; and God's Love We Deliver, which prepares and delivers meals to homebound people with AIDS, cancer, and other debilitating conditions. At Haring's memorial service, his sister Kay spoke about her brother's philanthropy: "His generous nature reached to touch virtually millions, and the canvas on which he drew became the whole world."[15]

Self-Disclosure, Medicines, and Care

Of all the places ravaged by AIDS, none is more affected than Africa, and perhaps nowhere has the stigma of this illness been greater.[16] Within Africa, the largest AIDS population is in South Africa, and there is extreme prejudice against people with the disease. When a

South African woman, Gugu Diamini, revealed that she was HIV-positive in 1998, her neighbors stoned and beat her to death. A memorial wall in Durban's Central Park was dedicated to Diamini in 2000, and there are now AIDS programs in South Africa. But the numbers of sick people are growing, the prejudice remains, and it is difficult to get medicine if you are HIV-positive and poor. Our next artists, a group of twelve women with AIDS, bravely exhibit their art about the illness and publicly tell their stories. Their work is a political statement to reduce the stigma of AIDS by putting personal faces on the pandemic. Through testimonials of their experience in images and words, they want other poor people to receive the medications so desperately needed for survival.

NOMAWETHU, NONDUMISO HLWELE, VICTORIA, NOLOYISO, BULELWA NOKWE, THOZAMA, BONGIWE, NTOMBIZODWA SOMLAYI, MARIA, NOMONDE, NCEDEKA, BABALWA CEKISO

Twelve South African women—Nomawethu (b. 1978), Nondumiso Hlwele (b. 1974), Victoria (b. 1968), Noloyiso (b. 1972), Bulelwa Nokwe (b. 1969), Thozama (b. 1981), Bongiwe (b. 1975), Ntombizodwa Somlayi (b. 1970), Maria (1965–2002 [she died in a traffic accident]), Nomonde (b. 1980), Ncedeka (b. 1977), and Babalwa Cekiso (b. 1975)—show their paintings and their photographs and write about their experience with AIDS in the book *Long Life . . . Positive HIV Stories*.[17] They come from Khayelitsha, the South African township hardest hit by AIDS, and are members of the Bambanani Women's Group, a support group for HIV-positive individuals. There is also a traveling exhibit of their paintings called *Body Maps*. I went from New York to Philadelphia to see their art and it is wonderful. The women do life-size images in water-based paints on large sheets of heavy brown wrapping paper, showing themselves in the foreground and a partner in the background. The partner's body is generally one color but their own bodies tell the story of a life with illness. They lie down on the paper, trace their body outlines, and then paint on the image, revealing how and where AIDS and its associated opportunistic illnesses have affected them. They paint difficulties such as skin problems, heart ailments, and tuberculosis, as well as their life experiences, showing pregnancy as a child in the womb. The artists add words around their self-portraits to give further information. All of the paintings are beautiful, original, and different from each other, and each one is a map of courage.

The work was created as part of the AIDS and Society Research Unit at the University of Cape Town. This outreach program, called the Memory Box Project, was directed by Jonathan Morgan and based on a project in Uganda called *Mapping Our Lives.* A combined form of art therapy, narrative therapy, and body work to relieve the stress of illness, it was originally intended to help people create a legacy for their children who would become orphans. But instead the South Africa project is called *Long Life* because the women look to the future rather than death, and with medications from MSF (Médecins sans Frontières—Doctors without Borders), they have increased hope. These women are among the fortunate few poor people who are receiving the much needed ARVs (antiretroviral medicines) against AIDS. Their documented experience counteracts the idea that poor individuals will not keep up the regimen of taking medicine. "This is the most important thing to us," insists Bulelwa Nokwe, "like air."[18]

The artists also assert that other low-income people need access to lifesaving medications. "When you're suffering," states Babalwa Cekiso, "it's a basic human right to get the right medicines."[19] Cekiso is a political activist who believes that people should speak out publicly about their illness and care. "I'm HIV-positive," she says, "and I believe we mustn't hide if we are one of the lucky ones to get treatment."[20] Their doctor, Herman Reuter, who is very dedicated to eradicating AIDS, takes care of the women's health and administers their ARVs. "We don't call him Herman," explains Victoria. "We call him Themba. It means 'hope' in Xhosa, and that is what he brings us."[21]

The stigma against AIDS is slowly starting to erode due to AIDS programs and because people like these artists are speaking out. When Bongiwe disclosed her condition in church, the congregation completely accepted her as an HIV-positive person. "It's not like that everywhere," admits Bongiwe. "I know of some girls who sleep in the streets because their families threw them out."[22] Providing medication to the poor that transforms AIDS from a death sentence into an illness that people can live with would further lessen the prejudice. It has given strength and hope to the artists of the Bambanani Women's Group. "We want to teach people living with HIV how to live with HIV," they say. "We want people outside to know that it is not the end of the world."[23]

Bravery and Vulnerability

Bravery despite vulnerability takes enormous courage. We see this in the Bambanani artists and also in Ernie Pepion, who said, "I am an artist, Blackfeet Indian, and am physically disabled."[24] In his art he exposes the prejudice toward both quadriplegics and people of color. "Some people in ignorance behave as though they are superior to those who are not of their race or who are disabled," he said. "They avoid interacting with those who are unlike them. Through painting I show my experience of these degradations."[25] Even his signature proclaims his condition. The artist combines the last three letters of "Pepion" into an image of a wheelchair.

ERNIE PEPION

When Eewokso Ernie Pepion (American, 1943–2005) returned from Vietnam, he was a decorated veteran with the Army Commendation Medal for his service.[26] Back home in Montana, Pepion thought life would continue on as it had before the war: working on the family ranch and riding in rodeos. But we can only presume what our life will be like, we can never predict it.

Four years later, in November 1971, Pepion was in the passenger seat of a car that crashed; his neck was broken, leaving him quadriplegic. After being treated in Montana, he was sent to the Long Beach, California, VA hospital that specializes in spinal cord injuries. It was there that he learned to paint from a man in an iron lung. The man, who had polio, could only be out of the iron lung for one hour a day, and he spent that hour making art. At first the hospital staff urged Pepion to use his left hand to work because it was stronger. "But I couldn't paint very good that way," he said,[27] so they made him a hand/forearm brace to support his right hand and help him hold a brush.

Returning home, Pepion found he was no longer interested in ranching. Instead, he enrolled as an art major in Montana State University, from which he graduated with honors and where he went on to earn a master of fine arts degree. Using a motorized easel made for him by the school's department of mechanical engineering, Pepion was able to create the large oil paintings that show his experiences as a quadriplegic and a Native American. "Women and children in my paintings tell of my unfulfilled dream for a family," he related.[28] No longer able to ride, he painted himself in a wheelchair with a wooden hobby horse between his knees, careening through the desert, winning a horse race, or hunting buffalo. In another painting he has become the buffalo, standing strong and flinging the wheelchair away. "When the

stick horse of my childhood appears in my painting the humor is obvious," he explained. "But as one looks deeper, the irony is apparent."[29]

In the last year of his life, Pepion's health began to fail, but two
weeks before he died, he was awarded the 2005 Montana Governor's
Award for the Arts. Pepion's work reveals his humor and his strength,
and is gaining a national reputation. "I am trying to show," he said,
"that even though we handicapped people may have physical limitations we can conquer anything mentally."[30]

Art Makes a More Beautiful World

Everyone who creates art contributes to the world, because art makes
the world more beautiful. By filling the world with beauty, art is like
flowers. There was a time on Earth, eons ago, before plants had flowers. The world proceeded and the plants reproduced. But then in the
late Jurassic period,[31] about 155 million years ago, the first flowers appeared and the world began to bloom with beauty. Our world could
go on without flowers or art, but it would not be the same. Teaching
others to make art and providing employment for artists keeps the
beauty alive for generations. This is what Eiichi Mitsui has done and
he has accomplished it through the challenge of his deafness.

EIICHI MITSUI

Eiichi Mitsui (Tamekichi III, Japanese, b. 1935) was born into a family
of ceramic artists and carries on their tradition of making ko-Kutani
ware, which is also known as old Kutani or classic Kutani.[32] This beautiful art form involves creating porcelain ceramics in a variety of shapes
and sizes and then painting the white porcelain surface with colorful
glazes to create birds, flowers, and landscapes, along with geometric
patterns. To form these images, a Kutani artist must be both classically

trained and an excellent observer of nature. Mitsui also goes by his professional name of Tamekichi III, a Japanese custom that shows he is the third master in a specific lineage of artists. The original Tamekichi was his grandfather. In addition to receiving traditional training within his family, Mitsui obtained a degree in ceramics from the Kanazawa Arts and Crafts University. He now heads the Sanmeido Company, which makes Kutani ware and oversees its artistic production; his wife, Nariko, who is also deaf, takes care of the business affairs. Most of their employees are deaf, because they want to provide opportunities for deaf individuals and have an atmosphere where people can communicate freely in Japanese Sign Language (JSL).

In addition to JSL, Eiichi and Nariko Mitsui have also learned American Sign Language (ASL). Leticia Arellano, a graduate of Gallaudet University in Washington, D.C., and a volunteer for the deaf in Japan, became their teacher. "They were the best ASL students that I ever had," she relates. "They also gave me many opportunities to learn about Japanese Sign Language, Deaf culture in Japan, moral values and more."[33] Using ASL Eiichi and Nariko Mitsui taught ceramic classes at the National Institute for the Deaf at the Rochester Institute of Technology and at Gallaudet University. Peggy Reichard, a Gallaudet ceramics instructor, welcomed Matsui, saying, "The students are privileged to learn this ancient art form."[34]

Mitsui has also taught at Ratchasuda College in Thailand. Winning great honors for his work, he donated a large group of ceramics to both the National Institute for the Deaf at the Rochester Institute of Technology and Gallaudet University for their permanent collections. Seeing his work on an ongoing basis is a continuing inspiration for the deaf art students at these schools. In 2005 Eiichi and Nariko Matsui were given the LCCF Edward Miner Gallaudet Award as international leaders working to benefit the deaf.

Helping Human and Nonhuman Animals

Our Earth is one great whole, and Temple Grandin helps both the human and nonhuman animals that comprise its wholeness. She accomplishes this by using abilities that come from her autism. Grandin lectures widely on autism, speaking about her personal experiences in an effort to help others, and is also a leading designer of humane animal handling facilities.

Grandin believes autism gives her insight into animal behavior, saying, "Animals with extreme talents are similar to autistic savants."[35] There are savants who may not be able to tell right from left or have severely impaired communication, yet they show splinter skills, which are islands of talent, usually in mathematics, art, music, or memory, that are far above those of an average person. Animals can also show extreme abilities. Grandin cites Arctic terns who learn and remember an 18,000-mile migration route and gray squirrels who remember when and where they bury hundreds of nuts for the winter. She feels that her deeper understanding of animals compensates for her difficulty with interpersonal skills as an autistic person. "Autism made school and social life hard," she reveals, "but it made animals easy."[36]

TEMPLE GRANDIN

Temple Grandin (American, b. 1947), who says she thinks in pictures, cannot remember phone numbers, learn foreign languages, or do algebra.[37] Yet she designs huge steel and concrete livestock-handling facilities in her mind, rotates them at any angle, and visualizes how the animals will walk through them. Her large, detailed floor plans of the structures that enable others to build them are so beautifully made that she exhibits these drawings as works of art. Grandin, who credits autism with giving her a strong ability to visualize, is now an associate professor of animal science at Colorado State University. She has written books and articles on autism and the treatment of animals, lectures widely, has her own business, and is constantly evolving as a human being. Autistic people usually resist change, but Grandin makes self-transformation a focus of her life.

With a goal of more humane treatment for animals, Grandin has designed more than half of all the livestock-handling equipment and facilities in the United States and Canada and has also designed facilities in Mexico, Europe, Australia, and New Zealand. She knows what will be most comfortable for the animals, because she has discovered that autistic people and animals see the world in similar ways. They both have a strong visual response to their environment and notice details that are not apparent to nonautistic human beings. While most people filter their environment and only see what they know, animals and autistic people lack this filter and see more of what is in front of them.

To provide a less stressful experience for animals, Grandin has designed a center track restrainer system that gently supports them and curved lanes for them to walk that use their natural inclination toward circling behavior. The scoring system she created to assess the handling of animals at meat plants locates instances of cruelty and promotes more humane treatment. Grandin advocates bringing ritual into slaughterhouses, such as a moment of silence as an act of respect for the animals. She thinks it would help to prevent people working in the plants from becoming callous or cruel. "I believe," she says, "that the place where an animal dies is a sacred one."[38]

Turning autism's capacity to focus into an intensity of work, Grandin dedicates her life to the humane treatment of animals and to reforming the care and education of people with autism. "I want to leave something behind," she says. "I want to make a positive contribution."[39]

Fighting Health Hazards Throughout the World

We are constantly exposed to toxins, but Monona Rossol is determined to protect us. As a chemist, an industrial hygienist, and one of the world's leading experts in health hazards and the arts, Rossol is the head of ACTS (Arts, Crafts, and Theater Safety), a nonprofit organization that exposes the multiple dangers to our well-being. But this was not her original path. Rossol was a ceramic artist and a singer until what doctors presumed was a terminal illness changed her life.

MONONA ROSSOL

By the time Monona Rossol (American, b. 1936) collapsed in the emergency room of St. Vincent's Hospital in New York, she had been sick for well over a year.[40] It was in the early 1970s, and her weight had dropped from 145 pounds to 103, but none of the doctors she saw knew what was wrong with her. When Rossol regained consciousness in the hospital, she had a flush characteristic of a rare cancer called carcinoid syndrome. A 5-hydroxyindoleacetic acid test found further evidence of the disease, as did the discovery of small masses throughout her body and the shadow in her brain near the pituitary. But one doctor at St. Vincent's disagreed with the general diagnosis. "So I went with the doctor who said I didn't have it," admits Rossol.[41] "He blocked all the surgery the other doctors wanted to perform." Instead, he gave her medications, trying to stabilize her heart, blood pressure, and endocrine system. "Nothing helped," explains Rossol, "so I gave up, went home, and waited to die." But somehow she recovered: "I was really kind of surprised when I lived."

At the time of her illness, Rossol was a ceramic artist and a teacher of ceramics, who also helped her students with safety issues. Her interest in health and safety began when she was working as a chemist in the 1960s to pay for graduate school in art. "I realized they were using the same chemicals in the art department that I was working with as a chemist," she says. But the chemists were protected, while the artists had no protection and no ventilation. "I didn't think that when you changed your major you became immune."[42] In 1977, a few years after her recovery, Rossol, along with Cate Jenkins and Michael McCann, started the Center for Occupational Hazards in New York, a nonprofit organization to protect visual artists. She also became an industrial hygienist, a professional concerned with occupational health and environmental problems.

In 1987 Rossol started her own nonprofit organization, ACTS (Arts, Crafts, and Theater Safety), incorporating her experience as both a visual artist and a performer. She has written seven books and numerous articles while publishing *ACTS FACTS*, a monthly newsletter on health hazards and the arts. Rossol's achievements result in better conditions for hundreds of thousands of people, from art students to union members, opera singers, theater audiences, paleontologists working on dinosaur bones, and aborigine painters in Australia.

Constantly traveling throughout the United States and the world to help others, Rossol describes herself as "a ball of fire." I am an officer on the board of directors for ACTS and have known Rossol for years, but her schedule still amazes me. I once asked her if she ever gets any rest. "Well, maybe for a few moments now and then," she replied, "just for contrast."[43]

Ancient Benefits of Illness

All of the artists in this chapter have consciously contributed to society, but artists may also make unconscious contributions. It is possible that at the dawn of human history certain aspects of our culture might have originated because of the challenges faced by individuals like Dane Bottino (American, b. 1990).[44] He is an autistic savant who is gifted in visual art and draws compulsively. At one point, Bottino copied styles of art across time, including prehistoric cave images. This behavior gave his neurologist, Dr. Bruce L. Miller, an interesting idea: What if autistic individuals with a compulsive need to draw were responsible for some of the first attempts at cave art?

I agree with Miller that this scenario is possible, and I propose that instances of prehistoric painting and sculpture may also have sprung from a desire to communicate by people who had no capacity for speech or who had difficulty speaking. Like spoken language, images are a form of communication. Around the time in early childhood when Dane Bottino lost the ability to speak, he began to communicate through images. Today, the teenage Bottino, who is capable of speech, still prefers visual communication.

Deaf children with visual talent and no verbal language also spontaneously communicate through art. In chapter 11 we saw how Harry R. Williams and Ann Silver drew pictures to converse with the hearing members of their family, and John Lewis Clarke made small sculptures to tell his family about the animals he saw near their home. All of them were deaf, and no one taught them to do this; they were natural and unprompted acts. So it is possible that in ancient times, people without spoken language may have used charcoal to draw or molded clay from the riverbank as a means of communication, resulting in cave art and prehistoric sculpture.

There is no proof for my conjectures or those of Miller, and prehistoric art appears to have emerged independently in many parts of the world and at different intervals. But it is possible that in some of these instances, it may have originated from the talents of challenged individuals.

Wholeness and Perfection

Challenges can inspire creativity and strength, yet we often view them as defects and long for a perfection that is impossible to attain. In Jungian psychology, perfection is an abstract concept, an unreachable goal, while wholeness is within us all the time.[45] Wholeness is our core self that cannot be destroyed, and when we access it through creativity the result is art. While perfection is an end, wholeness is ongoing and unique for each person. It is a place that transcends perfection, a natural force that physical illness cannot diminish or take away—and it is available to everyone. Nobody is perfect, yet all of us are whole.

By embracing our wholeness we realize there is a choice: We can focus on discomfort or we can transform. And when we change ourselves, we change our world.

Notes

To view work produced by artists in this book, please go to www. tobizausner.com and click on the book title *When Walls Become Doorways*. You will be directed to a list of websites showing the artists' work arranged alphabetically by name.

Introduction: My Story

1. Zhao Jin-Xiang, *Soaring Crane Qigong*, trans. Chen Hui-xian and Zhu An, comp. and ed. Maureen Goss (New York: Soaring Crane Qigong Institute, n.d.).

Chapter 1: What Is a Transforming Illness?

1. Mircea Eliade, *Shamanism: Archaic Techniques of Ecstasy*, trans. W. R. Trask (Princeton N.J.: Princeton University Press, 1974).

2. In his book *The Discovery of the Unconscious* Ellenberger concentrates on emotional illness, but the people he cites often have physical symptoms as well. He finds that illness changed the lives of five of the founders of modern psychology: Fechner, Freud, Jung, Steiner, and Nietzsche. Jung recognized his illness was associated with a time of transformation and noticed the same phenomenon in his colleague Richard

Wilhelm, the scholar of Chinese philosophy. He comments on this in Wilhelm's book *Secret of the Golden Flower.* Henri Ellenberger, *The Discovery of the Unconscious* (New York: Basic Books, 1970); C. G. Jung., foreword and commentary in Richard Wilhelm, *The Secret of the Golden Flower* trans. Cary F. Baynes (New York: Harcourt, Brace and World, 1962).

3. Julian Treuherz, "Introduction to Alma-Tadema," in *Sir Lawrence Alma-Tadema,* ed. Edwin Becker, Edward Morris, Elizabeth Prettejohn, and Julian Treuherz (New York: Rizzoli, 1996); obituary of Sir Lawrence Alma Tadema, 1836–1912, *Times* (London), June 26, 1912, *Victorian Art in Britain,* http://www.victorianartinbritain. co.uk/obituary/alma-tadema.htm.

4. Philip Sandblom, *Creativity and Disease* (New York: Marion Boyars, 1996), 115–16.

5. Diane Tepfer, "Janet Sobel at Gary Snyder," *Art in America,* July 2002, http://www.findarticles.com/p/articles/mi_m1248/is_7_90/ai_88582370; Gary Snyder, telephone communication, June 21, 2005; Alexi Worth, "Janet Sobel: Gary Snyder Fine Art," *ArtForum,* April 2002, http://www.findarticles.com/p/articles/ mi_m0268/is_8_40/ai_85459270.

6. Lynn Adele, *Spirited Journeys: Self-Taught Artists of the Twentieth Century* (Austin: University of Texas Press, 1997), 68–71.

7. Sandblom, *Creativity and Disease,* 20.

8. Rudolph Ballentine, *Radical Healing* (New York: Three Rivers Press, 1999), 437.

9. Ilya Prigogine and Isabelle Stengers, *Order Out of Chaos* (Toronto: Bantam Books, 1984).

10. Information on Dory Coffee is from personal communications, December 2 and December 7, 2005.

11. Ibid., December 2, 2005.

12. Ajit Mookerjee, *Tantra Art: Its Philosophy and Physics* (Paris: Ravi Kumar, 1966).

13. S. R. Maddi, "Hardiness Training at Illinois Bell Telephone," in *Health Promotion Evaluation,* ed. J. P. Opatz (Stevens Point, Wis.: National Wellness Institute, 1987), 101–15.

14. Karen Koenig, *Sacred Process* (New York: Kärelek Pres, 1993); Steven Koenig, M.D., personal communication, December 13, 2005.

15. Koenig, *Sacred Process,* 78.

16. Ibid., 78–79.

17. Salvatore R. Maddi, "Hardiness: An Operationalization of Existential Courage," *Journal of Humanistic Psychology* 44, no. 3 (July 2004): 279–98.

18. E. Katz, "Creativity, Art, and the Disabled Individual," *IJAM III* (Winter 1994): 30–33.

19. Florence Ludins-Katz and Elias Katz, *The Creative Spirit* (Richmond, Calif.: National Institute of Art and Disabilities, 1990), 3.

20. American Psychological Association, APA Online, Psychology Matters, "Turning Lemons into Lemonade: Hardiness Helps People Turn Stressful Circumstances into Opportunities," http://www.psychologymatters.org/hardiness.html.

21. Emmy Werner and Ruth S. Smith, *Overcoming the Odds: High Risk Children from Birth to Adulthood* (Ithaca, N.Y.: Cornell University Press, 1992); Emmy Werner and Ruth S. Smith, *Journeys from Childhood to Midlife: Risk, Resilience, and Recovery* (Ithaca, N.Y.: Cornell University Press, 2001).

22. Adele, *Spirited Journeys*, 64–67.

23. Ibid., 66.

24. Michael Rutter, "Psychosocial Resilience and Protective Mechanisms," *American Journal of Orthopsychiatry* 57, no. 3 (1987): 57.

25. Albert Bandura, *Self-Efficacy: The Exercise of Control* (New York: W. H. Freeman, 1997).

26. Adele, *Spirited Journeys*, 76–79.

27. Calvin Hall and Gardner Lindzey, *Theories of Personality* (New York: John Wiley and Sons, 1978), 52–53.

28. Mai-Mai Sze, trans. and ed., *The Mustard Seed Garden Manual of Painting by Chieh Tzu Yuan Chuan*, a facsimile of the 1887–88 Shanghai ed. (Princeton, N.J.: Bollingen Series, Princeton University Press, 1963), 17.

29. Henry P. Bowie, *On the Laws of Japanese Painting* (New York: Dover, 1952), 78–79.

30. Hayden Herrera, *Frida: A Biography of Frida Kahlo* (New York: Harper and Row, 1983), 75.

31. Mihaly Csikszentmihalyi, *Flow: The Psychology of Optimal Experience* (New York: Harper and Row, 1990); Mihaly Csikszentmihalyi, *Creativity: Flow and the Psychology of Discovery and Invention* (New York: HarperCollins, 1996).

32. Giorgio Vasari, *The Lives of the Artists*, trans. Gaston Du C. De Vere (1568; New York: Knopf, 1996), 937.

33. Ruth Richards, "The Arts and Self-Expression in Mental Health" (address at the Carter Center, Atlanta, Ga., March 16, 2004); Ruth Richards, "Introduction Part II: Everyday Creators: Psychological Problems and Creativity," in *Eminent Creativity,*

Everyday Creativity, and Health, ed. Mark Runco and Ruth Richards (Norwood, N.J.: Ablex, 1997), 97–98.

34. Carel van Mander, *Dutch and Flemish Artists*, trans. C. van de Wall (1604; New York: McFarlane, Warde, McFarlane, 1936), 61–63. The artist's name is spelled Quintijn Messijs.

35. Trenchard Cox, *David Cox* (London: Phoenix House, 1947), 18–19.

36. Celeste Rhodes, "Growth from Deficiency Creativity to Being Creativity," in Runco and Richards, *Eminent Creativity, Everyday Creativity, and Health*, 247–63.

37. Howard Gardner, *Art, Mind and Brain* (New York: Basic Books, 1982), 355.

38. George Tooker, personal communication, May 1999; Thomas H. Garver, *George Tooker* (San Francisco: Pomegranate Artbooks, 1992).

39. Information on Bluemner is from Judith Zilczer, *Oscar Bluemner* (Washington, D.C.: Smithsonian Institution Press, 1979); "Oscar Bluemner: American Modernist" (information accompanying an exhibition at Barbara Mathes Gallery, New York City, April 12–June 6, 1997).

40. Quoted in Jenny Hontz, "The Healing Canvas," *Los Angeles Times*, March 20, 2006, http://www.latimes.com/features/health/la-he-art20mar20,0,604786.story?coll=la-home-health.

41. Information on Wells is from Marc Alexander, *Artists Above All* (N.P.: Mouth and Foot Painting Artists, 2005), 184–86; promotional material from MFPA, Mouth and Foot Painting Artists.

42. Quoted in Alexander, *Artists Above All*, 184–85.

43. Information on Matisse is from Jack Flam, *Matisse: The Man and His Art* (Ithaca, N.Y.: Cornell University Press, 1986); Jack Flam, ed., *Matisse: A Retrospective* (New York: Park Lane, 1988); Jack Flam, ed., *Matisse on Art* (New York: E. P. Dutton, 1978); Henri Matisse, "Matisse Speaks" (Henri Matisse interviewed by E. Tériade), *Art News*, November 1951, in Flam, *Matisse: A Retrospective*, 27–28; Hilary Spurling, *The Unknown Matisse: A Life of Henri Matisse: The Early Years, 1869–1908* (Berkeley: University of California Press, 1998); Hilary Spurling, *Matisse the Master: A Life of Henri Matisse: The Conquest of Color, 1909–1954* (Berkeley: University of California Press, 1998); John Elderfield, *The Cut-Outs of Henri Matisse* (New York: George Braziller, 1978); François Gilot and Carlton Lake, *Life with Picasso* (New York: McGraw-Hill, 1964); Gotthard Jedlicka, "Die Matisse Kapelle in Vence" (1955), in Flam, *Matisse: A Retrospective*, 378–79; Alan Riding, "Starting with the Secular, Ending Up with the Divine," *New York Times*, June 5, 2002, E2.

44. Flam, *Man and His Art*, 26–29.

45. Matisse believed it was appendicitis, ulcerative colitis, or typhlitis. Sandblom and Flam call it appendicitis, and Spurling says it was a hernia. I think it may have been ulcerative colitis because the attacks seemed to come during times of stress.

46. Flam, *Man and His Art*, 27–28.

47. Ibid., 29.

48. Sandblom, *Creativity and Disease*, 32–33, 156.

49. Flam, *Matisse on Art*, 134.

50. Ibid.

51. Sandblom, *Creativity and Disease*, 32.

52. Gilot and Lake, *Life with Picasso*, 99.

53. Sandblom, *Creativity and Disease*, 156–57.

54. Flam, *Matisse on Art*, 108.

55. Riding, "Starting with the Secular," E2.

56. Flam, *Matisse on Art*, 84.

57. Jedlicka, "Die Matisse Kapelle in Vence," 378.

58. Ibid.

Chapter 2: Turning Poor Health into a Transforming Illness

1. Lisa Fittipaldi, *A Brush with Darkness: Learning to Paint after Losing My Sight* (Kansas City, Mo.: Andrews McMeel, 2004), x.

2. Information on Fittipaldi is from ibid.; her website, http://www.lisafittipaldi.com/; Mind's Eye Foundation, www.mindseyefoundation.org.

3. Fittipaldi, *Brush with Darkness*, x.

4. Ibid., 193.

5. Rolf E. Stenersen, *Edvard Munch—Close-Up of a Genius*, trans. and ed. Reidar Dittmann (1944; first English translation published 1969; Oslo: Sem & Stenersen A/S, 1994); Bente Torjusen, *Words and Images of Edvard Munch* (New York: Thames and Hudson, 1986); Per Amann, *Edvard Munch*, trans. Stephen Gorman (San Diego: Padre, 1990).

6. Reinhold Heller, *Munch: His Life and Work* (Chicago: University of Chicago Press, 1984), 20.

7. Carl Gustav Jung, *Symbols of Transformation*, trans. R. F. C. Hull (Princeton, N.J.: Bollingen Series, Princeton University Press, 1976), 180–81.

8. James G. Ravin and Christie Kenyon, "The Blindness of Edgar Degas," in *The Eye of the Artist*, ed. Michael F. Marmor and James G. Ravin (St. Louis: Mosby, 1997), 193–201.

9. Jan Greenberg and Sandra Jordan, *Chuck Close Up Close* (New York: DK Publishing, 1998), 27.

10. Ginny Ruffner (Artist Images lecture, University of Washington, Seattle campus), October 3, 2003).

11. Rosamond Bacou, *Odilon Redon Pastels*, trans. B. Rehl (New York: George Braziller, 1987), 14.

12. Ibid., 13–14.

13. All information and quotations are from personal communications with Pamela Mailman on March 24 and April 3, 2000, and October 11, 2005.

14. Richard Wilhelm, *The I Ching or Book of Changes*, trans. Cary F. Baynes (Princeton, N.J.: Bollingen Series, Princeton University Press, 1971), 104, 515.

15. Information on Nichols is from his website, http://michaelnicknichols.com/article/adventures and http://michaelnicknichols.com/article/philosophy, and from personal communications by telephone and e-mail with his son Ian Nichols, October 7, 2005.

16. Quoted at http://michaelnicknichols.com/article/philosophy.

17. Helen Evans Ramsaran, personal communications, February 17 and 22, 2006.

18. Mark H. Beers and Robert Berkow, eds., *The Merck Manual of Diagnosis and Therapy*, 17th ed. (Whitehouse Station, N.J.: Merck Research Laboratories, 1999), 1507–8; American Psychiatric Association, *DSM-IV-R: Diagnostic and Statistical Manual of Mental Disorders*, 3rd ed. (Washington, D.C.: American Psychiatric Association, 1994), 473–75.

19. I. Bergstrom, "Frida Kahlo: 'I'm a champion of the world when it comes to surgical interventions,'" *Lakartidningen* 101, no. 7 (February 12, 2004): 604–7.

20. Lori Sue Schmitt, *Even a Bird with Broken Wings Can Fly* (Otsego, Mich.: PageFree Publishing, 2004), 9; www.artbylori.net.

21. Information on Horan is from personal communication, May 26, 2006; "Meet the Artists: Carolyn (Lyons) Horan," Infinitec.org, http://www.infinitec.org/learn/art/horan.htm; "VSA Arts Announces a 2005 Call for Children's Arts," December 6, 2004, http://www.vsarts.org/x1109.xml.

22. "VSA Arts Announces a 2005 Call for Children's Arts."

23. Horan, personal communication, May 26, 2006.

24. Ibid.

Chapter 3: Creativity and the Transforming Illness

1. All quotes and information are from Phyllis Teiko, personal communication, May 15, 2006.

2. Darcy Lynn, personal communication, February 2002; Darcy Lynn, *Myself Resolved: An Artist's Experience with Lymphoma* (Philadelphia: Meniscus Health Care Communications, 1994).

3. Lynn, *Myself Resolved,* ix.

4. Lynn Adele, *Spirited Journeys: Self-Taught Artists of the Twentieth Century* (Austin: University of Texas Press, 1997), 57–58.

5. Information about Leonilson and Herring is from Holland Cotter, "Art in Review Projects' Oliver Herring and Leonilson," Museum of Modern Art, February 16, 1996, http://query.nytimes.com/gst/fullpage.html?res=9507E3D71239F935A25 751C0A960958260; Maria Bilske, *The Penelope,* 1993, at the Tate Museum, January 2005, http://www.tate.org.uk/servlet/ViewWork?cgroupid=999999874&workid=66774&searchid=7402&tabview=text; Mason Klein, Oliver Herring: Max Protech—New York, *ArtForum,* May 2002, http://www.findarticles.com/p/articles/mi_m0268/is_9_40/ai_86647191.

6. *Art: 21,* PBS interview, http://www.pbs.org/art21/artists/herring/clip2.html.

7. Information on Chihuly is from his website, http://www.chihuly.com; "Chihuly, Dale," *Current Biography,* August 1995, http://www.chihuly.com/essays/news_current biography.html. (Reprinted from *Current Biography,* August 1995 issue. Copyright © 1995 by The H.W. Wilson Company, used by permission of the publisher.)

8. "Chihuly, Dale."

9. Margaret Bourke-White, *Portrait of Myself* (New York: Simon and Schuster, 1963).

10. Cecilia Beaux, *Background with Figures* (New York: Houghton Mifflin, 1930); Tara Leigh Tappert, *Cecilia Beaux and the Art of Portraiture* (Washington, D.C.: Smithsonian Institution Press, 1995).

11. VSA Artists Registry, Rebecca Abell, http://www.vsarts.org/prebuilt/artists/registry/artistdetail.cfm?ArtistID=1774.

12. Information on Abell is from personal communication, May 28, 2006; VSA Artists Registry, Rebecca Abell.

13. Abell, May 28, 2006.

14. Ibid.

15. James Hamilton, *Turner* (New York: Random House, 1997), 378–81; A. J. Finberg, *The Life of J. M. W. Turner, R. A.*, rev. ed. (Oxford: Oxford University Press, 1967), 434–38; Jack Lindsay, *Turner: The Man and His Art* (New York: Franklin Watts, 1985), 157; John Gage, *J. M. W. Turner: A Wonderful Range of Mind* (New Haven, Conn.: Yale University Press, 1987), 243.

16. Kathleen Maclay, "A Painter Reinvents Herself: Art Professor Katherine Sherwood's Stroke Forced Her to Learn to Paint Left-handed." *Berkeleyan* 28, no. 10 (October 13–19, 1999), copyright 1999, the Regents of the University of California, http://www.berkeley.edu/news/berkeleyan/1999/1013/painter.html; Rona Marech, "Stroke of Luck: Debilitating Illness Changes Flow of UC Professor's Artwork," *San Francisco Chronicle*, August 31, 2001, http://www.sfgate.com/cgi-bin/article.cgi?file=/chronicle/archive/2001/08/31/EB232938.DTL.

17. Marech, "Stroke of Luck."

18. Maclay, "Painter Reinvents Herself."

19. Russel Ash, *Sir Edward Burne-Jones* (New York: Harry N. Abrams, 1993); Georgiana Burne-Jones, *Memorials of Edward Burne-Jones* (1904; New York: Benjamin Blom, 1971).

20. Burne-Jones, *Memorials*, 8.

21. Winona Laduke, *The Spirit Powers of Ojibwe and Odawa Art* (Washington, D.C.: Smithsonian National Museum of the American Indian, 2000), 19.

22. Frances Spalding, *Vanessa Bell* (New Haven, Conn.: Ticknor and Fields, 1983), 104–5.

Chapter 4: Childhood Illness as an Opportunity

1. Emmy Werner and Ruth S. Smith, *Overcoming the Odds: High Risk Children from Birth to Adulthood* (Ithaca, N.Y.: Cornell University Press, 1992).

2. Information on Warhol's childhood is from Victor Bockris, *The Life and Death of Andy Warhol* (New York: Bantam Books, 1989); Victor Bockris, *Warhol: The Biography*

(Cambridge, Mass.: Da Capo Press, 2003); Bob Colacello, *Holy Terror: Andy Warhol Close Up* (New York: Cooper Square Press, 2000).

3. Dan Boughner, assistant, the Andy Warhol Museum Education Department, personal communication, May 13, 2000.

4. Matt Wrbican, assistant archivist, the Andy Warhol Museum Education Department, personal communication, March 18, 2004.

5. Ernst Kris is cited in William G. Niederland, "Clinical Aspects of Creativity," *American Imaago* 24 (1967): 6–34.

6. Information on Ryder is from Elizabeth Brown, *Albert Pinkham Ryder* (Washington, D.C.: Smithsonian Institution Press, 1989); William Innes Homer and Lloyd Goodrich, *Albert Pinkham Ryder: Painter of Dreams* (New York: Harry N. Abrams, 1989); Lloyd Goodrich, *Albert P. Ryder* (New York: George Braziller, 1959); Alexander Eliot, *Three Hundred Years of American Painting* (New York: Time, 1957).

7. Smallpox was unfortunately prevalent in mid-nineteenth-century America, and by 1840 Ryder's hometown, the seaport of New Bedford, Massachusetts, was enforcing vaccinations in response to outbreaks of the disease. In addition to contact with local clusters of the illness in New England, the active seaport of New Bedford was also exposed to smallpox from foreign sources, because it was constantly receiving ships from around the world. See Leonard Bolles Ellis, *History of New Bedford and Its Vicinity, 1602–1892* (Syracuse, N.Y.: D. Mason, 1892), 145, 146, 264, 279, 377; Jonathan Tucker, *Scourge: The Once and Future Threat of Smallpox* (New York: Atlantic Monthly Press, 2001), 31–32. Ideally the vaccines given to a population are supposed to be identical, but they can vary, a condition more pronounced in the nineteenth century than today. As a result, some people may get a more severe reaction than others, and if that reaction goes to the eyes, there is a risk of blindness. Eye problems can also occur by touching the site of the smallpox vaccination and then touching the eyes, a behavior more common among children. See World Health Organization, "Smallpox: Historical Significance," fact sheet, http://www.who.int/mediacentre/factsheets/smallpox/en/.

8. Brown, *Albert Pinkham Ryder*, 10–13.

9. Information on Brady is from Mary Panzer, *Mathew Brady and the Image of History* (Washington, D.C.: Smithsonian Institution Press, 1997). Quote appears on page 7.

10. Ibid., 14.

11. Ibid., 18.

12. All quotations from Blaine are from personal communications, March 1996.

13. Information on Blaine is from Blaine, personal communications, March 1996; Marticia Sawin, *Nell Blaine: Her Art and Life* (New York: Hudson Hills Press, 1998); Pat Van Gelder, "Close to Home," *American Artist* (February 1990): 28–35, 69–71; *Nell Blaine: Recent Oils, Watercolors, Drawings, April 6 through May 6, 1995* (catalog for the exhibition at Fischbach Gallery, New York City).

14. Ilya Prigogine and Isabelle Stengers, *Order Out of Chaos* (Toronto: Bantam Books, 1984).

15. Information on Basquiat is from Phoebe Hoban, *Basquiat: A Quick Killing in Art* (New York: Viking Press, 1998); Richard Marshall, *Jean-Michel Basquiat* (New York: Whitney Museum of American Art/Harry N. Abrams, 1992).

16. Quoted in Hoban, *Basquiat*, 17.

17. Ibid.

18. Information on Tony Smith is from Robert Storr, *Tony Smith: Architect, Painter, Sculptor* (New York: Museum of Modern Art, 1998); Harriet F. Senie, "Re-Approaching Tony Smith," *Sculpture* 17, no. 9 (November 1998), available on-line at International Sculpture Center, http://sculpture.org/documents/scmag98/tsmith/sm-tsmth.shtml; Michael Kimmelman, "A Life's Discoveries in the Geometric," *New York Times*, July 3, 1998, E29, E33. Quote appears on page 12 of Storr.

19. Storr, *Tony Smith*, 12.

20. A. W. Rossalbi, *Max Ernst*, ed. David Larkin (New York: Ballantine Books, 1975).

21. Ernst's diaries are quoted in ibid.

22. Information on O'Keeffe is from Roxana Robinson, *Georgia O'Keeffe* (New York: Harper and Row, 1989); Anita Pollitzer, *A Woman on Paper: Georgia O'Keeffe* (New York: Simon and Schuster, 1988).

23. Information on Redon is from Odilon Redon, *To Myself: Notes on Life, Art, and Artists*, trans. Mira Jacob and Jeanne L. Wasserman (New York: George Braziller, 1986; original work published as *A soi-même*, 1979); Douglas W. Druick and Peter Kort Zegers, "Painful Origins," in *Odilon Redon, Prince of Dreams*, ed. Douglas W. Druick (Chicago: Art Institute of Chicago, 1994), 13–24; Douglas W. Druick and Peter Kort Zegers, "Under a Cloud," in Druick, *Odilon Redon*, 25–72; Rosamond Bacou, *Odilon Redon Pastels*, trans. B. Rehl (New York: George Braziller, 1987); Fred

Leeman, "Redon's Spiritualism and the Rise of Mysticism," in Druick, *Odilon Redon,* 215–36.

24. Redon, *To Myself,* 10.

25. Ibid., 10–11.

Chapter 5: Early Accidents as a Turning Point

1. Information on Kahlo is from Hayden Herrera, *Frida: A Biography of Frida Kahlo* (New York: Harper and Row, 1983); Hayden Herrera, *Frida Kahlo: The Paintings* (New York: HarperCollins, 1993); Carlos Fuentes and Sarah M. Lowe, *The Diary of Frida Kahlo: An Intimate Self-Portrait* (New York: Harry N. Abrams, 1995).

2. The psychologist Danielle Knafo believes that Kahlo's careful method of painting was a result of restricted movement, but this is not the case. Her arms, wrists, and hands were unaffected by illness, and she filled her diary with looser and more calligraphic works. Kahlo, who was capable of a variety of styles, chose to work in an elegant and precise method of painting on canvas. Illness influenced the size of her works rather than their style. Her paintings are not large because smaller canvases are easier to manage for an artist who is lying in bed or sitting in a wheelchair. Danielle Knafo, "In Her Own Image: Self-Representation in the Art of Frida Kahlo and Anna Mendieta," *Art Criticism* 11, no. 2 (1996): 4. Kahlo's freely drawn sketches can be seen in Fuentes and Lowe, *Diary of Frida Kahlo.*

3. Herrera, *Frida,* 63.

4. Spina Bifida Association of America, "Facts about Spina Bifida," http://www.sbaa.org/html/sbaa_facts.html; Queensland Clinical Genetics Service, http://www.spinabifida.org/occulta.htm.

5. Cited in Philip Sandblom, *Creativity and Disease* (New York: Marion Boyars, 1996), 12–13.

6. Stephen Conrad, M.D., orthopedic surgeon and chief of staff, Seton Medical Center, Daly City, Calif., telephone communication, May 28, 2004.

7. Herrera, *Frida,* 76.

8. Cited in Sandblom, *Creativity and Disease,* 13.

9. Information on Thurber is from Burton Bernstein, *Thurber* (New York: Dodd, Mead, 1975); Harrison Kinney, *James Thurber: His Life and Times* (New York: Henry Holt, 1995); Thomas Fensch, ed., *Conversations with James Thurber* (Jackson: University Press of Mississippi, 1989).

10. "Sympathetic Ophthalmia," University of Utah, John A. Moran Eye Center, http://insight.med.utah.edu/opatharch/uvea/sympathetic_ophthalmia.htm.

11. Fensch, *Conversations with James Thurber,* 38–39.

12. Quoted on his failing eyesight in *Newsweek,* June 16, 1958, http://www.bartleby.com/63/91/5391.html.

13. Information on Schonzeit is from Ben Schonzeit, personal communications, May 15–16 and 24, 2006, May 27, 1996, March 18, 1995 (studio visit); Charles A. Riley II, *Ben Schonzeit Paintings* (New York: Harry N. Abrams, 2002).

14. Schonzeit, March 18, 1995.

15. Ibid., May 15, 2006.

16. Ibid., May 24, 2006.

17. Riley, *Ben Schonzeit Paintings,* 11.

18. Schonzeit, March 18, 1995.

19. Information on Vanderpoel is from *A Memorial Collection of Works by John H. Vanderpoel Exhibited from February 28, 1912, in the Art Institute of Chicago* (Chicago: Art Institute of Chicago, 1912); Jimmie Lee Buehler, "Beverly's Foremost Art Figure, John H. Vanderpoel," *Beverly Review History Issue* (August 12, 1987), 25; Jimmie Lee Buehler, personal communication, March 17, 2000; William H. Klug, *The John H. Vanderpoel Memorial Gallery: The Catalog of the John H. Vanderpoel Art Association* (Chicago, 1935); Jules Guerin, "In Chicago's Studios: Sketch of Professor John Vanderpoel's Life and Work," *Chicago Post,* January 30, 1891; "Stimulating Interest in Art: What Vanderpoel Art Association Is Doing and Hopes to Accomplish," *AIC Scrapbook* 43 (January 1922–September 1922): 61; "In Memoriam," *Bulletin of the Art Institute of Chicago* (July 1911): 3; Vanderpoel Memorial Collection, c. 1970s, John H. Vanderpoel Art Association, Chicago.

20. Buehler, March 17, 2000.

21. Quoted in Klug, *Memorial Gallery,* 5.

22. John H. Vanderpoel, *The Human Figure* (Mineola, N.Y.: Dover Publications, 1958).

23. Jimmie Lee Buehler, personal communication, May 11, 2000.

24. Quoted in Roxana Robinson, *Georgia O'Keeffe* (New York: Harper and Row, 1989), 52.

25. Information on Goltzius is from Carel van Mander, *Dutch and Flemish Artists,* trans. C. van de Wall (1604; New York: McFarlane, Warde, McFarlane, 1936), 355–

73; Huigen Leeflang and Ger Luitjen, eds., *Hendrick Goltzius (1558–1617): Drawings, Prints and Paintings* (Zwolle, Netherlands: Waanders Publishers, 2003). Quotes from Van Mander appear on page 368.

26. Information on Aertzoon is from van Mander, *Dutch and Flemish Artists,* 218–19.

27. Ibid., 218.

Chapter 6: Challenged Walking

1. Information on Toulouse-Lautrec is from Julia Frey, *Toulouse-Lautrec: A Life* (New York: Viking, 1994); Beverly B. Conrad, "Henri de Toulouse-Lautrec: A Fresh Explanation for His Artistic Giftedness" (paper presented at the 106th Annual Convention of the American Psychological Association, August 1998); Beverly B. Conrad, "Testing a Pathogenic Belief as Part of the Creative Process of Henri de Toulouse-Lautrec (1864–1901)" (XIVth Congress of International Association of Empirical Aesthetics, Prague, Czech Republic, August 1–4, 1996); P. Huisman and M. G. Dortu, *Lautrec by Lautrec* (New York: Viking, 1964); Giles Néret, *Henri de Toulouse-Lautrec* (Cologne: Benedikt Taschen Verlag, 1994).

2. Néret, *Henri de Toulouse-Lautrec,* 18.

3. P. Maroteaux and M. Lamy, "The Malady of Toulouse-Lautrec," *Journal of the American Medical Association* 191 (1965): 715–17; Bruce D. Gelb, Jacob G. Edelson, and Robert J. Desnick, "Linkage of Pycnodysostosis to Chromosome 1q21 by Homozygosity Mapping," *Nature Genetics* 10, no. 2 (1995): 235–37; M. H. Polymeropoulos, "The Gene for Pycnodysostosis Maps," *Nature Genetics* 10, no. 2 (1995): 238–39.

4. Stanley M. Elmore, "Pycnodysostosis: Review," *Journal of Bone and Joint Surgery* 49-A (January 1967): 153–62; Gelb, Edelson, and Desnick, "Linkage of Pycnodysostosis to Chromosome 1q21," 235–37; Polymeropoulos, "Gene for Pycnodysostosis Maps," 238–39; Frey, *Toulouse-Lautrec,* 58–60, 77–83.

5. Frey, *Toulouse-Lautrec,* 115.

6. Huisman and Dortu, *Lautrec by Lautrec,* 23.

7. Ibid.

8. Ellen Robbins, "Reminiscences of a Flower Painter," pt. 1 *New England,* n.s., 14 (March/August 1896): 440.

9. Information on Robbins is from Robbins, "Reminiscences," pt. 1: 440–51, pt. 2: 532–45; Maud de Leigh Hodges, "Ellen Robbins World," in *Crossroads on the Charles: A History of Watertown, Massachusetts* (Canaan, N.H.: Phoenix Publications, 1980), 103; "Watercolor Paintings at Library," *Watertown Sun*, 1973; *American Women Artists 1830–1930 at the National Museum of Women in the Arts* (catalalog for the exhibition, Washington, D.C., 1987).

10. Robbins, "Reminiscences," pt. 1, 446.

11. Mark H. Beers and Robert Berkow, eds., *The Merck Manual of Diagnosis and Therapy*, 17th ed. (Whitehouse Station, N.J.: Merck Research Laboratories, 1999), 2220; "Pediatric Development and Behavior: Selected Conditions of Young Children with Disabilities: Club Foot," http://www.dbpeds.org/conditions/conditions.cfm?Abbrev=clubfoot; "Club Foot," Cincinnati Children's Hospital Medical Center, http://www.cincinnatichildrens.org/health/info/orthopaedics/diagnose/club-foot.htm.

12. Robbins, "Reminiscences," pt. 1, 442.

13. Ibid., pt. 2, 540.

14. Information on Mackintosh is from Alan Crawford, *Charles Rennie Mackintosh* (New York: Thames and Hudson, 1995); Barbara Bernard, "Introduction," in *Mackintosh Architecture*, ed. Jackie Cooper (London: Academy Editions, 1977); Wendy Kaplan, ed., *Charles Rennie Mackintosh* (New York: Abbeville Press, 1975); Alison Filippo, *Charles Rennie Mackintosh as a Designer of Chairs* (Woodbury, N.Y.: Barron's, 1977).

15. Crawford, *Charles Rennie Mackintosh*, 9.

16. Quoted at Painter's Keys, "Resource of Art Quotations," http://www.painterskeys.com/auth_search.asp?name=Charles%20Rennie%20Mackintosh.

17. Information on Demuth is from Betty Fahlman, *Pennsylvania Modern: Charles Demuth of Lancaster* (Philadelphia: Philadelphia Museum of Art, 1983); Barbara Haskell, *Charles Demuth* (New York: Whitney Museum of American Art, 1987); Alvord Eiseman, *Charles Demuth* (New York: Watson-Guptill, 1982); Emily Farnham, *Charles Demuth: Behind a Laughing Mask* (Norman: University of Oklahoma, 1971).

18. Quoted in a footnote to "Demuth's Voyage" in Farnham, *Charles Demuth*, 41.

19. Ibid., 41.

20. Beers and Berkow, *Merck Manual*, 2341–43.

21. JoniMitchell.com, http://www.jonimitchell.com/bio/bio.cfm?id=230.

22. Alfred Adler, *The Individual Psychology of Alfred Adler*, edited and annotated by Heinz Ansbacher and Rowena Ansbacher (New York: Basic Books, 1956), 22–30.

23. Information on Lange is from Milton Meltzer, *Dorothea Lange: A Photographer's Life* (New York: Farrar, Straus and Giroux, 1978); Therese Thau Heyman, Sandra S. Phillips, and John Szarkowski, *Dorothea Lange: American Photographs* (San Francisco: San Francisco Museum of Art/Chronicle Books, 1994); *Dorothea Lange* (book accompanying an exhibition at the Museum of Modern Art, with an introductory essay by George P. Elliott; New York: Museum of Modern Art/Doubleday, 1966).

24. Meltzer, *Dorothea Lange*, 6.

25. Ibid., 12.

26. Ibid., 7.

27. Quoted in the Dorothea Lange Archive at the Oakland Museum of California, http://www.museumca.org/lange.html.

28. Mathias Oppersdorff, personal communication, May 18, 1999.

29. Information on Oppersdorff is from Mathias Oppersdorff, personal communications, May 1999 through December 2004; Mathias Oppersdorff, *Under the Spell of Arabia* (Syracuse, N.Y.: Syracuse University Press, 2001); Mathias Oppersdorff, *People of the Road: The Irish Travelers* (Syracuse, N.Y.: Syracuse University Press, 1997).

30. Oppersdorff, May 18, 1999.

31. Ibid., December 1, 2004.

32. Ibid., May 18, 1999.

33. Information on Pearson is from Marguerite Stuber Pearson Papers, Archives of American Art, Smithsonian Institution, New York City, microfilm reels 2391 and 2392, n.p.; Guild of Boston Artists, *New England's Women Painters: Works from 1900–1930* (Boston: 1993; catalog of the exhibition); Patricia Jobe Pierce and John Douglas Ingraham, *Marguerite S. Pearson, American Painter, 1898–1978* (Pierce Galleries; catalog of the exhibition); Paul E. Sternberg Sr., *Art by American Women: Selections from the Collection of Louise and Alan Sellars* (catalog for the exhibition at Brenau College, Gainesville, Ga., April 20–June 15, 1991; copyright 1991, Louise and Alan Sellars Collection of Art by American Women); Sue Rice, curator, Louise and Alan Sellars Collection of Art by American Women, telephone communication, June 17, 2000; Judith A. Curtis, "Exponents of the Boston School," *American Art Review* 12, no. 2 (2000): 186–93.

34. Marguerite Stuber Pearson Papers, reel 2392: Peter Olson, "Artist Paints Old, New Scenes She Likes," 1971.

35. Ibid., reel 2392: "Portraits, Spinets, Star Boats."

36. Madith Mantyla, personal communication, December 11, 2004.

Chapter 7: The Learning Disorders of Leonardo da Vinci

1. Frederick Hartt, *History of Italian Renaissance Art* (New York: Harry N. Abrams, 1987), 430; Giorgio Vasari, *The Lives of the Artists,* trans. Gaston Du C. De Vere (1568; New York: Knopf, 1996), 1:625–40.

2. Alan A. Beaton, *Dyslexia, Reading, and the Brain* (Hove, UK: Psychology Press, 2004), 256–60.

3. Edward M. Hallowell and John J. Ratey, *Driven to Distraction: Recognizing and Coping with Attention Deficit Disorder from Childhood through Adulthood* (New York: Simon and Schuster, 1995), 164.

4. Thomas G. West, *In the Mind's Eye: Visual Thinkers, Gifted People with Dyslexia and Other Learning Difficulties, Computer Images and the Ironies of Creativity* (Amherst, N.Y.: Prometheus Books, 1997); P. G. Aaron, Scott Phillips, and Steen Larsen, "Specific Reading Disability in Historically Famous Persons," *Journal of Learning Disabilities* 21, no. 9 (November 1988): 523–38.

5. This makes mirror writing different from scripts such as Hebrew and Arabic, and Eastern languages such as Chinese and Japanese. While these languages are written from right to left, their letters are not reversed.

6. Theodore Andrea Cook, *The Curves of Life* (1914; New York: Dover, 1979), 370–71. Cook found that Leonardo reversed his sketch of a landscape in Amboise, France.

7. Carmen C. Bambach, "Leonardo, Left-Handed Draftsman and Writer," in *Leonardo da Vinci: Master Draftsman,* ed. Carmen C. Bambach (New Haven, Conn.: Yale University Press, in association with the Metropolitan Museum of Art, 2003), 51–52.

8. West, *In the Mind's Eye,* 64–69; Margaret B. Rawson, "Louise Baker and the Leonardo Syndrome," *Annals of Dyslexia* 32 (1982): 289–304.

9. Charles Nicholl, *Leonardo da Vinci: Flights of the Mind* (New York: Penguin, 2004), 58, 96.

10. Augusto Marinoni, "The Writer: Leonardo's Literary Legacy," in *The Unknown Leonardo,* ed. Ladislao Reti (New York: McGraw-Hill, 1974), 60.

11. Bambach, "Leonardo, Left-Handed Draftsman and Writer," 44–45; Nicholl, *Leonardo da Vinci*, 58; Marinoni, "Writer," 60.

12. Carlo Vecce, "Word and Image in Leonardo's Writing," in Bambach, *Leonardo da Vinci*, 62; Bambach, "Leonardo, Left-Handed Draftsman and Writer," 45.

13. Aaron, Phillips, and Larsen, "Specific Reading Disability," 534–37.

14. Giuseppe Sartori, "Leonardo da Vinci, Omo Sanza Lettere: A Case of Surface Dysgraphia?" *Cognitive Neuropsychology* 4, no. 1 (February 1987): 1–10.

15. International Dyslexia Association, http://www.interdys.org/.

16. Vecce, "Word and Image in Leonardo's Writing," 59–61; Nicholl, *Leonardo da Vinci*, 54.

17. Aaron, Phillips, and Larsen, "Specific Reading Disability," 534–37.

18. Bambach, "Leonardo, Left-Handed Draftsman and Writer," 49.

19. Ibid., 45–48.

20. Sartori, "Case of Surface Dysgraphia?" 4–5.

21. Vasari, "Michelangelo," in *Lives of the Artists*, 2:642–768.

22. Vasari, "Leonardo da Vinci," in *Lives of the Artists*, 1:625.

23. Marinoni, "Writer," 62; Sartori, "Case of Surface Dysgraphia?" 6–8; Aaron, Phillips, and Larsen, "Specific Reading Disability," 536.

24. Leonardo da Vinci, *The Notebooks of Leonardo da Vinci*, trans. and ed. Jean Paul Richter (1489–1519; New York: Dover, 1970), 1:14–15.

25. Vecce, "Word and Image in Leonardo's Writing," 50; Nicholl, *Leonardo da Vinci*, 54.

26. Sartori, "Case of Surface Dysgraphia?" 9–10.

27. Sara Denning, psychologist specializing in ADD, personal communication, September 14, 2005.

28. Quoted in Kenneth Clark, *Leonardo da Vinci: An Account of His Development as An Artist* (Harmondsworth, UK: Penguin, 1971), 84.

29. Leonardo da Vinci, *Notebooks*, vols. 1 and 2, trans. and ed. Richter; Leonardo da Vinci, *The Notebooks of Leonardo da Vinci*, trans. and ed. Edward MacCurdy (1489–1519; Garden City, N.Y.: Garden City Publishing, 1941–42).

30. Ritchie Calder, *Leonardo and the Age of the Eye* (New York: Simon and Schuster, 1970), 214–21.

31. Benoit Mandelbrot, *The Fractal Geometry of Nature* (San Francisco: W. H. Freeman, 1977), C3.

32. Leonardo da Vinci, *Notebooks*, vol. 1, trans. and ed. Richter; Leonardo da Vinci,

Notebooks, trans. and ed. MacCurdy; Leonardo da Vinci, *Leonardo on Painting*, ed. Martin Kemp, trans. Martin Kemp and Margaret Walker (New Haven, Conn.: Yale University Press, 1989).

33. Leonardo da Vinci, *Anatomical Drawings from the Royal Library Windsor Castle* (catalog for an exhibition at the Metropolitan Museum of Art; New York: Metropolitan Museum of Art, 1984); Leonardo da Vinci, *Leonardo on the Human Body*, trans. and ed. Charles D. O'Malley and J. B. de C. M. Saunders (1489–1519; New York: Dover, 1983); Leonardo da Vinci, *Notebooks*, trans. and ed. MacCurdy.

34. Bruce F. Pennington, *Diagnosing Learning Disorders: A Neuropsychological Framework* (New York: Guilford Press, 1991), 97–98; Hallowell and Ratey, *Driven to Distraction*, 6.

35. Patricia O. Quinn, "Neurobiology of Attention Deficit Disorder," in *A Comprehensive Guide to Attention Deficit Disorder in Adults: Research, Diagnosis, Treatment*, ed. Kathleen G. Nadeau (New York: Brunner/Mazel, 1995), 18–31; Pennington, *Diagnosing Learning Disorders*, 4, 12–18.

36. Hallowell and Ratey, *Driven to Distraction*, 165.

37. Dale R. Jordan, *Attention Deficit Disorder: ADHD and ADD Syndromes* (Austin, Tex.: Pro-ed, 1998), 46.

38. American Psychiatric Association, *DSM-IV-R: Diagnostic and Statistical Manual of Mental Disorders*, 3rd ed. (Washington, D.C.: American Psychiatric Association, 1994), 78–84.

39. Vasari, "Leonardo da Vinci," 1:638.

40. Andre Chastel, *The Genius of Leonardo da Vinci*, trans. Ellen Callman (New York: Orion Press, 1961), xii.

41. Hartt, *History of Italian Renaissance Art*, 444.

42. Bonnie Cramond, "Attention Deficit Hyperactivity Disorder and Creativity—What Is the Connection?" *Journal of Creative Behavior* 28, no. 3 (1994): 193–210; Bonnie Cramond, "The Coincidence of Attention Deficit Hyperactivity Disorder and Creativity" (University of Georgia, March 1995), complete paper at http://borntoexplore.org/adhd.htm.

43. Lynn Weiss, *A.D.D. and Creativity: Tapping Your Inner Muse* (Lanham, Md.: Taylor Trade Publishing, 1997); Cramond, "Attention Deficit Hyperactivity Disorder and Creativity," 193–210; Cramond, "Coincidence of Attention Deficit Hyperactivity Disorder and Creativity"; Hallowell and Ratey, *Driven to Distraction*, 176–78.

44. Leonardo da Vinci, *Leonardo on Painting*.

45. Hartt, *History of Italian Renaissance Art*, 430.

46. Carmen C. Bambach, "Introduction to Leonardo and His Drawings," in Bambach, *Master Draftsman*, 4–5.

47. Vasari, "Leonardo da Vinci," 1:625–26.

48. Denning, September 14, 2005.

49. Vasari, "Leonardo da Vinci," 1:625–39; quote appears on page 625.

50. The psychologist Bonnie Cramond distinguishes between these two types of restlessness in the creative person; see "Coincidence of Attention Deficit Hyperactivity Disorder and Creativity."

51. Bambach, "Introduction to Leonardo and His Drawings," 4–5; Jane Roberts, "The Drawings and Manuscripts," in *Leonardo da Vinci: Artist, Scientist, Inventor* (London: Yale University Press, 1989), 17.

52. Bambach, "Introduction to Leonardo and His Drawings," 13.

53. Marinoni, "Writer," 82; Leonardo da Vinci, *Notebooks*, vols. 1 and 2, trans. and ed. Richter.

54. Edward M. Hallowell and John J. Ratey, *Answers to Distraction* (New York: Bantam Books, 1996), 97–98.

55. Leonardo da Vinci, *Leonardo on Painting*, 39.

56. Denning, September 14, 2005.

57. Edward DeBono, *New Think: The Use of Lateral Thinking in the Generation of New Ideas* (New York: Basic Books, 1967). It is also known as divergent thinking, radial thinking, and jumping mental tracks. See also Bob Seay, "How Are We Different? How Different Are We?" *ADDitude*, http://www.bobseay.com/littlecorner/newurl/differ.html#RADIAL; Jordan, *Attention Deficit Disorder*, 33–34.

58. Vasari, "Leonardo da Vinci," 1:638.

59. Kenneth D. Keele, "Leonardo da Vinci the Anatomist," in Leonardo da Vinci, *Anatomical Drawings from the Royal Library Windsor Castle*, 12.

60. Hallowell and Ratey, *Driven to Distraction*, x.

61. Clark, *Leonardo da Vinci*, 90.

62. Hartt, *History of Italian Renaissance Art*, 441–44.

63. Alan J. Zametkin, Thomas E. Nordahl, Michael Gross, Catherine King, William E. Semple, Judith Rumsey, Susan Hamburger, and Robert M. Cohen, "Cerebral Glucose Metabolism in Adults with Hyperactivity of Childhood Onset," *New England Journal of Medicine* 323 (November 15, 1990): 1361–1366; Hallowell and Ratey, *Answers to Distraction*, 207–8.

64. The theoredtical foundation for the Mozart effect comes from X. Leng and

G. L. Shaw, "Toward a Neural Theory of Higher Brain Functioning Using Music as a Window," *Concepts in Neuroscience* 2 (1991): 229–58. That Mozart's *Sonata for Two Pianos in D Major*, K. 448, was more effective than a relaxation tape or silence was demonstrated by F. H. Rauscher, G. L. Shaw, and K. N. Ky in "Music and Spatial Task Performance," *Nature* 365 (1993): 611. The discovery that spatial performance was enhanced when people listened to what they preferred, either to music or words, is from K. M. Nantais and E. G. Schellenberg, "The Mozart Effect: An Artifact of Preference," *Psychological Science* 10, vol. 4 (1999): 370–73. For an overview of the research on the Mozart effect and an experiment indicating that arousal is the factor in performance, see Martin H. Jones, Stephen D. West, and David B. Estell, "The Mozart Effect: Arousal, Preference, and Spatial Performance," *Psychology of Aesthetics, Creativity, and the Arts* S, no. 1 (2006): 26–32.

65. Vasari, *Lives of the Artists*, 1:632.

66. Leonardo da Vinci, *Notebooks*, vol. 1, trans. and ed. Richter, no. 508, 254.

67. Hallowell and Ratey, *Answers to Distraction*, 209.

68. Vasari, *Lives of the Artists*, 1:625–28.

69. Leonardo da Vinci, *Notebooks*, vol. 1, trans. and ed. Richter, no. 508, 254.

70. Bambach, "Introduction to Leonardo and His Drawings," 21–22.

71. Cramond, "Coincidence of Attention Deficit Hyperactivity Disorder and Creativity."

72. Margaret Cheney, *Tesla: Man Out of Time* (New York: Barnes and Noble Books, 1981), 12.

73. Calder, *Leonardo and the Age of the Eye*, 121.

74. Leonardo da Vinci, *Notebooks*, vol. 1, trans. and ed. Richter; Calder, *Leonardo and the Age of the Eye*; Leonardo da Vinci, *Notebooks*, trans. and ed. MacCurdy.

75. Calder, *Leonardo and the Age of the Eye*, 107.

76. Ibid., 211–17.

77. "No work shall tire me," "Death before weariness," and "God, sellest us all good things at the price of labor" are from Istituto Geografico De Agostini S.p.A., *Leonardo da Vinci* (New York: Reynal, 1956), 171.

78. Angela Tzelepis, Howard Schubiner, and Lawrence H. Warbasse III, "Differential Diagnosis and Psychiatric Comorbidity Patterns in Adult Attention Deficit Disorder," in Nadeau, *Comprehensive Guide to Attention Deficit Disorder in Adults*, 37–39.

Chapter 8: Artists and Learning Difficulties

1. The International Dyslexia Association, http://www.interdys.org/.

2. Richard Schickel, *The Disney Version* (Chicago: Elephant Paperbacks, 1997); Paul Jerome Croce, "A Clean and Separate Space: Walt Disney in Person and Production," *Journal of Popular Culture* 25, no. 3 (1991): 91–103; Christopher Finch, *The Art of Walt Disney: From Mickey Mouse to Magic Kingdom* (New York: Harry N. Abrams, 1995); Walt Disney Family Museum, *Walt's Biography*, http://disney.go.com/disneyatoz/family museum/collection/biography/marceline/index.html. Information on Disney's early years is from the biographical sections on Kansas City and Laugh-O-Grams.

3. Howard Gardner, *Frames of Mind: The Theory of Multiple Intelligences* (New York: Basic Books, 1985), x.

4. Maxime de la Falaise McKendry, "Robert Rauschenberg Talks to Maxime de la Falaise McKendry," *Interview* 6, no. 5 (May 1976): 34.

5. Robert S. Mattison, *Robert Rauschenberg: Breaking Boundaries* (New Haven, Conn.: Yale University Press, 2003), 37.

6. Robert Hughes, "The Most Living Painter," *Time*, November 29, 1976, 59.

7. Mattison, *Robert Rauschenberg*, 34–40.

8. McKendry, "Robert Rauschenberg," 34.

9. Mattison, *Robert Rauschenberg*, 32–40.

10. Quoted in Grace Glueck, "With All Due Immodesty," *New York Times*, December 16, 1990, 49.

11. Patrick O'Brian, *Pablo Ruiz Picasso: A Biography* (New York: W. W. Norton, 1976); Roland Penrose, *Picasso: His Life and Work* (Berkeley: University of California Press, 1981); John Richardson with Marilyn McCully, *A Life of Picasso*, vol. 1, 1881–1906 (New York: Random House, 1991).

12. All information and quotes from Rossol are from personal communications, October 28, 2000, May 29, 2005, and May 30, 2005.

13. Richard E. Cytowic, "Synesthesia: Phenomenology and Neuropsychology: A Review of Current Knowledge," *PSYCHE* 2, no. 10, July 1995, http://psyche.cs. monash.edu.au/v2/psyche-2-10-cytowic.html.

14. International Dyslexia Association.

15. Thomas G. West, "A Future of Reversals: Dyslexic Talents in a World of Computer Visualization," *Annals of Dyslexia* 42 (1992): 124–39.

16. Its full name is Academia Rodinensis Pro Remediatione (Rodin Remediation Academy) at the Institute of Medical Psychology, part of the Medical Faculty at the University of Munich, http://www.imp-muenchen.de/Rodin_Remediation_Ac.350.0.html.

17. Information on Rodin is from Bernard Champigneulle, *Rodin* (New York: Oxford University Press, 1967); Frederic V. Grunfeld, *Rodin: A Biography* (New York: Da Capo Press, 1987); Anne Leslie, *Rodin: Immortal Peasant* (New York: Prentice Hall, 1937).

18. Quoted in Champigneulle, *Rodin*, 14.

19. Jan Greenberg and Sandra Jordan, *Chuck Close Up Close* (New York: DK Publishing, 1998), 6.

20. Ibid., 5–10.

21. Chuck Close, telephone communication, June 30, 2005.

22. Greenberg and Jordan, *Chuck Close Up Close*, 6.

23. John Guare, *Chuck Close: Life and Work, 1988–1995* (New York: Thames and Hudson, 1995), 32.

24. Greenberg and Jordan, *Chuck Close Up Close*, 5.

25. Prosopagnosia Research Center, Harvard University, Ken Nakayama, Ph.D., and Bradley C. Duchaine, Ph.D., http://www.faceblind.org/; Ruth Daniels, "The Coexistence of Artistic Talent and Dyslexia" (copyrighted unpublished manuscript), 1996.

26. Greenberg and Jordan, *Chuck Close Up Close*, 11.

27. Ruth Daniels, "Art and Dyslexia: Chuck Close" (paper presented at the 104th Annual Convention of the American Psychological Association, Toronto, Ontario, 1996).

28. Greenberg and Jordan. *Chuck Close Up Close*, 11.

29. Oliver Sacks, *The Man Who Mistook His Wife for a Hat and Other Clinical Tales* (New York: HarperCollins, 1987), 8–22.

30. Greenberg and Jordan, *Chuck Close Up Close*, 10.

31. Information on Bonheur is from Anna Klumpke, *Rosa Bonheur: The Artist's (Auto)biography*, trans. Gretchen van Slyke (Ann Arbor: University of Michigan Press, 1997); Dore Ashton, *Rosa Bonheur: A Life and a Legend* (New York: Viking Press, 1981); Mariann Smith, *Rosa Bonheur, "The Horse Fair,"* Albright Knox Gallery, http://www.albrightknox.org/ArtStart/Bonheur.html.

32. Klumpke, *Rosa Bonheur*, 112–113.

33. The match of *b* for bull is from an English translation of the artist's autobiography. In French the word for bull is *taureau*. Ibid., 87.

34. Abby Cohen, "Brushed by Talent: Down Syndrome Didn't Limit Raymond Hu's Artistic Vision," *San Francisco Chronicle*, June 30, 2000, http://www.sfgate.com/cgi-bin/article.cgi?file=/chronicle/archive/2000/06/30/CC48827.DTL.

35. Information on Hu is from Raymond Hu, personal communication, June 20, 2000; Margaret Hu, personal communication, June 20, 2000; Raymond Hu, *The Eyes of Raymond Hu: Brush Paintings by Raymond Hu* (Chicago: Art Media Resources, 1996); Raymond Hu home page, http://www-atdp.berkeley.edu/1623/students/jason/Raymond.html; Cohen, "Brushed by Talent."

36. Mark H. Beers and Robert Berkow, eds., *The Merck Manual of Diagnosis and Therapy*, 17th ed. (Whitehouse Station, N.J.: Merck Research Laboratories, 1999), 2233–36.

37. Cohen, "Brushed by Talent."

38. Raymond Hu, June 20, 2000.

39. Cohen, "Brushed by Talent."

40. American Psychiatric Association, *DSM-IV-R: Diagnostic and Statistical Manual of Mental Disorders*, 3rd ed. (Washington, D.C.: American Psychiatric Association, 1994), 66–71; "Autism Spectrum Disorders (Pervasive Developmental Disorders)," NIMH, National Institute of Mental Health, http://www.nimh.nih.gov/publicat/intro and http://www.nimh.nih.gov/healthinformation/autismmenu.cfm.

41. Temple Grandin, keynote speech for the symposium "Pure Visionaries: Artists on the Spectrum," Cooper Union, New York, November 4, 2005; Temple Grandin, *Thinking in Pictures: And Other Reports from My Life with Autism* (New York: Doubleday, 1995).

42. Clara Park, *Exiting Nirvana: A Daughter's Life with Autism* (Boston: Little, Brown, 2001), 4.

43. Ibid.; Clara Park, *The Siege: The First Eight Years of an Autistic Child* (Boston: Little, Brown, 2001); Clara Park and Jessica Park, speech for the symposium "Pure Visionaries: Artists on the Spectrum"; Emmanuelle Delmas-Glass, "Painting the World with a Rainbow," *Folk Art Messenger* 17, no. 2 (Fall/Winter 2004), http://www.folkart.org/mag/park/park.html.

44. Information on Castle is from Tom Trusky, director, Hemingway Western Studies Center, Idaho Center for the Book, personal communication, November 29,

2005; Tom Trusky, *James Castle: His Life and Art* (Boise, Idaho: Idaho Center for the Book, 2004); Tom Trusky, "Found and Profound: The Art of James Castle," *Folk Art* (Winter 1999/2000): 39–48; Tom Trusky, *The Art Books of James Castle* (catalog for the exhibition "Reputedly Illiterate: The Art Books of James Castle" at the AIGA Design Center, New York, May 2000); Tom Trusky, *James Castle and the Book* (Boise, Idaho: Idaho Center for the Book, 1999); Tom Trusky, "James Castle and the Burden of Art," *Raw Vision*, July 1, 2000, http://www.rawvision.com/back/castle/castle.html; Cornelia H. Butler, "The Still Life of Objects," in *A Silent Voice: Drawings and Constructions of James Castle* (catalog for the exhibition at Fleisher/Ollman Gallery, New York, 1998), 2–6; *Dreamhouse: The Art and Life of James Castle* (documentary film written and directed by Tom Trusky and Peter Lutze; Boise, Idaho: Painted Smiles Press, 1999); Jay Tobler, *James Castle: House Drawings* (catalog for the exhibition at the Drawing Center, New York, March 4–May 4, 2000), 5–7.

45. Trusky, *James Castle: His Life and Art*, 5.

46. Stephen Wiltshire is discussed in Oliver Sacks, *An Anthropologist on Mars* (New York: Vintage Books, 1996), 196–222, 228–43.

47. Craig Hou, Bruce L. Miller, Jeffrey L. Cummings, Michael Goldberg, Paula Mychack, Vivian Bottino, and D. Frank Benson, "Artistic Savants," *Neuropsychiatry, Neuropsychology, and Behavioral Neurology* 13, no. 1 (2000): 29–38.

48. Ellen Winner, *Invented Worlds: The Psychology of the Arts* (Cambridge, Mass.: Harvard University Press, 1982).

49. J. V. Field, *The Invention of Infinity: Mathematics and Art in the Renaissance* (Oxford: Oxford University Press, 1997); Samuel Y. Edgerton, *The Heritage of Giotto's Geometry* (Ithaca, N.Y.: Cornell University Press, 1991); John White, *The Birth and Rebirth of Pictorial Space* (Boston: Boston Book and Art Shop, 1967).

50. In her book review of Lorna Seife, *Nadia: A Case of Extraordinary Drawing Ability in an Autistic Child* (London: Academic Press, 1977), Clara Park cites Seife's observation that young children draw in schemas and E. H. Gombrich, who says children draw what they know, not what they see. This is not true of autistic children, who draw what they see.

51. Temple Grandin, personal communication, November 30, 2005.

52. Clara Park, *Exiting Nirvana*, 4.

53. Allan Snyder, Homayoun Bahramali, Tobias Hawker, D. John Mitchell. "Savant-like Numerosity Skills Revealed in Normal People by Magnetic Pulses," *Perception* 35, no. 6 (May 3, 2006): 837–45.

Chapter 9: Vision Challenges and Visual Art

1. Michael F. Marmor, "Munch and Visions from within the Eye," in *The Eye of the Artist*, ed. Michael F. Marmor and James G. Ravin (St. Louis: Mosby, 1997), 204–12.

2. Ibid., 208.

3. Charles R. Knight, "Autobiography of an Artist" (unpublished manuscript written between 1898 and 1953; covers the years 1874–1898; photocopy in the Special Collections Department, American Museum of Natural History, New York); Gregory S. Paul, "The Art of Charles R. Knight," *Scientific American* 274, no. 6 (June 1996): 86–93; Rhoda Steele Kalt (Rhoda Knight Steele), "Toppy and Me" (unpublished manuscript; photocopy in the American Museum of Natural History Library, New York, 1980); Sylvia Massey Czerkas and Edwin H. Glut, *Dinosaurs, Mammoths, and Cavemen: The Art of Charles R. Knight* (New York: E. P. Dutton, 1982).

4. Charles R. Knight, "Autobiography of an Artist" (handwritten draft of unpublished manuscript written between 1898 and 1953; original in draft box 5 F.1, Manuscripts Division of the New York Public Library), 3.

5. Charles R. Knight, *Before the Dawn of History* (New York: McGraw-Hill, 1935); Charles R. Knight, *Life through the Ages* (New York: Knopf, 1946).

6. Mark H. Beers and Robert Berkow, eds., *The Merck Manual of Diagnosis and Therapy*, 17th ed. (Whitehouse Station, N.J.: Merck Research Laboratories, 1999), 731; James G. Ravin and Christie Kenyon, "The Blurred World of Georgia O'Keeffe," in Marmor and Ravin, *Eye of the Artist*, 216.

7. Ravin and Kenyon, "Blurred World of Georgia O'Keeffe," 216; James G. Ravin and Christie Kenyon, "The Blindness of Edgar Degas," in Marmor and Ravin, *Eye of the Artist*, 194–95.

8. Ravin and Kenyon, "Blindness of Edgar Degas," 193–201; Patrick Trevor-Roper, *The World through Blunted Sight*, 2nd ed. (London: Penguin, 1988), 39.

9. Quoted in Ravin and Kenyon, "Blindness of Edgar Degas," 195.

10. Ian Dunlop, *Degas* (New York: Harper and Row, 1979), 214–16.

11. Roxana Robinson, *Georgia O'Keeffe* (New York: Harper and Row, 1989), 514–15.

12. Ravin and Kenyon, "Blurred World of Georgia O'Keeffe," 213–22.

13. Georgia O'Keeffe, *Georgia O'Keeffe* (New York: Viking, 1976), plate 104.

14. Lisa Mintz Messinger, "Georgia O'Keeffe," *Metropolitan Museum of Art Bulletin* 42, no. 2 (Fall 1984): 29.

15. O'Keeffe, *Georgia O'Keeffe*, n.p.

16. Messinger, "Georgia O'Keeffe," 58.

17. Trevor-Roper, *World through Blunted Sight*, 2nd, 93–95.

18. James G. Ravin, "Artistic Vision in Old Age: Claude Monet," in Marmor and Ravin, *Eye of the Artist*, 168–80; James G. Ravin and Christie Kenyon, "Artistic Vision in Old Age: Claude Monet and Edgar Degas," in *Creativity and Successful Aging: Theoretical and Empirical Approaches*, ed. Carolyn E. Adams-Price (New York: Springer, 1998), 251–67; Daniel Wildenstein, "Monet's Giverny," in *Monet's Years at Giverny: Beyond Impressionism* (New York: Metropolitan Museum of Art, 1978), 15–40.

19. Quoted in Ravin, "Artistic Vision in Old Age: Claude Monet," 170.

20. James G. Ravin, "Cataracts, Diabetes, and Radium: The Case of Mary Cassatt," in Marmor and Ravin, *Eye of the Artist*, 181–86.

21. Quoted in Ravin, "Artistic Vision in Old Age: Claude Monet," 178.

22. Wildenstein, "Monet's Giverny," 36.

23. Quoted in Ravin, "Artistic Vision in Old Age: Claude Monet," 179.

Chapter 10: Art and the Way We See the World

1. Temple Grandin and Catherine Johnson, *Animals in Translation: Using the Mysteries of Autism to Decode Animal Behavior* (New York: Scribner, 2005), 44.

2. A. Hyatt Mayor, "Rembrandt and the Bible," *Metropolitan Museum of Art Bulletin* (Winter 1978/1979): 46.

3. James Ravin, personal communication, July 11, 2005.

4. Patrick Trevor-Roper, *The World through Blunted Sight* (Indianapolis: Bobbs-Merrill, 1970), 75–86.

5. James G. Ravin and Philippe Lanthony, "An Artist with a Color Vision Defect: Charles Meryon," in *The Eye of the Artist*, ed. Michael F. Marmor and James G. Ravin (St. Louis: Mosby, 1997), 101–7.

6. The neurobiologists Margaret S. Livingstone and Bevil R. Conway have another hypothesis about Rembrandt's vision and its influence on his work. They believe that Rembrandt's eyes did not converge normally. This means that instead of staring straight ahead with both eyes, Rembrandt had strabismus, or what is sometimes called "a lazy eye" that at times drifted out of alignment. As a result, they think he lacked normal stereoscopic vision and did not have depth perception. The oph-

thalmologists Michael F. Marmor and Saad Shaikh find this premise to be in error, and I agree with them. They say artists will often misalign eyes in portraits. This may be due to the way artists fix their gaze as they paint first one eye and then the other, or it may be artistic style. In an earlier writing on divergent eyes in art, the ophthalmologist Patrick Trevor-Roper finds that most painters give the people in their portraits a slight degree of eye divergence, either consciously or unconsciously. Even though I disagree with the Livingstone-Conway premise, I think they have done us a service by saying that major artists could have eye problems and that these difficulties may enhance their work. There are other theories that have been found to be in error, such as attributing astigmatism to El Greco. His elongated figures are now accepted to be a decision of artistic style rather than astigmatic painting. Other misattributions of astigmatism were made about Hans Holbein the Younger, Lucas Cranach the Elder, and Amedeo Modigliani. Like El Greco, their images were a choice of artistic style rather than the result of a vision difficulty. Margaret S. Livingstone and Bevil R. Conway, "Was Rembrandt Stereoblind?" *New England Journal of Medicine* 351, no. 12 (September 16, 2004): 1264–65; Michael F. Marmor and Saad Shaikh, "Was Rembrandt Stereoblind?" letter to the editor, *New England Journal of Medicine* 352, no. 6 (February 10, 2005): 631–32; Trevor-Roper, *World through Blunted Sight*, 115.

7. James Ravin, personal communication, March 25, 2005.

8. Mayor, "Rembrandt and the Bible," 46.

9. Oliver Sacks, *An Anthropologist on Mars* (New York: Vintage, 1996).

10. Ibid., 38; Grandin and Johnson, *Animals in Translation*, 43; Trevor-Roper, *World through Blunted Sight*, 99.

11. Oliver Sacks, *Island of the Colorblind* (New York: Knopf, 1997), 3–57.

12. Quoted in ibid., 44.

13. Etching is a process of incising lines on a metal plate. The lines are then filled with ink and the metal plate is pressed on paper, producing a print called an etching.

14. K. G. Boon, *Rembrandt: The Complete Etchings* (New York: Harry N. Abrams, n.d.), n.p.

15. Michael F. Marmor, "The Eye and Art: Visual Function and Eye Disease in the Context of Art," in Marmor and Ravin, *Eye of the Artist*, 19; Diana H. Heath, M.D., ophthalmologist, "Color Blindness," http://www.toledo-bend.com/colorblind/aboutCB.html.

16. Information on Kollwitz is from Kaethe Kollwitz, *The Diary and Letters of Kaethe Kollwitz*, ed. Hans Kollwitz, trans. Richard and Clara Winston (Chicago: Henry

Regnery, 1955); Herbert Bittner, *Kaethe Kollwitz: Drawings* (New York: Thomas Yoseloff, 1959); Elizabeth Prelinger, "Käthe Kollwitz Reconsidered," in *Käthe Kollwitz,* by Elizabeth Prelinger, Alessandra Comini, and Hildegard Bachert (Washington, D.C.: National Gallery of Art; New Haven, Conn.: Yale University Press, 1992), 13–88; Carl Zigrosser, introduction to *Kaethe Kollwitz* (New York: H. Bittner and Company, 1946).

17. Kollwitz, *Diary and Letters,* 39.

18. Ibid., 40.

19. Ravin and Lanthony, "Artist with a Color Vision Defect: Charles Meryon," 101–7.

20. Quoted in ibid., 107.

21. Marmor, "Eye and Art," 19–20.

22. Information on Michael Wainwright is from personal communication, September 7, 2005, and his website, http://www.michaelwainwright.com.

23. Trevor-Roper, *World through Blunted Sight,* 85.

24. Carel van Mander, *Dutch and Flemish Artists,* trans. C. van de Wall (1604; New York: McFarlane, Warde, McFarlane, 1936), 400–403.

25. Laurence Sickman and Alexander Soper, *Art and Architecture of China* (London: Penguin, 1956), 184–86.

26. Laurence Binyon, *Painting in the Far East* (New York: Dover, 1969), 142.

27. Ibid., 193–94.

28. Sickman and Soper, *Art and Architecture of China,* 295–97.

29. John M. Kennedy, *Drawing and the Blind; Pictures to Touch* (New Haven, Conn.: Yale University Press, 1993).

30. Quoted in Alison Motluk, "Senses Special: The Art of Seeing without Sight," *New Scientist,* no. 2484, January 29, 2005, http://www.newscientist.com/channel/being-human/mg18524841.700.

31. Jacques Derrida, *Memoirs of the Blind: The Self-Portrait and Other Ruins,* trans. Pascale-Anne Brault and Michael Naas (Chicago: University of Chicago Press, 1993), 3.

32. Kennedy, *Drawing and the Blind,* 258.

33. Helen Fukuhara, personal communication, June 13, 2006.

34. Ibid.; Christine Ellen Leahey, "The Reciprocal Gaze," in *The View from Here* (catalog for the exhibition "The View from Here: Visual Art by Artists Who Are

Visually Impaired and Blind," LA Artcore, February 1–28, 2004); Christine Ellen Leahey, curator and director of "The View from Here," director of Visitor Services, Santa Monica Museum of Art, personal communications, July 26–27, 2005; Duane Noriyuki, "The Artist Within: An Exhibit at the LA Artcore Center Explores the Nature of Blindness and the Relationship between Sight and Art, February 1–28, 2004," *Los Angeles Times*, February 12, 2004.

35. Quoted in Noriyuki, "Artist Within."

36. Fukuhara, June 13, 2006.

37. Bonnie Britton, "Documentary Shares Artist's Blind Journey," *Indianapolis Star*, July 13, 2000, E1, E2; Rick Del Vecchio, "Blind Photographer's Vision Extends Beyond Her Eyes," *San Francisco Chronicle*, February 18, 2005, http://www.sfgate.com/cgi-bin/article.cgi?file=/c/a/2005/02/18/EBG90B98SE1.DTL; Wendy Edelstein, "In the Eye of the Beholder; Berkeley Art Museum and the Townsend Center Take a Closer Look at Art and Visual Impairment in 'Blind at the Museum' Exhibit," *UC Berkeley News*, March 2, 2005, http://www.berkeley.edu/news/berkeleyan/2005/03/02_blind.shtml.

38. Edelstein, "In the Eye of the Beholder."

39. Del Vecchio, "Blind Photographer's Vision Extends Beyond her Eyes."

40. John Dugdale, personal communication, September 7, 2005; John Wessel, Wessel + O'Connor Fine Art, personal communication, December 21, 1999; Christopher Mason, "Fearless Vision Brings an Artist Home," *New York Times*, November 25, 1999, F1, F7; Catherine Edelman Gallery, artist information, http://www.edelmangallery.com/dugdale.htm; Scheinbaum & Russek Ltd, gallery, artist information, http://www.photographydealers.com/siteindex.html.

41. Dugdale, September 7, 2005.

42. Catherine Edelman Gallery.

43. Alison Ulman, personal communication, June 2005. Ulman received the 2002 Outstanding Artist Award for *A Coffee Table Is Work*, Honduran mahogany, bronze, 29 × 27 in × 6 ft, http://www.lighthouse-sf.org/activities/insights/RoseResnick LightHouseUlman_ACoffeeTableisWork.php.

44. Alison Ulman, http://www.endlessprocess.com/spiritmovement.html.

45. Bob Pool, "Loss of Sight Focuses His Artistic Vision," *Los Angeles Times*, January 6, 2005, front page California section; Michael Richard, artist statement for

"The View from Here" exhibit at Photo San Francisco 2005, the sixth annual San Francisco Photographic Art Exposition; http://www.announceart.net/photosf/2005/welcome.html.

46. Jeffrey Cooper and Rachel Cooper, "All about Amblyopia (Lazy Eye), 2001–2005," Optometrists Network, http://www.strabismus.org/amblyopia_lazy_eye.html.

47. Pool, "Loss of Sight Focuses His Artistic Vision."

48. Information on Armagan is from Motluk, "Senses Special"; Esref Armagan, http://www.esrefarmagan.com/ and http://www.armagan.com/; Cara Feinberg, "Old Brain, New Tricks," *Boston Globe*, January 15, 2006, http://www.boston.com/news/globe/ideas/articles/2006/01/15/old_brain_new_tricks/?p1.

49. Cited in Feinberg, "Old Brain, New Tricks."

Chapter 11: Deafness and the Creative Process

1. Harlan Lane, *A Deaf Artist in Early America: The Worlds of John Brewster, Jr.* (Boston: Beacon Press, 2004), xv, 86–88.

2. An additional summary of research in the adaptation of deaf brains can be found in Bruce Bower, "The Brain Spreads Its Sights in the Deaf," *Science News* 158 (September 23, 2000). Conversely, blind people have been shown to have better hearing than sighted people. They allocate part of the brain usually used for vision to distinguish sound; see Patrice Voss, Maryse Lassonde, Frederic Gougoux, Madeleine Fortin, Jean-Paul Guillemot, and Franco Lepore, "Early- and Late-Onset Blind Individuals Show Supra-Normal Auditory Abilities in Far-Space," *Current Biology* 14 (October 5, 2004): 1734–38.

3. D. Bavelier, A. Tomann, C. Hutton, T. V. Mitchell, D. P. Corina, G. Liu, and H. J. Neville, "Visual Attention to the Periphery Is Enhanced in Congenitally Deaf Individuals," *Journal of Neuroscience* 20 (2000): 1–6.

4. The total U.S. population that has hearing problems, which includes both deaf and hard of hearing, is 20,295,000, or 8.6 percent. Gallaudet University Library, Deaf-Related Resources, http://library.gallaudet.edu/dr/faq-statistics-deaf-us.html.

5. Dr. Janice Berchin-Weiss, director of the Institute for Mediated Learning at the Lexington School for the Deaf, personal communication, September 26, 2005.

6. Rusty Freeman, interview with Tin Ly, Duane Hanson's longtime assistant, in *Duane Hanson: Portraits from the Heartland*, ed. Erika Doss, Wesla Hanson, and Tin Ly (Fargo, N. Dak.: Plains Art Museum in collaboration with New Rivers Press, 2004).

7. Lane, *Deaf Artist in Early America.*

8. Ibid., 45.

9. Quoted in ibid., 10.

10. Deborah Sonnenstrahl, *Deaf Artists in America: Colonial to Contemporary* (San Diego: Dawn Sign Press, 2003), 8–12.

11. "Ear Trumpets," John Q. Adams Center for the History of Otolaryngology—Head and Neck Surgery, American Academy of Otolaryngology—Head and Neck Surgery, http://www.entnet.org/museum/exhibits/hearingaids_eartrumpets.cfm.

12. Quoted in Martin Postle, ed., *Joshua Reynolds: The Creation of Celebrity* (London: Tate Gallery, 2005), 172.

13. Information on Reynolds is from ibid.; Derek Hudson, *Sir Joshua Reynolds: A Personal Study* (London: Geoffrey Bles, 1968); William B. Boulton, *Joshua Reynolds, P. R. A.* (New York: E. P. Dutton, 1905); Tate Gallery, "Joshua Reynolds: The Creation of Celebrity" (exhibition, May 26–September 18, 2005), http://www.tate.org.uk/britain/exhibitions/reynolds/roomguide4.shtm.

14. The poet and playwright Oliver Goldsmith said about Reynolds: *"To COX-COMBS AVERSE, yet most civilly steering; When they JUDGED without Skill, he was still Hard of Hearing."* Tate Gallery, "Joshua Reynolds: The Creation of Celebrity." See also Ian McIntyre, *Joshua Reynolds: The Life and Times of the First President of the Royal Academy* (London: Allen Lane, 2003).

15. Paul E. Sternberg Sr., *Art by American Women: Selections from the Collection of Louise and Alan Sellars* (catalog for the exhibition at Brenau College, Gainesville, Ga., April 20–June 15, 1991; copyright 1991, Louise and Alan Sellars Collection of Art by American Women), 31; Sue Rice, curator, Louise and Alan Sellars Collection of Art by American Women, telephone communication, June 17, 2000; Sonnenstrahl, *Deaf Artists in America*, 43–47; Charlotte Streifer Rubinstein, *American Women Artists* (Farmington Hills, Mich.: G. K. Hall, 1982), 58–60; "One's Best Work Over at Eighty? Nonsense, Says Mrs. Charlotte Coman," *New York Herald*, magazine section, January 12, 1913, 7.

16. Information on Goya is from Pierre Gassier, *Goya: Biographical and Critical Study*, trans. James Emmons (New York: Skira, 1986); Evan S. Connell, *Francisco Goya* (New

York: Perseus Books, 2004); Anthony H. Hull, *Goya: Man Among Kings* (New York: Hamilton Press, 1987); Xavier de Salas, *Goya*, trans. Arnoldo Mondadori (New York: Mayflower Books, 1981); James G. Ravin and Chuck Close, "Art and Ophthalmology" (invited address at Weil Medical College of Cornell University, New York City, March 10, 2005); Pierre Descargues, *Goya* (New York: Crescent Books, 1979).

17. Quoted in Robert Hughes, *Goya* (New York: Knopf, 2004), 130.

18. Jonathan Brown, *The Golden Age of Painting in Spain* (New Haven, Conn.: Yale University Press, 1991), 58–60; Rosemarie Mulcahy, "Navarrete, Juan Fernández de (Mudo, El)," in *The Grove Dictionary of Art*, ed. Jane Turner (New York: Oxford University Press, 1996); Lane, *Deaf Artist in Early America*.

19. Information on Hockney is from Peter Webb, *Portrait of David Hockney* (New York: E. P. Dutton, 1988); Sonnenstrahl, *Deaf Artists in America*; Charles A. Riley, "A Higher Tone," *WE* (September–October 1998): 36–41; Bernard Weinraub, "Enticed by Bright Light: A Show of Hockney's Photocollages," *New York Times*, August 15, 2001, E3; Matthew Gurewitsch, "Stravinsky, Featuring Hockney: A Met Mix," *New York Times*, October 12, 2003, AR33; David Hockney, *The Colors of Music* (film directed by Maryte Kavaliauskas and Seth Schneidman; produced by Chantal Bernheim, 2005), http://www.davidhockneythecolorsofmusic.com/javascript.

20. Quoted in Weinraub, "Enticed by Bright Light," E3.

21. Hockney, *Colors of Music*.

22. Quoted in Webb, *Portrait of David Hockney*, 186.

23. Quoted in Gurewitsch, "Stravinsky, Featuring Hockney," AR33.

24. Sonnenstrahl, *Deaf Artists in America*.

25. *Deaf Way II: Featured Visual Artists* (catalog for the exhibition at Gallaudet University; Washington, D.C.: Gallaudet University Press, 2002), 57; "20 Deaf Artists: Common Motifs" (exhibit of Deaf Artists at Deaf Studies VI Conference, ProArts Gallery, Oakland, Calif.), Deaf View/Image. Art (De'VIA), http://www.deafart.org/Biographies/Orkid_Sassouni/orkid_sassouni.html.

26. *Deaf Way II*, 57.

27. Information and a manifesto for De'VIA can be found on the Deaf View/Image Art website as "What Is Deaf Art?" http://www.deafart.org/Deaf_Art_/deaf_art_.html.

28. L. K. Elion, essay in Charles Crawford Baird, *Chuck Baird 35 Plates* (San Diego: Dawn Sign Press, 1993), 13.

29. Sonnenstrahl, *Deaf Artists in America*, 324–29; *Deaf Way II*, 61.

30. Quoted in Sonnenstrahl, *Deaf Artists in America*, 326.

31. Ibid., 330–35.

32. Mary Thornley, foreword to *Deaf Way II*, 3–4.

33. Quoted in Sonnenstrahl, *Deaf Artists in America*, 332.

34. Elion, essay, 9–10; Sonnenstrahl, *Deaf Artists in America*, 313.

35. Sonnenstrahl, *Deaf Artists in America*, 311–17; Baird, *Chuck Baird 35 Plates*; *Deaf Way II*, 12.

36. Quoted in *Deaf Way II*, 12.

37. Quoted in Elion, essay, 11.

38. Sonnenstrahl, *Deaf Artists in America*, 318–23; Harry R. Williams website, http://www.geocities.com/camijerosa/index.htm.

39. Williams, http://www.geocities.com/camijerosa/index.htm.

40. Sonnenstrahl calls the painting *Coffin Door II*, while on the website dedicated to Harry R. Williams by his brother, the painting is called *Prophesy*.

41. Lane, *Deaf Artist in Early America*, 56–61.

42. National Institute on Deafness and Other Communication Disorders (NIDCD), part of the National Institutes of Health, http://www.nidcd.nih.gov/health/hearing/coch.asp.

43. John Horgan, "The Forgotten Era of Brain Chips," *Scientific American* (October 2005), 72; Berchin-Weiss told me of the increasing popularity of cochlear implants, September 26, 2005.

44. Sonnenstrahl, *Deaf Artists in America*, 139–43; Smithsonian Institution Libraries, file on John Lewis Clarke, assorted references.

45. Sonnenstrahl, *Deaf Artists in America*, 140.

46. "Bear Didn't Pose but Somehow Indian Artist Got Perfect Portrait in Wood: Deaf and Dumb Native Artist Discovered by U.S. at Last," *Washington Daily News*, January 27, 1934, 10; "Deaf, Dumb Indian Carver to Exhibit Work at Festival," *Kalispell (Montana) Inter Lake*, May 20, 1955.

47. Oliver Sacks, *Seeing Voices* (New York: HarperPerennial, 1990).

48. Ibid., 136.

49. Bob Keefer, "Carving a Way Out," *Register-Guard*, July 24, 1992, 1D, 2D; Bob

Keefer, personal communication, November 22, 2005; Tommy Griffin, curator, Presentation Design Group, personal communication, November 22, 2005; "For Year of Disabled Hospital to Show Sculptor's Work," *Oregonian*, November 16, 1981, C4; Ted Wimmer, "Russell Childers" (biographical essay; Jamison Thomas Gallery, Portland, Ore.).

50. Keefer, November 22, 2005; Keefer, "Carving a Way Out," 1D, 2D.

51. Quoted in Keefer, "Carving a Way Out," 1D.

Chapter 12: Cancer and Creativity

1. "Cancer Facts and Figures 2005," National Cancer Institute, http://www.cancer.org/downloads/STT/CAFF2005f4PWSecured.pdf.

2. All information and quotations are from Vincent Desiderio, personal communication, October 4, 2005.

3. Information on breast cancer is from the National Breast Cancer Foundation, http://www.nationalbreastcancer.org/.

4. All information and quotations are from Nancy Fried, personal communication, October 8, 2005.

5. Cited by Fried, October 8, 2005.

6. All information and quotations are from Anne Thulin, personal communication, October 9, 2005.

7. All information and quotations are from Martha Jane Bradford, personal communication, October 3, 2005.

8. Bradford's instructions are at http://www.marthavista.com/Digitaldrawings areoriginalart.pdf and her home page is http://www.marthavista.com.

9. American Cancer Society, "Tobacco Control Front and Center at International Conferences: 1 Billion Tobacco Deaths Possible If Current Trends Continue," July 7, 2006, http://www.cancer.org/docroot/NWS/content/NWS_2_1x_Tobacco_ Control_Front_and_Center_at_International_Conferences.asp.

10. Hilton Kramer, "Over the Line: The Art and Life of Jacob Lawrence," *Art & Antiques* 24, no. 9 (October 2002): 110–11; Elizabeth Hutton Turner, ed., *Jacob Lawrence: The Migration Series* (Washington, D.C.: Rappahannock Press/Phillips Collection, 1993).

11. Peter T. Nesbett, Michelle DuBois, and Stephanie Ellis-Smith, *Jacob Lawrence; Paintings, Drawings, and Murals (1935–1999), A Catalog Raisonné* (Seattle: University of

Washington Press, 2000); Jacob and Gwen Knight Lawrence Virtual Resource Center of Jacob and Gwendolyn Lawrence Foundation, http://www.jacoband gwenlawrence.org.

12. Jacob and Gwen Knight Lawrence Virtual Resource Center, http://www. jacobandgwenlawrence.org/teaching00.html.

13. Ibid., http://www.jacobandgwenlawrence.org/artandlife02.html.

14. Michael Kimmelman, "Simplicity Can Be Complicated: Jacob Lawrence Found Emotional Authenticity in Art and Life," *New York Times*, June 14, 2000, 3.

15. Jacob and Gwen Knight Lawrence Virtual Resource Center, http://www. jacobandgwenlawrence.org/artandlife00.html.

16. Dodie Kazanjian, "Freeing the Spirit," *Vogue* (October 2005): 352–57, 396; Carol Kino, "A Visit with the Modern's First Grandmother," *New York Times*, October 2, 2005, AR30.

17. Quoted in Kazanjian, "Freeing the Spirit," 396.

18. Ibid., 352.

19. Quoted in Kino, "Visit with the Modern's First Grandmother," AR30.

20. Elizabeth Murray, "The Aftermath: Clinging to Belief in Art," *New York Times*, September 23, 2001, AR29.

21. Joel Kupferman, New York Environmental Law and Justice Project, personal communication, December 2, 2005.

22. Joan Reibman, Shao Lin, Syni-An A. Hwang, Mridu Gulati, James A. Bowers, Linda Rogers, Kenneth I. Berger, Anne Hoerning, Marta Gomez, and Edward F. Fitzgerald, "The World Trade Center Residents' Respiratory Health Study: New-Onset Respiratory Symptoms and Pulmonary Function," *Environmental Health Perspectives* 113, no. 4 (April 2005), http://ehp.niehs.nih.gov/members/2004/7375/7375.html; P. Landrigan, P. Lioy, G. Thurston, et al., "Health and Environmental Consequences of the World Trade Center Disaster," *Environmental Health Perspectives* 112 (2004): 731–39, http://ehp.niehs.nih.gov/members/2004/6702/6702.html.

23. Quoted in Kazanjian, "Freeing the Spirit," 396.

24. Hannah Wilke, *Hannah Wilke: A Retrospective*, ed. Thomas H. Kochheiser (Columbia: University of Missouri Press, 1989); Hannah Wilke, *Intra Venus/Hannah Wilke* (New York: Ronald Feldman Fine Arts, 1995); Hannah Wilke, *Hannah Wilke, 1940–1993* (Katalogredaktion und Lektorat, Stefanie Kreuzer; in *Zusammenarbeit mit Wibke Behrens et al.*; Berlin: Neue Gesellschaft für Bildende Kunst, 2000).

25. Monona Rossol, personal communication, October 16, 2005.

26. Wilke, *Hannah Wilke, 1940–1993,* 149.

27. Information on Arneson is from Sandra Shannonhouse, widow of Robert Arneson, personal communication, November 4, 2005; Jonathan Fineberg, "Humor at the Frontier of the Self," in *Robert Arneson: Self Reflections,* ed. Gary Garrels and Janet Bishop (exhibition catalog; San Francisco: San Francisco Museum of Modern Art, 1997), 10–22; Neal Benezra, *Robert Arneson: A Retrospective* (exhibition catalog; Des Moines, Iowa: Des Moines Art Center, 1985), 43–79; Gary Garrels, "Chemo I and Chemo II," in Garrels and Bishop, *Robert Arneson,* 68; Rachel Rosenfield Lafo, *Robert Arneson: Self Portraits and Drawings* (exhibition catalog; Lincoln, Mass.: De Cordova Museum and Sculpture Park, 1999).

28. Quoted in *Revolution of the Wheel, Part IV* (film directed and edited by Scott Sterling; produced by Kathleen Garfield, 1997).

29. Monona Rossol, personal communication, October 21, 2005.

Chapter 13: Difficulties with Hands, Arms, Legs, and Feet

1. Carel van Mander, *Dutch and Flemish Artists,* trans. C. van de Wall (1604; New York: McFarlane, Warde, McFarlane, 1936), 342–43.

2. Information on Martin Wong is from personal communication with his mother, Florence Wong Fie, June 10, 2006, and from Jason Murison of the PPOW Gallery in New York, June 9, 2006; the video (*Martin Wong,* by Charlie Ahearn, 1998); and the exhibition *Sweet Oblivion: The Urban Landscape of Martin Wong* at the New Museum in New York, May 27–September 13, 1998.

3. James G. Ravin, "Renoir's Maladies: The Medical Tribulations of an Impressionist," in *The Eye of the Artist,* ed. Michael F. Marmor and James G. Ravin (St. Louis: Mosby, 1997), 38–42.

4. Quoted in ibid., 39.

5. Joseph E. Sniezek, Centers for Disease Control and Prevention (CDC), "Emerging Public Health Strategies for Arthritis: Population-Based Approaches for the Leading Cause of Disability in the United States (paper presented at the International Conference for the Bone and Joint Decade 2000–2010, Tokyo, April 2002), http://www.boneandjointdecade.org/countries/japan/abstracts/3_1_sniezek.pdf.

6. Mark H. Beers and Robert Berkow, eds., *The Merck Manual of Diagnosis and Ther-*

apy, 17th ed. (Whitehouse Station, N.J.: Merck Research Laboratories, 1999), 409–23.

7. Jean Renoir, *Renoir, My Father,* trans. Randolph Weaver and Dorothy Weaver (Boston: Little, Brown, 1958), 26–28, 348–458.

8. Ibid., 28.

9. Ibid., 452.

10. Quoted in Philip Sandblom, *Creativity and Disease* (New York: Marion Boyars, 1996), 4.

11. Laurence Binyon, *Painting in the Far East* (New York: Dover, 1969), 141–46; Laurence Sickman and Alexander Soper, *Art and Architecture of China* (London: Penguin, 1956), 233–34.

12. Beers and Berkow, *Merck Manual,* 2402–3; National Institute of Arthritis and Musculoskeletal and Skin Diseases (NIAMS), National Institutes of Health (NIH), "Questions and Answers about Juvenile Rheumatoid Arthritis," http://www.niams.nih.gov/hi/topics/juvenile_arthritis/juvarthr.htm#3.

13. Information on Lewis is from Lance Woolaver, *The Illuminated Life of Maud Lewis,* photographs by Bob Brooks (Halifax, NS: Nimbus Publishing/Art Gallery of Nova Scotia, 1995); Lance Woolaver, *Christmas with Maud Lewis,* photographs by Bob Brooks (Fredericton, NB: Goose Lane Editions, 1997); Bernard Riordan, director, Art Gallery of Nova Scotia, personal communication, March 1999; Laurie Hamilton, *The Painted House of Maud Lewis: Conserving a Folk Art Treasure* (Halifax, NS: Art Gallery of Nova Scotia, 2001); *Maud Lewis: An Intimate Look at the Life and Work of One of Nova Scotia's Best Loved Folk Artists* (CD; Art Gallery of Nova Scotia, 1997); *Maud Lewis: A World without Shadows* (video directed by Diane Beaudry; produced by Kathleen Shannon; National Film Board of Canada, 1997).

14. Quoted in Woolaver, *Christmas with Maud Lewis,* 112.

15. Ibid.

16. Ibid., 12.

17. Mihaly Csikszentmihalyi, *Flow: The Psychology of Optimal Experience* (New York: Harper and Row, 1990), 204.

18. Paul Camic, "Expanding Treatment Possibilities for Chronic Pain Through the Expressive Arts," in *Medical Art Therapy with Adults,* ed. C. Malchioiti (London and Philadelphia: Jessica Kingsley, 1999), 43–61.

19. Norman Cousins, *Anatomy of an Illness* (New York: W.W. Norton, 1979).

20. Lee S. Berk, David L. Felten, Stanley A. Tan, Barry B. Bittman, and James Westengard, "Modulation of Neuroimmune Parameters During the Eustress of Humor-Associated Mirthful Laughter," *Alternative Therapies* 7, no. 2 (March 2001): 62–76.

21. Elizabeth Ferrer, *The True Poetry: The Art of Maria Izquierdo* (New York: Americas Society Art Gallery, 1997).

22. Nell Blaine, personal communications, March 1996; Marticia Sawin, *Nell Blaine: Her Art and Life* (New York: Hudson Hills Press, 1998); Pat Van Gelder, "Close to Home," *American Artist* (February 1990): 28–35, 69; *Nell Blaine: Recent Oils, Watercolors, Drawings, April 6 through May 6, 1995* (catalog for the exhibition at Fischbach Gallery, New York City).

23. Quoted in Sawin, *Nell Blaine*, 70.

24. Quoted in Van Gelder, "Close to Home," 69.

25. Ibid., 33.

26. Information on Wyant is from Eliot Candee Clark, *Alexander Wyant* (New York: privately printed, 1916); Eliot Candee Clark, *Sixty Paintings by Alexander H. Wyant, Described by Eliot Clark* (New York: privately printed, 1916); Robert S. Olpin, essay in *Alexander Helwig Wyant* (catalog for the exhibition at the Utah Museum of Fine Arts, University of Utah, Salt Lake City, March 3–31, 1968; Paragon Press, 1968), n.p.

27. Mark Etkind, *Boris Kustodiev—Paintings, Graphic Works, Book Illustrations, Theatrical Designs*, trans. Ashkhen Mikoyan and Vladimir Vezey (New York: Harry N. Abrams; Leningrad: Aurora Art Publishers, 1983), 256–69; Dmitri Shostakovich, *The Memoirs of Dmitri Shostakovich*, ed. Solomon Volkov, trans. Antonina W. Boisnyk (New York: Harper and Row, 1979), 16–20.

28. Etkind, *Boris Kustodiev*, 257.

29. Ibid., 258.

30. Shostakovich, *Memoirs*, 20.

31. Cited in Etkind, *Boris Kustodiev*, 264.

32. Information on Drake is from Jill Beute Koverman, personal communication, February 2000; Jill Beute Koverman, ed., *I Made This Jar . . . : The Life and Works of the Enslaved African-American Potter, Dave* (Columbia: McKissick Museum/University of South Carolina, 1998); *Pottery, Poetry and Politics Surrounding the Enslaved African-American Potter, Dave* (proceedings of the symposium at the McKissick Museum, April 25, 1998; Columbia: McKissick Museum/University of South Carolina, 1998); Tom

Mack, "Dave the Potter" (Aiken: University of South Carolina, October 5, 1999), http://www.usca.edu/aasc/davepotter.htm.

33. This work is in the collection of the Atlanta History Center, Atlanta, Ga.

34. John A. Burrison, "Dave, the Potter and His Place in American Ceramics History," in *Pottery, Poetry and Politics*, 26–29.

35. Aaron De Groft, "Pottery, Poetry, or Protest: The Work of the Slave, 'Dave the Potter,'" in *Pottery, Poetry and Politics*, 51–62.

36. Burrison, "Dave, the Potter," 26. This work was made on April 14, 1859, but its current collection is unknown.

37. Orville Vernon Burton, "Edgefield, South Carolina; Home to Dave the Potter," in Koverman, *I Made This Jar*, 46.

38. This work is in the collection of Tony and Marie Shank.

39. This work was made on August 16, 1857, and is in the collection of Larry Carlson.

Chapter 14: Working with Quadriplegia and Beyond

1. Information on Close is from Chuck Close, telephone communication, June 30, 2005; John Guare, *Chuck Close: Life and Work, 1988–1995* (New York: Thames and Hudson, 1995); Jan Greenberg and Sandra Jordan, *Chuck Close Up Close* (New York: DK Publishing, 1998); Sheila Farr, "The Art of Overcoming," *Atlantic*, November 18, 1998, http://www.theatlantic.com/unbound/criticaleye/ce981118.htm#farr.

2. Guare, *Chuck Close*, 46.

3. Greenberg and Jordan, *Chuck Close Up Close*, 40.

4. *Chuck Close: Recent Paintings* (catalog for an exhibition at PaceWildenstein Gallery, New York, May 10–June 18, 2005).

5. Greenberg and Jordan, *Chuck Close Up Close*, 40.

6. Information on Callahan is from John Callahan, *Don't Worry, He Won't Get Far on Foot* (New York: Vintage Books, 1990); John Callahan, *Will the Real John Callahan Please Stand Up? Lurid Revelations, Shocking Rejections, Irate Letters* (New York: William Morrow, 1998).

7. Callahan, *Don't Worry*, 155.

8. Ibid., 158.

9. Ibid., 217.

10. The review is at http://www.bbc.co.uk/ouch/features/filmfest.shtml.

11. Karl Pribram, "The Neurophysiology of Remembering," *Scientific American* (January 1969): 73–86; Daniel Goleman, "Holographic Memory: Karl Pribram Interviewed by Daniel Goleman," *Psychology Today* 12, no. 9 (February 1979): 71–74. For an excellent and readable book on holograms and our world, see Michael Talbot, *The Holographic Universe* (New York: HarperCollins, 1991).

12. Information on Bernhardt is from Cindi Bernhardt, personal communication, January 5, 2006; Marc Alexander, *Artists Above All* (N.p.: Mouth and Foot Painting Artists, 2005), 61–62; promotional material from MFPA, Mouth and Foot Painting Artists; two websites featuring her work and her life: http://www.infinitec.org/learn/art/bernhardt.htm and http://www.newla.com/cindibernhardt.

13. Quoted in Alexander, *Artists Above All,* 62.

14. Ibid.

15. Bernhardt, January 5, 2006.

16. Quoted in Alexander, *Artists Above All,* 62.

17. Information on Wikstrom is from his website, http://www.bromwikstrom.com/; VSA arts, http://www.vsarts.org/x548.xml and http://www.vsarts.org/prebuilt/showcase/gallery/exhibits/permanent/artists/bwikstrom.html; mailings from the Association of Mouth and Foot Painting Artists (AMFPA).

18. From Wikstrom's biography on his website, http://www.bromwikstrom.com/orleans.html.

19. Ibid.

20. Ibid.

21. Ibid.

22. Quoted in Alexander, *Artists Above All,* 138.

23. Ibid., 139.

24. From Wikstrom's biography, http://www.bromwikstrom.com/disch.html.

25. Ibid.

26. Information on Chun is from her husband, Elroy Chun, personal communication, March 30, 2006; her daughter-in-law Kimi Morton Chun, personal communication, April 2006; her website, http://www.peggychun.com.

27. All Chun quotes are from http://www.peggychun.com.

Chapter 15: Accidents, Hazards, Injuries, and Art

1. "Transformation: The Art of Joan Brown" (exhibition at the Oakland Museum of California, September 1998), http://www.museumca.org/exhibit/exhi_joan_brown.html.

2. Monona Rossol, "Popular Toronto Artist Dies," *ACTS FACTS* (monthly newsletter from Arts, Crafts, and Theater Safety [ACTS]), November 2005, 4.

3. Monona Rossol, *The Artist's Complete Health and Safety Guide* (New York: Watson-Guptill, 2001).

4. Department of Health and Human Services (National Institute of Occupational Safety and Health), "Direct Blue 6, Direct Black 38, and Direct Brown 95 Benzidine Derived Dyes, Epidemiological and Medical Studies—Benzidine-Based Dyes," *Current Intelligence Bulletin* 24, April 17, 1978, http://www.cdc.gov/niosh/78148_24.html.

5. Information on the Radium Girls is from Claudia Clark, *Radium Girls: Women and Industrial Health Reform, 1910–1935* (Chapel Hill: University of North Carolina Press, 1997); Bill Kovarik, "The Radium Girls," http://www.radford.edu/~wkovarik/envhist/radium.html (originally published as chap. 8 in *Mass Media and Environmental Conflict: America's Green Crusades*, ed. Mark Neuzil [Thousand Oaks, Calif.: Sage Publications, 1996]).

6. Information on Hanson comes from Martin H. Bush, *Sculptures by Duane Hanson* (Wichita, Kans.: Edwin A. Ulrich Museum of Art/Wichita State University, 1985); Erika Doss, Wesla Hanson, and Tin Ly, *Duane Hanson: Portraits from the Heartland* (Fargo, N. Dak.: Plains Art Museum/New Rivers Press, 2004); Christine Giles, Elizabeth Hayt, and Katherine Plake Hough, *Duane Hanson: Virtual Reality* (Palm Springs, Calif.: Palm Springs Desert Museum, 2000); Kirk Varnedoe, *Duane Hanson* (New York: Harry N. Abrams, 1985).

7. Quoted in Bush, *Sculptures by Duane Hanson*, 15.

8. Information on polyvinyl acetate is from Monona Rossol, personal communication, January 31, 2006.

9. Bush, *Sculptures by Duane Hanson*, 75.

10. Ibid., 4.

11. Ibid., 15.

12. Information on DeFeo is from Leah Levy, executor of the Jay DeFeo estate,

personal communications, February 6 and 8, 2006; Bill Berkson, "Jay DeFeo: The Romance of the Rose," in *Jay DeFeo: Selected Works, 1952–1989* (catalog for the exhibition at The Galleries at Moore, Moore College of Art and Design, Philadelphia, September 6–October 20, 1996), http://thegalleriesatmoore.org/publications/defeocl.shtml; Jane Green and Leah Levy, eds., *Jay DeFeo and the Rose* (Berkeley: University of California Press/New York: Whitney Museum of American Art, 2003); Dean Smith, "DeFeo, Conner Papers Add to Bancroft's Beat Collection," *Bancroftiana* 112 (Spring 1998), http://bancroft.berkeley.edu/events/bancroftiana/112/defeo.html; Eve Strickman, "Jay DeFeo's Deadly Rose," *NY Arts*, http://nyartsmagazine.com/pages/nyam_document.php?nid=46&did=595.

13. Quoted in Berkson, "Jay DeFeo."

14. Ibid.

15. Jay DeFeo, *Out of My Own Head: Photographs by Jay DeFeo* (catalog for the exhibit at Mills College Art Museum, September 2005), n.p.

16. Quoted in Green and Levy, *Jay DeFeo and the Rose*, 37.

17. Information on Blackburn is from Tesia Blackburn, personal communication, February 12, 2006; Tesia Blackburn, "Poisoned by Painting: The Problem of Toxic Art-Supplies" (Independent Arts and Media, Expo, August 10, 2001), http://www.artsandmedia.net/cgi-bin/dc/expo/2001/08/10_oilpaints; Tesia Blackburn, website, http://www.blackburnfineart.com.

18. Quotes from Blackburn, "Poisoned by Painting."

19. Information on Day is from Rebecca Dobkins with Carey T. Caldwell and Frank R. LaPena, *Memory and Imagination: The Legacy of Maidu Indian Artist Frank Day* (Oakland: Oakland Museum of California, 1997); Frank Day, quotes from the exhibition "Memory and Imagination: The Legacy of Maidu Indian Artist Frank Day," National Museum of the American Indian, New York, February–March 1998; "The Life, Art, and Legacy of Maidu Indian Artist Frank Day," panel discussion at the exhibition "Memory and Imagination: The Legacy of Maidu Indian Artist Frank Day," National Museum of the American Indian, New York, February 12, 1998 (panelists included Rebecca Dobkins, exhibition curator and professor of anthropology, Willamette University; Carey Caldwell, chief curator of history at the Oakland Museum of California; Harry Fonseca, Native American artist; Judith Lowry, Native American artist).

20. Quote from the exhibition "Memory and Imagination."

21. Quoted in Rebecca Dobkins, "The Life and Art of Frank Day," in Dobkins, Caldwell, and LaPena, *Memory and Imagination*, 9.

22. Ibid., 1.

23. Information on di Suvero is from James Monte, *Mark di Suvero* (New York: Whitney Museum of American Art, 1975); Mark di Suvero, *Mark di Suvero: Open Secret: Sculpture 1990–92* (New York: Gagosian Gallery in association with Richard Bellamy/Rizzoli, 1993); Irving Sandler, *Mark di Suvero at Storm King Art Center* (New York: Storm King Art Center/Harry N. Abrams, 1996); David Taffet, "Nasher Shapes Dallas Art Scene"; DeCordova Museum and Sculpture Park, Mark di Suvero, http://www.decordova.org/ . . . /sculp_park/di_suvero.html; "Modern Sculpture Center's Comprehensive Collection, Impeccable Design to Have Global Significance," *Dallas Voice*, http://www.dallasvoice.com/articles/dispArticle.cfm?Article_ ID=3646.

24. Sandler, *Mark di Suvero at Storm King Art Center*, 98.

25. Quoted in Monte, *Mark di Suvero*, 12.

26. Howardena Pindell, personal communication, October 30, 2005; Howardena Pindell, "Johannesburg Biennale and Interview with Olu Oquibe," *International Review of African American Art* 15, no. 3 (1998): 12–19; Howardena Pindell, "Numbering: Counting on My Fingers and Toes," *International Review of African American Art* 19, no. 3 (2004): 42–43; Mira Schor, "Contemporary Feminism: Art Practice, Theory, and Activism—an Intergenerational Perspective," *Art Journal* 58, no. 4 (Winter 1999): 8–29; Howardena Pindell, "Autobiography: Water/Ancestors Middle Passage/ Family Ghosts," Legacy Project, Visual Arts Library, http://www.legacy-project .org/arts/display.html?ID=961.

27. Pindell, October 30, 2005.

28. Quoted in Schor, "Contemporary Feminism," 24.

29. Pindell, October 30, 2005.

30. Ibid.

31. Ibid.

32. Information on Ruffner is from Ginny Ruffner, personal communication, February 7, 2006; Bonnie Gangelhoff, "Eternal Sunshine," *Southwest Art* 34, no. 12 (May 2005): 114–17; Ellen Pall, "Starting from Scratch," *New York Times Magazine*, September 24, 1995; Regina Hackett, "Ginny Ruffner's Flowering Tornado," *Art Guide Northwest!* (2006), http://www.artguidenw.com/Ruffner.html; Frances

DeVuono, "A Conversation with Ginny Ruffner, Artist," *Artweek* 29, no. 17 (October 1998); Jan Garden Castro, "Cultivating Her Garden: Ginny Ruffner," *Sculpture* 19, no. 2 (March 2000): 10–11.

33. Hackett, "Ginny Ruffner's Flowering Tornado."

34. Ruffner, February 7, 2006.

35. Pall, "Starting from Scratch."

36. Ruffner, February 7, 2006.

37. Pall, "Starting from Scratch."

38. Ruffner, February 7, 2006.

39. Sheila Farr, "The Art of Overcoming," *Atlantic* (November 18, 1998), http://www.theatlantic.com/unbound/criticaleye/ce981118.htm#farr.

40. Information on Pippin is from Judith E. Stein, *I Tell My Heart: The Art of Horace Pippin* (Philadelphia: Pennsylvania Academy of Fine Arts/Universe Publishing, 1993); Romare Bearden, "Horace Pippin," in *Horace Pippin* (exhibition catalog; Washington, D.C.: Phillips Collection, 1976), n.p.; Alexander Eliot, *Three Hundred Years of American Painting* (New York: Time, 1957), 200–201; Stephen May, "Horace Pippin: World War I Veteran and Artist," *Military History* (February 1998), http://historynet.com/mh/blhoracepippin/; "African American Military History," http://www.ritesofpassage.org/mil_wwone.htm.

41. "African-American Military History."

42. Stein, *I Tell My Heart*, 4.

43. May, "Horace Pippin."

44. Information on Sudek is from Zdenek Kirschner, *Josef Sudek* (Prague: Takarajima Books/Museum of Decorative Arts, 1993), n.p.; Charles Sawyer, "Josef Sudek," *Creative Camera*, no. 190 (April 1980), http://www.people.fas.harvard.edu/~sawyer/Sudek.htm; Anna Farkova, *Josef Sudek*, trans. Michael Knight (Munich: Gina Kehayoff Verlag, 1999).

45. Sawyer, "Josef Sudek."

46. Information on Léger is from Robert L. Delavoy, *Léger: Biographical and Critical Study*, trans. Stuart Gilbert (Paris: Albert Skira, 1962); Jack Flam, "Fernand Léger," in *Fernand Léger* (catalog for the exhibition at the Acquavella Galleries, October 23–December 12, 1987; New York: Acquavella Galleries, 1987); Katherine Kuh, *Léger* (Urbana: University of Illinois Press, 1953); Carolyn Lanchner, *Fernand Léger* (New York: Museum of Modern Art, 1998); Werner F. L. Schmalenbach, *Fernand Léger* (Salzburg: Museum Moderner Kunst, Rupertinum, 2002).

47. Quoted in Flam, "Fernand Léger," 13.

48. Rebecca Holland, School of Chemistry, University of Bristol, UK, http://www.bris.ac.uk/Depts/Chemistry/MOTM/mustard/mustard.htm.

49. Quoted in Flam, "Fernand Léger," 15.

50. Schmalenbach, *Fernand Léger,* 18.

51. Information on Beuys is from Peter Nesbit, "Crash Course: Remarks on a Beuys Story," in *Joseph Beuys: Mapping the Legacy* (New York: Dap Publishers; Sarasota, Fla.: John and Mable Ringling Museum of Art, 2001); Benjamin H. D. Buchloh, "Beuys: Twilight of the Idol: Preliminary Notes for a Critique," *Artforum* 18, no. 5 (January 1980): 35–43; Joan Rothfuss, curator, Walker Art Center, "Joseph Beuys: A Brief Biography," http://www.walkerart.org/archive/4/9C43FDAD069C47F36167.htm; Deborah Schultz, "Joseph Beuys, at the Tate Modern, London," *Art Monthly,* no. 285 (April 2002): 21–22.

52. Quote from a 1979 interview with Frans Hak appears in "Ecovention: Current Art to Transform Ecologies," Section 9: Artists' Philosophical Statements, http://www.greenmuseum.org/c/ecovention/sect9.html.

53. Information on Francis is from William C. Agee, *Sam Francis: Paintings, 1947–1990* (Los Angeles: Museum of Contemporary Art, 1999); Peter Selz, *Sam Francis,* rev. ed., with essays on his prints by Susan Einstein and Jan Butterfield (New York: Harry N. Abrams, 1982); Luke Elwes, "A Floating World" (written for the exhibition "Selected Paintings, 1955–1990" at the Broadbent Gallery, London, 2001, http://www.broadbentgallery.com/francis/francis_article1.html.

54. Selz, *Sam Francis,* 20.

55. Sam Francis, *Saturated Blue: Writings from the Notebooks* (Santa Monica, Calif.: privately published in association with Lapis Press, 1995), n.p.

Chapter 16: Michelangelo's Problems and Perseverance

1. Biographical information on Michelangelo comes from Giorgio Vasari, *The Lives of the Artists,* trans. Gaston Du C. De Vere (1568; New York: Knopf, 1996), 2:642–769; Ascanio Condivi, *The Life of Michelangelo,* trans. Alice Sedgwick Wohl, ed. Hellmut Wohl (1553; University Park: Pennsylvania State University Press, 1999); Howard Hibbard, *Michelangelo* (New York: Harper and Row, 1974); Linda Murray, *Michelangelo: His Life, Work and Times* (New York: Thames and Hudson, 1984).

2. Vasari, *Lives of the Artists,* 2:643.

3. Nathan Leites, *Art and Life: Aspects of Michelangelo* (New York: New York University Press, 1986).

4. Murray, *Michelangelo*, 15–16; Charles H. Morgan, *The Life of Michelangelo* (New York: Reynal and Company, 1960), 33–34.

5. Condivi, *Life of Michelangelo*, 108.

6. Quoted in Benvenuto Cellini, *The Autobiography of Benvenuto Cellini*, trans. George Bull (1558–66; London: Penguin, 1956), 31.

7. Morgan, *Life of Michelangelo*, 33–34.

8. Michelangelo, *Complete Poems and Selected Letters of Michelangelo*, trans. Creighton Gilbert, ed. Robert N. Linscott (1496–1563; Princeton, N.J.: Princeton University Press, 1963), 142 (madrigal 253).

9. Ibid., 151 (terza-rima stanzas 265).

10. Leites, *Art and Life*, 26–27.

11. William G. Niederland, "Clinical Aspects of Creativity," *American Imaago* 24 (1967): 23.

12. Information on Michelangelo's artistic style is from Vasari, "Michelangelo," in *Lives of the Artists*, 2:642–768; Peter Bencivenga, "Michelangelo: The Effects of Pain on Artistic Style" (unpublished manuscript, New School University, New York, 1994); Hibbard, *Michelangelo*, 99–147; Frederick Hartt, *History of Italian Renaissance Art* (New York: Harry N. Abrams, 1987), 487–503.

13. Previously, it was thought that one of the influences on Michelangelo's changing style might be an ancient statue called *Laocoön* presumed to have been discovered in 1506. But Lynn Catterson of Columbia University believes the statue was actually sculpted by Michelangelo and passed off as an antique to raise money during a time when he was in financial straits. Jennifer Grogan, "The Ultimate Art History Whodunit: A Michelangelo Forgery or a Classical Antiquity?" Columbia News Service, May 3, 2005, http://jscms.jrn.columbia.edu/cns/2005-05-03/grogan-michelangelo forgery.

14. Condivi, *Life of Michelangelo*, 58.

15. Michelangelo, *Complete Poems and Selected Letters*, 5–6.

16. Bencivenga believes that Michelangelo's eye problems may have resulted in a looser style of painting. He quotes Hibbard, who says that at the beginning of the project, when Michelangelo transferred his drawing of a figure onto the ceiling of the chapel in order to paint it, he carefully followed the outlines he had drawn. But later, the artist painted more freely and sometimes improvised around his original

drawing. This may be due to eye problems, but I think it is more likely that Michelangelo's later looser style came as a result of creating his increasingly dynamic figures.

17. Carlos Hugh Espinel, "Michelangelo's Gout in a Fresco by Raphael," *Lancet* 354 (December 18–25, 1999): 2149–52.

18. Michelangelo, *Complete Poems and Selected Letters*, 202.

19. Ibid., 211.

20. Garabed Eknoyan, personal communications, January 6 and 9, 2006; Garabed Eknoyan, "Michelangelo: Art, Anatomy, and the Kidney," *Kidney International* 57 (March 2000): 1190–1201.

21. This is the most common title, but Condivi calls this image *The Congregation of the Waters* (*Life of Michelangelo*, 44).

22. Eknoyan points out that although Vasari attributes the phrase to Michelangelo, it originates with the classical scholar Angelo Poliziano (1454–1494); see "Michelangelo: Art, Anatomy, and the Kidney," 1200.

23. There is another anatomical reference in a Sistine Chapel ceiling panel. Next to the *Separation of Land from Water* is Michelangelo's most famous image, *The Creation of Adam*, which shows God reaching out his hand to bring Adam to life. It also may encode a reference to anatomy, but this image resembles a brain instead of a kidney. And while it implies Michelangelo's thoughts on the creative process rather than his physical problems, it supports Eknoyan's theory by suggesting additional anatomical symbolism in the fresco. Here again God is flying through the sky in a great mantle, but his garments, the angels, and his mantle are different. In "An Interpretation of Michelangelo's Creation of Adam Based on Neuroanatomy," *Journal of the American Medical Association* 264 (1990): 1837–41, Frank Lynn Meshberger, an obstetrician and gynecologist at St. John's Medical Center in Anderson, Indiana, finds that the outline of God's mantle is in the shape of a brain, and the figures within the mantle correspond to the brain's inner structures, such as the sulcus cinguli, vertebral artery, pons, spinal cord, pituitary, optic nerve, optic chasm, and optic tract. Although the image is acknowledged as God giving life to Adam, Meshberger believes it also symbolizes an awakening of the intellect and creative consciousness. He says the idea that creativity first starts in the mind and is later expressed by the hands is found in Michelangelo's poetry and cites a line in one of the artist's poems: "Only after the intellect has planned the best and highest can the ready hand take up the brush and try all things received."

24. Quoted in Condivi, *Life of Michelangelo*, 106.

25. Eknoyan, "Michelangelo: Art, Anatomy, and the Kidney," 1198.

26. Eknoyan, January 6, 2006.

27. Vasari, *Lives of the Artists*, 2:697.

Chapter 17: Creativity, Illness, and Identity

1. Information on Kubota is from Itchiku Kubota, "A Personal Chronology by Itchiku Kubota," in *Opulence: The Kimonos and Robes of Itchiku Kubota*, ed. Tomoyuki Yamanobe (Tokyo: Kodansha International, 1984), 128–30; Yamanobe, *Opulence*; "To Dye For: Portraying Nature on Silk," *Landscape Architecture* 86 (March 1996): 20–22.

2. Kubota, "Personal Chronology," 128. Today, *yūzen* is referred to as *Yuzen*, but I have used the older spelling because it is given that way in Kubota's autobiographic personal chronology in *Opulence*.

3. "A Short History of Yuzen Dyeing," Sei-Sen-Kyo Ueno Textile Design Lab., Kyoto, Japan, http://web.kyoto-inet.or.jp/people/yuzen/en/yuzen.html.

4. Kubota, "Personal Chronology," 129.

5. Ibid.

6. Information on Tanner is from Dewey Mosby with Darryl Sewell and Ray Alexander-Minter, *Henry Ossawa Tanner* (Philadelphia: Philadelphia Museum of Art; New York: Rizzoli, 1991); Marcia M. Mathews, *Henry Ossawa Tanner: American Artist* (Chicago: University of Chicago Press, 1994); "Henry Ossawa Tanner," Springfield Museum of Art, permanent collection, http://www.spfld-museum-of-art.org/collection/tanner.html.

7. Quoted in Mathews, *Henry Ossawa Tanner*, 13–14.

8. Ibid., 248.

9. Information on Yarde is from Richard Yarde, personal communication, January 30, 2006; Kathleen Koman, "Walking in the Valley of the Shadow," *Hope Magazine: Humanity Making a Difference* (August 1997): 18–25; Christine Temin, "Death and Transfiguration—the Art of Richard Yarde," *Bostonia, the Alumni Quarterly of Boston University* (Summer 1997): 83–85; "Worcester Art Museum Exhibition Features New Work by Richard Yarde," Worcester Art Museum, Worcester, Mass., museum press release, http://www.worcesterart.org/Information/PR/Past/6-5-03.html; "Visionary

Anatomies" (exhibition at the National Academy of Sciences, Washington, D.C.), http://www7.nationalacademies.org/arts/Yarde_Visionary_Anatomies.html.

10. Quoted in Koman, "Walking in the Valley of the Shadow," 20.

11. Quoted in artist biography, Rosenbaum Fine Art, http://www.rosenbaum fineart.com/yarde.jsp.

12. Yarde, January 30, 2006.

13. Information on Abbott is from Greystone Abbott, personal communication, February 22, 2006; Greystone Abbott's website, http://www.greystoneabbott.com; VSA arts (formerly Very Special Arts), http://www.vsarts.org/prebuilt/artists/registry/artistdetail.cfm?ArtistID=1871.

14. Abbott, February 22, 2006.

15. Stephen M. Edelson, Ph.D., "Scotopic Sensitivity Syndrome and the Irlen Lens System," Center for the Study of Autism, Salem, Ore., http://www.autism.org/irlen.html.

16. Abbott, February 22, 2006.

17. Ibid.

18. Ibid.

19. Information on Neel is from Patricia Hill, *Alice Neel* (New York: Harry N. Abrams, 1995); Cherry Smyth, "Alice Neel: Victoria Miro Gallery, London," *Art Monthly*, no. 278 (July/August 2004): 38; Sara London, "Alice Neel Looks at the Family: Smith College Museum of Art/Northampton," *Art New England* 19, no. 3 (April/May 1998): 36; Peter Gallo, "Firehouse Center for the Visual Arts/Burlington: Alice Neel: Women Drawn," *Art New England* 24, no. 5 (August/September 2003): 34; Avis Berman, "When Artists Grow Old," *Art News* (December 1983): 76–83.

20. Quoted in Berman, "When Artists Grow Old," 77.

21. Quote from Alice Neel's website, http://www.aliceneel.com.

22. Quoted in Berman, "When Artists Grow Old," 77.

23. Quoted in Hill, *Alice Neel*, 179.

24. Emily Carr, *The Complete Writings of Emily Carr* (Vancouver: Douglas and McIntyre; Seattle: University of Washington Press, 1997), 887.

25. Information on Carr is from Carr, *Complete Writings*; Maria Tippett, *Emily Carr: A Biography* (Toronto: Oxford University Press, 1979); Bennett Schiff, "Canada's National Treasure," *Smithsonian Magazine* 29, no. 12 (March 1999): 102–11; Doris

Shadbolt, *Emily Carr* (Vancouver: Douglas and McIntyre; Seattle: University of Washington Press, 1980); "Emily Carr," BC Heritage Branch, Province of British Columbia, http://collections.ic.gc.ca/Emilycarrhomework/gallery/gallmain.htm.

26. Emily Carr, *Growing Pains: The Autobiograhy of Emily Carr* (Vancouver: Douglas and McIntyre, 2005), 257.

27. Quoted in Tippett, *Emily Carr*, 258.

28. Carr, *Complete Writings*, 88.

29. Information on Dürer is from Albrecht Dürer, *The Writings of Albrecht Dürer*, trans. and ed. William Martin Conway (1506–1528; New York: Philosophical Library, 1958); Fedja Anzelewsky, *Dürer: His Art and Life*, trans. Heide Grieve (New York: Alpine Fine Arts, 1980); Jane Campbell Hutchinson, *Albrecht Dürer: A Biography* (Princeton, N.J.: Princeton University Press, 1990).

30. Dürer, *Writings*, 118.

31. "Malaria and the Netherlands," Royal Tropical Institute (Koninklijk Instituut voor de Tropen—KIT), http://www.kit.nl/frameset.asp?/specials/html/ma_special_features.asp&frnr=1&.

32. Quoted in Hutchinson, *Albrecht Dürer*, 184.

33. Vincent van Gogh, *The Complete Letters of Vincent van Gogh: With Reproductions of All the Drawings in the Correspondence*, 3 vols. (Boston: New York Graphic Society, 1978), 2:620 (letter 514).

34. Information on van Gogh and acute intermittent porphyria is from van Gogh, *Complete Letters*, vols. 1–3; Wilfred N. Arnold, *Vincent Van Gogh: Chemicals, Crises, and Creativity* (Boston: Birkhäuser, 1992); Loretta Loftus and Wilfred Niels Arnold, "Vincent van Gogh's Illness: Acute Intermittent Porphyria?" *British Medical Journal* 303 (December 21–28, 1991): 1589–91; Wilfred Niels Arnold, "The Illness of Vincent Van Gogh," *Journal of the History of Neurosciences* 13, no. 1 (March 2004): 22–43; Philip Sandblom, review of *Vincent van Gogh: Chemicals, Crises, and Creativity*, in *New England Journal of Medicine* 329, no. 15 (October 7, 1993): 1133.

35. Van Gogh appears to have had emotional difficulties in addition to AIP. One theory suggests that he was schizophrenic and another that he had bipolar disorder. For evidence suggesting schizophrenia, see Ellen Winner, *Invented Worlds: The Psychology of the Arts* (Cambridge, Mass.: Harvard University Press, 1982), and for evidence suggesting bipolar disorder, see Kay Redfield Jamison, *Touched with Fire* (New York: Macmillan, 1993), and A. Carota, G. Iaria, A. Berney, and J. Bogousslavsky, "Understanding Van Gogh's Night: Bipolar Disorder," in Julien Bogousslavsky and François

Boller, eds., *Frontiers of Neurology and Neuroscience*, vol. 19, *Neurological Disorders in Famous Artists* (Basel, Switzerland: Karger, 2005), 121–31. It is also possible that van Gogh's poor impulse control, ability to hyperfocus while working, and constant moving (he had thirty different homes in his thirty-seven years) may have been caused by attention-deficit/hyperactivity disorder (ADHD), which might exist along with the previous conditions. Although Arnold does not mention ADHD, he gives a chart showing van Gogh's thirty homes (see Arnold, *Vincent Van Gogh*, 30.)

36. Some scientists have suggested that Friedrich Wilhelm I of Prussia and King George III of England may also have had AIP, and that George suffered from it during the time of the American Revolution, influencing the course of the war. See Christoph Handschin, Jiandie Lin, James Rhee, Anne-Kathrin Peyer, Sherry Chin, Pei-Hsuan Wu, Urs A. Meyer, and Bruce M. Spiegelman, "Nutritional Regulation of Hepatic Heme Biosynthesis and Porphyria Through PGC-1," *Cell* 122 (August 26, 2005): 505–15, http://www.biozentrum.unibas.ch/meyer/documents/Hand-Cell-05.pdf.

37. Paul L. Wolf says that van Gogh's being treated with digitalis for presumed epilepsy is the reason for a great deal of yellow in his paintings. I believe the use of yellow in his works is a stylistic choice rather than the result of medication. Although van Gogh favored yellow and it is prominent in his paintings, the other colors in his work appear unaltered; that is, they show no change or yellowing, which would be the case if the artist was seeing a world shifted toward yellow. Wilfred N. Arnold also believes that yellow was an artistic preference rather than the result of illness or medication. See Paul L. Wolf, "The Effects of Diseases, Drugs, and Chemicals on the Creativity and Productivity of Famous Sculptors, Classic Painters, Classic Music Composers, and Authors," *Archives of Pathology and Laboratory Medicine* 129, no. 11 (2005), 1457–64, http://arpa.allenpress.com/arpaonline/?request=get-document&doi= 10.1043%2F15432165(2005)129%5B1457:TEODDA%5D2.0.CO%3B2; Arnold, *Vincent van Gogh*, 238.

38. Sandblom, review, 1133.

39. Ibid.

40. In *Vincent van Gogh: Chemicals, Crises, and Creativity*, 32, 36, Arnold dates van Gogh's decision to become an artist to letter 134, August 20, 1880, and he notes that it was also in 1880 that the artist's father wanted to commit him to a mental hospital.

41. Van Gogh, *Complete Letters*, 2:485.

42. Ibid., 3:143–44.

43. For information about the chemistry of absinthe and terpenes and their effect on van Gogh, see Wilfred Niels Arnold, "Vincent Van Gogh and the Thujone Cononection," *Journal of the American Medical Association* 260, no. 20 (November 25, 1988): 3042–44. For a history and discussion of the toxicity of absinthe, see A. Dettling, H. Grass, A. Schuff, G. Skopp, P. Strohbeck-Kuehner, and H.-Th. Haffner, "Absinthe: Attention Performance and Mood under the Effect of Thujone," *Journal of Studies on Alcohol* 65, no. 5 (September 2004): 573–81.

44. Arnold, *Vincent van Gogh*, 152.

45. Van Gogh, *Complete Letters*, 2:198.

46. Information on frontotemporal dementia and Wightman, Chang, and Adams is from Bruce L. Miller, personal communication, March 30, 2006; Bruce L. Miller, "Portraits of Artists: Creativity in Dementia" (presented by the Penn Humanities Forum and Penn Institute on Aging at the University of Pennsylvania, March 1, 2006); the UCSF Memory and Aging Patient Art Gallery, http://memory. ucsf.edu/Art/gallery.htm, which leads to the separate Web pages for each artist; Bruce L. Miller and Craig E. Hou, "Portraits of Artists: Emergence of Visual Creativity in Dementia," *Neurological Review*, repr. in *Archives of Neurology* 61, no. 6 (June 2004): 842–44; Bruce L. Miller, J. Cummings, F. Mishkin, K. Boone, F. Prince, M. Ponton, and C. Cotman, "Emergence of Artistic Talent in Frontotemporal Dementia," *Neurology* 51 (1998): 978–82; Ulrich Kraft, "Unleashing Creativity: Moments of Brilliance Arise from Complex Cognitive Processes," *Scientific American* 16, no. 1 (April 2005): 16–23; Jennifer O'Brien, "The Art of Disease," *UCSF Magazine* 23, no. 2 (June 2003), http://pub.ucsf.edu/magazine/200306/art_of_disease.html.

47. O'Brien, "Art of Disease."

48. Quoted in Kraft, "Unleashing Creativity," 18.

Chapter 18: Using Illness to Benefit Others

1. Stephen G. Post, "Altruism, Happiness, and Health: It's Good to Be Good," *International Journal of Behavioral Medicine* 12, no. 2 (2005): 66–77: Allan Luks, "Helper's High: Volunteering Makes People Feel Good, Physically and Emotionally," *Psychology Today* (October 1988): 39, 42; Ervin Staub, "The Roots of Goodness: The Fulfillment of Basic Human Needs and the Development of Caring, Helping and Non-aggression, Inclusive Caring, Moral Courage, Active Bystandership, and Altruism Born of Suffering," *Nebraska Symposium on Motivation* 51 (2005): 33–72.

2. Hollis Sigler, *Hollis Sigler's Breast Cancer Journal* (New York: Hudson Hills Press, 1999), 26.

3. Sylvano Arieti, *Creativity: The Magic Synthesis* (New York: Basic Books, 1976), 413.

4. Information on Sigler is from Sigler, *Breast Cancer Journal*; Susan Fisher Sterling, "Steven Scott Collects," *Women in the Arts* (Summer 2005): 19–21; tribute to Hollis Sigler in memoriam, WomanMade Gallery, http://www.womanmade.org/tribute.html.

5. Sigler, *Breast Cancer Journal*, 26.

6. Ibid., 33.

7. Ibid., 28.

8. Ibid., 33.

9. Information on Savage is from Dan Savage, personal communications, May 2004–October 2005; Daniel Savage, "Alluding to Illness in Art: The Pursuit of Catharsis" (diss., University of Lancaster, Lancaster, UK, 2004); Sheena Hastings, "My Illness, My Art, and My Hope," *Yorkshire Post*, April 12, 2004, 11.

10. Savage, "Alluding to Illness in Art."

11. Hastings, "My Illness, My Art, and My Hope," 11.

12. Information on Haring is from John Gruen, *Keith Haring: The Authorized Biography* (New York: Prentice Hall, 1991); the Keith Haring website, http://www.haring.com; David Sheff, "Keith Haring, An Intimate Conversation," *Rolling Stone* (August 10, 1989), http://www.haring.com/archives/journals/index.html; Keith Haring, *Keith Haring Journals* (New York: Viking, 1996).

13. Quoted in Gruen, *Keith Haring*, 213.

14. Ibid., 187.

15. Ibid., 220.

16. Allen F. Roberts, "'Break the Silence': Art and HIV/AIDS in KwaZulu-Natal," *African Arts* 34, no. 1 (Spring 2001): 36–39, 93–94; Gregg Bordowitz, "Network Society," *Art Journal* 59, no. 4 (Winter 2000): 5–7.

17. Information on the Bambanani Women's Group artists and their work is from Jonathan Morgan and the Bambanani Women's Group, *Long Life . . . : Positive HIV Stories* (Cape Town, South Africa: Double Storey Press, 2003); *Body Maps: South African Women & HIV-AIDS*, Annenberg Scholars Program in Culture and Communication at the Annenberg School for Communication, University of Pennsylvania, Philadelphia; David Krut Fine Art, New York City.

18. Morgan and the Bambanani Women's Group, *Long Life*, 85.

19. Ibid., 169.

20. Ibid., 167.

21. Ibid., 53.

22. Ibid., 117.

23. Ibid., 5.

24. Ernie Pepion, "Artist's Statement," in *Ernie Pepion: Dreams on Wheels* (Missoula, Mont.: Missoula Museum of the Arts, 1993), n.p.

25. Ibid.

26. Information on Pepion is from Pepion, "Artist's Statement," "One Vet to Another," an interview with Tom Kumpf, and an essay by Lucy Lippard in Pepion, *Ernie Pepion;* VSA arts Permanent Collection, Ernie Pepion, *Buffalo Hunter,* http://www.vsarts.org/prebuilt/showcase/gallery/exhibits/permanent/artists/epepion. html; "Quadriplegic Blackfeet Painter Pepion Dies at 61," *Billings Gazette,* Associated Press, January 16, 2005, http://www.billingsgazette.com/newdex.php?display=rednews/2005/01/16/build/state/70-pepion-painter.inc; Dan Carter, "Paraplegic Shares Life from His Point of View," BillingsGazette.com, September 27, 2003, http://www.billingsgazette.com/newdex.php?display=rednews/2003/09/27/build/local/26-pepion.inc.

27. Quoted in "One Vet to Another," in Pepion, *Ernie Pepion.*

28. Pepion, "Artist's Statement."

29. Quoted in the essay by Lucy Lippard in Pepion, *Ernie Pepion.*

30. Carter, "Paraplegic Shares Life."

31. The earliest known fossil of a flower is from the late Jurassic period, approximately 155 million years ago, according to Ge Sun, David L. Dilcher, Shaoling Zheng, and Zhekun Zhou, "In Search of the First Flower: A Jurassic Angiosperm, *Archaefructus,* from Northeast China," *Science* (November 27, 1998): 1692–95.

32. Information about Mitsui is from biographical material from the National Technical Institute for the Deaf, Rochester Institute of Technology, Rochester, New York; *Deaf Way II: Featured Visual Artists* (catalog for the exhibition at Gallaudet University; Washington, D.C.: Gallaudet University Press, 2002); Rochester Institute of Technology, "Kutani Porcelain on Permanent Exhibit in SRC," *CRTL Newsletter* 3, no. 5 (January 1995), http://www.rit.edu/~490www/Newslet/1-95news.html; Robert Baker, National Technical Institute for the Deaf, Rochester Institute of Technology, personal communications, April 14 and 17, 2006; Kutani Ware, Japan Atlas Traditional Crafts, http://web-japan.org/atlas/crafts/cra13.html.

33. Michele Scheib, "Opening Eyes to the World: Volunteer Teaching (Japan)," Mobility International USA, http://www.miusa.org/ncde/stories/arellano.

34. Rochester Institute of Technology, "Kutani Porcelain on Permanent Exhibit."

35. Temple Grandin and Catherine Johnson, *Animals in Translation: Using the Mysteries of Autism to Decode Animal Behavior* (New York: Scribner, 2005), 1.

36. Ibid.

37. Information on Grandin is from Temple Grandin, personal communications, 2005; Temple Grandin and Margaret M. Scariano, *Emergence: Labeled Autistic* (New York: Warner Books, 2005); Temple Grandin, *Thinking in Pictures: And Other Reports from My Life with Autism* (New York: Doubleday, 1995); Grandin and Johnson, *Animals in Translation*; Temple Grandin, keynote speech for the symposium "Pure Visionaries: Artists on the Spectrum," Cooper Union, New York, November 4, 2005; Oliver Sacks, *An Anthropologist on Mars* (New York: Vintage, 1996), 244–96.

38. Grandin, *Thinking in Pictures*, 206.

39. Sacks, *Anthropologist on Mars*, 296.

40. Information on Rossol is from Monona Rossol, personal communications from 1990 to the present, with interviews on October 20, 2005, April 25, 2006, and April 29, 2006; "About Monona Rossol," ACTS website, http://www.artscrafts theatersafety.org/bio.html.

41. Rossol, April 25, 2006.

42. Ibid.

43. Rossol, October 20, 2005.

44. Bruce L. Miller, personal communication, March 30, 2006; Bruce L. Miller, "Portraits of Artists: Creativity in Dementia" (presented by the Penn Humanities Forum and Penn Institute on Aging at the University of Pennsylvania, March 1, 2006); UCSF Memory and Aging Patient Art Gallery, Dane Bottino, http://memory .ucsf.edu/Art/Patient%20Art/pat_art_bottinod.html.

45. C. G. Jung, *Psyche and Symbol* (Garden City, N.Y.: Doubleday, 1958), 58–59; Marion Woodman, *Addiction to Perfection: The Still Unravished Bride* (Toronto: Inner City Books, 1982), 51.

Index

spine
    abnormalities of, 66–67
    diseases of, 219–20, 255
    trauma to, 66, 72, 245, 254–55
    sports accidents, 20, 71–73, 231
Steiner, Rudolf, 311n.1
stem cell transplant, 30
stigma. See prejudice
strabismus, 164, 336–37n.6
Stravinsky, Igor, 175
stream-of-consciousness, 114
strength, 12–13, 26–27, 140–41
stress, 10, 11, 12, 27, 130, 197
    creativity as relief from, 14, 36, 65, 214
stroke, 42, 78, 162, 218
Sudek, Josef, 250, 251–52
surface dysgraphia, 98
surrealism, 39, 61, 181
symbolism, 43, 180, 181
sympathetic ophthalmia, 68–69
synesthesia, 124
syphilis, 78, 172

Tamekichi III, 303
Tanner, Henry Ossawa, 275, 276–77
team creativity, 39, 56
Teiko, Phyllis, 35–36
Tesla, Nikola, 114
testicular cancer, 295–96
theatrical design, 175–76, 220
Third of May, 1808, The (Goya), 173, 178–79
Thornley, Mary, 178–79, 182
Thulin, Anne, 191, 193, 194–95
Thurber, James, 68–69
tipping brushes, 238–39
tiredness, 3, 4, 13, 29
Titian, 149, 174
tonsillectomy, 57
Tooker, George, 19
touch, sense of, 159, 160, 184
Toulouse-Lautrec, Henri de, 16, 76–78
toxins, 4, 172, 201–2, 203, 205, 238–43,
    306–7
traffic accidents, 29, 32, 39, 58–60, 246–49,
    301
transformation, definition of, 34
transformational coping, 11
transforming illness, 3–4, 7–27, 34, 35
    in childhood, 45, 49–64
    definition of, 8
    See also creativity; specific conditions
travel, 74, 75, 80, 82, 88, 90, 104

Trevor-Roper, Patrick, 140, 147, 151,
    337n.6
trophic ulcers, 67
tuberculosis, 27, 60
    of hip, 83
    of spine, 219–20, 255
Turner, Joseph Mallord William, 41–42
turpentine, 242–43, 287
typhoid fever, 31

ulcerative colitis, 19, 21
Ulman, Alison, 160, 163, 165
unconscious
    ambient sound and, 108
    artistic expression of, 270
    fear and, 198
    projection and, 15
    repressed emotions and, 28
urinary tract problems, 266–69

vaccines, 53, 76
Vanderpoel, John Henry, 61, 71–73
van Gogh, Theo, 286, 287
van Gogh, Vincent, 285–87
Van Mander, Carel, 73
Vasari, Giorgio, 99, 106, 261, 262, 266,
    273
vasculitis, 27
ventilator, 234, 235
Vermeer, Jan, 149, 151
Verocchio, Andrea del, 98
Verrio, Antonio, 146–47
veterans, war injuries and 250–55
viral infections, 162
vision intensification, 167–68, 175
vision problems, 3–4, 11, 131, 139, 140–48,
    265–66, 336–37n.6
    as artistic challenge, 10, 14, 27, 28, 29,
        39, 53–58, 72–73
    blindness and, 146, 158–66, 186
    children with, 54–55, 56
    color perception and, 148, 149–58
    correction of, 56–58, 147, 148
    creative process and, 54–58, 70–71,
        140–41
    dyslexia and, 125
    eye loss and, 68–71
    light sensitivity and, 279–80
    touch and, 159, 160, 184
visual cortex, 166
visualization, 165–66, 194, 304–5
visual stimulation, 59–61